DESKTOP PUBLISHER'S EASY TYPE GUIDE

The 150 Most Important Typefaces

Rockport Publishers • Rockport, Massachusetts
Distributed by North Light Books
Cincinnati, Ohio

First published in the United States of America by:
Rockport Publishers, Inc.
P.O. Box 396, Five Smith Street
Rockport, Massachusetts 01966
Telephone: (508) 546-9590
Fax: (508) 546-7141
Telex: 5106019284 ROCKORT PUB

Distributed to the book trade in the U.S. and Canada by:
North Light, an imprint of
F & W Publicatons
1507 Dana Avenue
Cincinnati, Ohio 45207
Telephone: (513) 531-2222

First published in 1992 in Germany by:
Nippan
Nippon Shuppan Hanbai Deutschland GmbH
Krefelder Str. 85
D-4000 Dusseldorf 11 (Heerdt)
Telephone: (0211) 5048089
Fax: (0211) 5049326

Other Distribution by:
Rockport Publishers, Inc.
Rockport, Massachusetts 01966

ISBN 1-56496-007-2

Design: Stephen Bridges

Typographic Production: Desktop, Inc.,
Watertown, Massachusetts

Print Production: Barbara States

Printed in the United States of America

DESKTOP PUBLISHER'S EASY TYPE GUIDE

The 150 Most Important Typefaces

Don Dewsnap

Contents

This book was produced on a desktop publishing system using fonts produced by Adobe Systems International. All typefaces listed in the Similar Styles page are available from Adobe Systems International.

The text of this book comprises various typefaces in the ITC Stone Serif and ITC Stone Sans families.

Further information on the production of this book is available from the publisher.

Further information on the typefaces in this book is available from Adobe Systems International (address on page 172).

Introduction

There are thousands of different styles of type available to the owners of desktop publishing systems. How does one choose which to purchase? This book will not only help you make those decisions, but will show you how to get the most benefit from the type styles you choose.

The type styles in this book, representing less than five percent (5%) of all those available, will suffice for over 90%, and in many cases 100%, of all the work you will need to do. You may not need all 150 right away, so comments are included with each typeface to help you fit them to your needs.

While it is true that graphic designers and professional typographers may cringe at some of the conclusions in this book, the fact is that the vast majority of readers are not graphic designers or typographers. This book is about reality. What are the major differences in type styles, and what are the major effects they create? Those are the questions answered here.

As you learn more about type, and according to the demands of your clients, you will no doubt add more types styles to your library. Until then, this book will get you off to a running start.

While this book's cover refers to the 150 most important typefaces, it would probably be more accurate to refer to the most important type families.

A family of typefaces can range in number from two to over thirty, combining roman (vertical) and italic (slanted) forms, different weights (light, regular, bold, extra bold), and different widths (normal, condensed, expanded). Not all members of a family are as useful—as "important"—as all the others.

Unfortunately, in the PostScript® world, type is usually sold in packages (called "volumes" for reasons best known to some marketing department), so you have to buy some faces you might not buy normally, to get what you want. (This is changing, fortunately. Even now, you can buy a CD-ROM with an entire library on it, and pay to have individual faces unlocked for your equipment.) This is mentioned because in this book, not all the faces in a family may be included, if it is felt they are not of great use. In other cases, some faces in a family are included with decidedly negative comments, because they are unavoidable and it is good to know how to deal with them. So not all 150 faces herein are individually "important."

Actually, determining which families to include was the hardest part of creating this book. What makes a typeface "important"?

Seven families were easy, as they have been around a long time, have proven their value in millions of uses, and are generally familiar. These include Helvetica, Optima, Times Roman, Palatino, Garamond, Century, and Baskerville.

The next level of importance had to be based on significant differences, choosing one representative of a specific type "style." The typeface chosen in these cases had to be the easiest to set, and the easiest to read, or the best combination of the two available, in that "style." This level includes most of the balance of the faces in the book.

Finally, some special faces are important, both for variety and because sometimes nothing else will do. This category includes four script faces, Zapf Dingbats, Copperplate, and Friz Quadrata. Other than the Dingbats, you may not need these but once in a year. When you do, though, nothing else will do.

The choices of typefaces and the comments offered about each one are solely the responsibility and based on the experience of the author. These choices and comments were not made lightly but legitimate disagreement is possible.

It is important to keep in mind that type is but one aspect of a printed piece. It works with the artwork, with the words, and with the medium in which it is reproduced. No general suggestions or guidelines can rule every usage of a typeface. Feel free to experiment when some unusual design seems to demand an unusual solution. Sometimes it will work, sometimes it won't. All this book can do is give you a starting point.

Above all, try to enjoy it. Choosing (and then using) typefaces is not a necessary evil: it is an act of creation, and/or helping another to create. It is an assist to communication which consists of far more than mere words. (If words were all that mattered, there would only be one typeface.)

Seeing a printed piece that really communicates what it is supposed to do, with the power it needs, will be your reward for the time you spend on learning about type. It's a great feeling. May you have it often.

NOTE: There is a glossary at the end of the book which explains all the typesetting terminology used in this book. It is very important *that you not go past any words you don't know, but look them up when you meet them, to get the most out of this book.*

Broad Characteristics

There is a major division among typefaces: *Serif* versus *Sans Serif*. Other categories, such as Script, Ornamental, or Casual, make up a small percentage of the total number. It is most important, therefore, to understand the underlying principles of the two categories into which most typefaces fall.

In general, serif typefaces are the best to use for large blocks of text, such as books, brochures, magazines, newspapers. In large quantities, serif faces are easier to read than sans serif. This is a physiological phenomenon, involving eye muscles and how much they have to work, not a design principle or an opinion.

Accordingly, serif faces are best used in smaller sizes, up to fifteen point. Above that range, they are increasingly difficult to read.

Sans serif typefaces are easier to read in two circumstances: in larger type sizes, and in smaller quantities. Children are first taught to read—and write—"block letters." I.e., sans serif. The style is familiar and comfortable to most people. But only when *very visible*. As in BIG.

In smaller sizes in sans serif type, letters tend to blur together: they're not as distinct. The mind has to work a little bit harder to recognize words. In small quantities—say descriptions in a catalogue, or in a chart where a lot of space surrounds each column—this isn't a big problem, even in smaller sizes.

In larger sizes, as in headlines, sans serif type affords much greater flexibility than serif type in adjusting the space between letters to maximize word-recognition. Serifs hold letters apart, and can create the impression of gaps in a word. These gaps can be avoided with sans serif type, so words can be made to appear more cohesive, more instantly recognizable. Word-recognition is, after all, the essence of legibility.

For the smallest sizes, below eight point, keep reality in mind. Very small sizes are generally used for 1) required but not intrinsic-to-the-message data (copyrights, etc.), or 2) for information not intended to be read easily (the famous "small print" of a contract). It doesn't matter very much whether serif or sans serif type is used. If people want to read it, they will. Just so you know, however, in smaller sizes legibility depends on the reproduction process used as much as the typeface. For rough processes, such as copiers, laser printers, or printing, sans serif is better (serifs may not even print). With high quality printing, serif type is still more legible than sans serif in small sizes.

Within each major group, the serifs and the sans serifs, there are hundreds of typefaces, but they fall into a much smaller number of subgroups of similar characteristics.

The serifs easily divide into *four* groups: hard, medium, soft, and square.

"Hard" serif faces are those with a lot of contrast in their lines, such as Bodoni. Each character is made up of very thin or much thicker lines. The serifs on hard serif faces are abrupt; they look "stuck on" to the ends of the letters.

This kind of face is used mainly for its aesthetic value. Because of the thin strokes it is best used in larger sizes, 10-point to 15-point. It is not the most legible group of typefaces, but does produce a light, airy appearance, overall. This is a sophisticated look, thus appropriate to sophisticated subject matter for upper-end readers.

"Medium" serif faces have less contrast in their strokes, are more gently curved, and have serifs that look more naturally like a part of the letter. This is the most legible group of typefaces, and most used. The three faces most representative of this group are Times, Century, and Garamond.

"Soft" serif faces are more rounded, "comfortable." Souvenir is the best example. Using a soft serif suggests a less formal, more familiar approach to both the subject and to the reader. *Or,* they can be used for an artistic effect. In any case, they are also somewhat less legible than the medium group.

Square serifs—also known as "slab" serifs—have an even stroke thickness, and rigidly formal curves and angles. Memphis is a good example. Their use is limited to highly structured messages, to emphasize the importance of that structure. While not intrinsically very legible, square serif faces if set with a lot of white space can make a strong statement. The stress of it is on practicality rather than creativity.

Sans serif faces are not so easily categorized. There are perhaps two main divisions: functional and artistic.

"Functional" means designed specifically for greatest legibility. Helvetica and Optima lead this category.

"Artistic" faces try to convey some emotion. They are not so easy to read, so should not be used for large amounts of type.

Beyond serif and sans serif, there are ornamental and script faces, just a few of which are commonly used. Most of these faces are application-specific, to be obtained as needed or requested.

Dingbats are a collection of odd characters used in printing—stars, little hands, arrows, etc.

Most typefaces have two versions—roman and italic. Sometimes, especially with medium-serif faces, the italic version is designed completely anew, with flourishes and swooping curves. Other italic faces are little more than slanted versions of the roman design. In either case, italics are used for *emphasis*. A word may be stressed to indicate importance, urgency, or verbal stress. A sentence can have very different meanings depending on which word in it is stressed.

In general, italics are not very legible, so should be used sparingly. Overuse dilutes their impact.

Most typefaces also come in a variety of weights—sometimes just two, up to eight. Helvetica, for instance, commonly comes in Light, Regular, Medium, Bold, Heavy, and Black, and has been produced in even lighter weights, Thin and Ultra-Thin, by some type manufacturers.

As the weight of the type increases, it picks up mass. It becomes heavier. With very bold type, a little goes a long way. Because of the thickness of the strokes, the characters move away from standard lettershapes, so legibility decreases a bit, though if used for just a few words, not enough to matter.

Very light type is harder to read than a normal weight, and should only be used in large sizes; certainly no smaller than

12-point. Light type is used mainly to make a design work, where a heavier or even a normal face would create a disturbingly dark area where the design doesn't allow for it.

Some typefaces are designed in condensed or extended versions. With only a few exceptions, these can be considered specialty faces and not for general use. Most typesetting programs allow you to compress or expand a face electronically, which will usually serve the purpose.

Each of the type families shown in this book is representative of a class. At the end of the book there is a list of other faces in each class. Thus if your client asks you for a typeface you don't have, you can offer an alternative which will serve much the same function. Sometimes, of course, only a specific typeface will do, so your library will grow.

Within a year, if you are setting type for a varied clientele, you will probably use all 150 and have added a few more.

A Short Introduction to Each Type Family

Americana The author's favorite typeface, whispering of Beacon Hill and soft conversations in upper-class venues. There is an understated strength to Americana, and it should be used for understated messages in smaller sizes than one might normally use. No other face approaches Americana's feel of wealth and power without the need to show it off.

Avant Garde No adequate justification for this face exists, yet it is used a lot and often requested by clients. It is included herein only for that reason. Once in a while, its geometrically perfect circularity may be appropriate to a specific application, and nothing else will do. Like it or not, it should be in your repertoire.

New Baskerville The most modern version of an old and venerable typeface, this face has a lot of contrast in its design and is very legible. Its importance lies in its distinction and delicacy, as other serif faces are just as legible, but in comparison look a bit "klunky." Basically it is unprepossessing, but self-possessed.

Bodoni The classic "old-fashioned" look, harking back to the days of musty books in dusty libraries, and the warm sweet smell of Grandmother's attic in summer. This is the face of doomed love. It gives a patina to the messages it carries. In other words, it's perfect for romance, for history, for providing a sense of continuity. "In business for over 100 years," and this typeface proves it. Other, similar faces carry some of this feel, but none so well as Bodoni.

ITC Century To some degree, Century is redundant to Times and Garamond, also serving as a common text face. It falls between the two on the conservative-to-artistic scale, wherein lies its greatest value. There are many variations of

Century, with ITC Century embodying the major design elements and not much more. This is a "safe" face if you're not sure of a client's taste or needs.

Clearface This face earns inclusion for two reasons: it is narrow, so it is useful when space is at a premium, and it is friendly, with various blips and globs in its characters that prove it doesn't take itself overly seriously. When a personal touch is needed, but not total informality, Clearface is an excellent choice.

Copperplate The tiny serifs of this face are specific to its original use, implied by its name. It was used for engraved type (popular to display wealth, social standing, prestige, or the significance of an event), and the serifs held the corners of the characters during the process. Today it is used as an affectation to the same purpose. Its serifs do assist it in today's thermograving process, which is how it is often reproduced.

Eurostile Almost a class unto itself, Eurostile serves one function and serves it well: it is rock solid. Not very legible in quantity, you'll use it in logos, in stationery, in headlines. It has no best size range, unlike most faces. Eurostile is a deceptively useful face, brilliant in its concept and design. It's a face to experiment with, because it is so hard to predict when it will work. It can look very silly when misused.

Friz Quadrata This is a funny face, existing in only two weights and flouting many design principles. Yet it works, particularly for "artistic" pieces, or when something a bit out of the mainstream is appropriate to the message. You might not use it often, but you'll enjoy it when you do.

Frutiger Of the many alternatives to

Helvetica as a basic sans serif face, Frutiger provides the clearest choice. It is clean to the point of being stark, but designed with agreeable curves so is not harsh. Most other sans serifs attack; Frutiger infiltrates. This face needs air, and will not carry a ponderous message well.

ITC Garamond The history of this typeface deserves a book of its own, if it doesn't have one. In its evolution over 400 years, and its hundreds of variations, its basic strength of design has maintained. Its quality lies in the distinctive shapes of its serifs, the manner in which its stroke weights echo and reinforce the shapes of the characters for ease of recognition, with an underlying sense that says "type is more than functional; it's also beautiful." Not every variation of Garamond works as well as every other, and ITC Garamond is not the prime example. The advantage to ITC Garamond is that it has a wide range of weights. Adobe Garamond is a version designed to reproduce better on laser printers than ITC Garamond does, so may be more appropriate to your circumstances. While not appropriate to the most conservative applications, and not quite as legible as Times or Century, Garamond is the most interesting and aesthetic typeface for general purpose text use.

Goudy Perhaps the crowning achievement of its designer, Frederic Goudy, this text face is graceful, eminently readable, and a work of art. Its low x-height means it can be set without a lot of line space, so it is economical. It is not a conservative face, and should not be used for most jobs, but when a sophisticated and slightly liberal look is needed, this is your man.

Helvetica Arguably the most-used

English typeface in the world, Helvetica embodies the classic alphabet, but with enough subtle flair to soften its appearance. Most sans serif faces are much harsher and more "mathematical." There are little curves and almost imperceptible variations in Helvetica's stroke thickness that "humanize" the face, and make it easy to read. As with any sans serif type, large quantities of Helvetica become tiring to the eye, but for a catalogue or advertisement which needs a clean uncomplicated look, Helvetica will usually do admirably.

Memphis The square serifs of Memphis and similar faces contain the sense of stability of Eurostile without its solidity. Square serifs can be hard to work with, *in re* letterspacing, so it may not look evenly set without a lot of work, but to generate a sense of firm intention, nothing can beat it. Memphis's overriding importance lies in its strength, and the strength it helps a message convey. Obviously not appropriate to every message.

Optima While a sans serif face, Optima's lines are thin at the middle and thicken at the end, giving it qualities reminiscent of a serif. It has been called the world's most readable typeface, but that is very arguable at smaller sizes. However, it probably does have the widest useful range of sizes of any type family, and a wide range of weights, so can be used for an entire brochure without looking forced or getting boring. Optima would be preferred to Helvetica when a more "interesting" or "artistic" look is desired.

Palatino A very popular typeface, imbuing classic form with dash and vigor. There's nothing outlandish about it, but it has enough idiosyncrasies to keep it alive and vibrant. Palatino is very easy to read, but perhaps a bit outre for the most conservative applications. It does need more line space than most serif faces, so is not economical in the sense of space-usage. At headline sizes, it tends to look a bit unnatural and not flow well. In sum, an excellent, interesting text face.

Souvenir Once a very popular, even over-used typeface, Souvenir for whatever design community whim has fallen into an undeserved disfavor. It is a bit more artsy than other serif faces, and incorporates a soft rounded serif, so doesn't stand up to hard use. For a pleasant, sit-down-and-chat feel, however, it is much better than more angular, sharp typefaces.

Stone Serif/Stone Sans the designer of this recent and popular typeface intended to create a "conversational" face, appropriate to less formal correspondence. It has not passed the test of time, but is included herein because it is increasingly requested. It seems to be appearing most often in magazines and journals and brochures that attempt to interact with their readers, where a more formal typeface would add distance, make them less approachable. This family may very well turn into a classic, if it is not used to death early. Ask me in five years.

Times Roman The workhorse of text faces, Times Roman was designed specifically for maximum legibility at text sizes (around 10 point). It is a short face, so doesn't need much if any extra line space to visually separate the lines, so can be set compactly. Its serifs are strong, though not muscular. Since it is much-used, its legibility is enhanced by its familiarity. When space is at a premium and legibility a prime concern, Times Roman is the way to go.

Trump Another text face, Trump is an

odd combination, almost a mongrel face, having elements of old and new, artistic and conservative. Somehow, it works, producing a block of text that looks attractive and is easy to read. Over 11-point, it begins to fall apart, and it does need a point or two more line space than some serif faces, but it carries a mood of quiet confidence that no other face can duplicate.

ABCDEFGHIJKLMNOPQRSTUVWXYZ
abcdefghijklmnopqrstuvwxyz
0123456789&?!$%“”.,/;()

8 point type, 9 point linespace

The alphabet is firmly fixed in the shapes of its letters. Three-year-olds recognize letterforms. Yet there are on the order of 50,000 typefaces in existence, each different. Subtle and not-so-subtle variations in the thickness of the lines, the curves and angles, the shapes of the serifs, the relative sizes of the parts of the letters, and other design features, all add up to individualities. The alphabet is firmly fixed in the shapes of its letters. Three-year-olds recognize letterforms. Yet there are on the order of 50,000 typefaces in existence, each different. Subtle and not-so-subtle variations in the thickness of the lines, the curves and angles, the shapes of the serifs, the relative sizes of the parts of the letters, and other design features, all add up to individualities. The alphabet is firmly fixed in the shapes of its letters. Three-year-olds recognize letterforms. Yet there are on the order of 50,000 typefaces in existence, each different. Subtle and not-so-subtle variations in the thickness of the lines, the curves and angles, the shapes of the serifs, the relative sizes of the parts of the letters, and other design features, all add up to individualities. The alphabet is firmly fixed in the shapes of its letters. Three-year-olds recognize letterforms. Yet there are on the order of 50,000 typefaces in existence, each

10 point type, 11 point linespace

The alphabet is firmly fixed in the shapes of its letters. Three-year-olds recognize letterforms. Yet there are on the order of 50,000 typefaces in existence, each different. Subtle and not-so-subtle variations in the thickness of the lines, the curves and angles, the shapes of the serifs, the relative sizes of the parts of the letters, and other design features, all add up to individualities. The alphabet is firmly fixed in the shapes of its letters. Three-year-olds recognize letterforms. Yet there are on the order of 50,000 typefaces in existence, each different. Subtle and not-so-subtle variations in the thickness of the lines, the curves and angles, the shapes of the serifs, the relative sizes of the parts of the letters, and other design features, all add up to individualities. The alphabet is firmly fixed in the shapes of its letters. Three-year-olds recognize letterforms. Yet

12 point type, 13 point linespace

The alphabet is firmly fixed in the shapes of its letters. Three-year-olds recognize letterforms. Yet there are on the order of 50,000 typefaces in existence, each different. Subtle and not-so-subtle variations in the thickness of the lines, the curves and angles, the shapes of the serifs, the relative sizes of the parts of the letters, and other design features, all add up to individualities. The alphabet is firmly fixed in the shapes of its letters. Three-year-olds recognize letterforms. Yet there are on the order of 50,000 typefaces in existence, each different. Subtle and not-so subtle variations in the thickness of the lines,

This high-bodied, graceful face exemplifies elegance. No, it's not very readable in large quantities, but to express a sense of self-worth and even a touch of justified arrogance, it makes a heckuva letterhead. Kind of snobby, overall.

ABCDEFGHIJKLMNOPQRSTUVWXYZ
abcdefghijklmnopqrstuvwxyz
0123456789&?!$%“”.,/;()

8 point type, 9 point linespace

The alphabet is firmly fixed in the shapes of its letters. Three-year-olds recognize letterforms. Yet there are on the order of 50,000 typefaces in existence, each different. Subtle and not-so-subtle variations in the thickness of the lines, the curves and angles, the shapes of the serifs, the relative sizes of the parts of the letters, and other design features, all add up to individualities. The alphabet is firmly fixed in the shapes of its letters. Three-year-olds recognize letterforms. Yet there are on the order of 50,000 typefaces in existence, each different. Subtle and not-so-subtle variations in the thickness of the lines, the curves and angles, the shapes of the serifs, the relative sizes of the parts of the letters, and other design features, all add up to individualities. The alphabet is firmly fixed in the shapes of its letters. Three-year-olds recognize letterforms. Yet there are on the order of 50,000 typefaces in existence, each different. Subtle and not-so-subtle variations in the thickness of the lines, the curves and angles, the shapes of the serifs, the relative sizes of the parts of the letters, and other design features, all add up to individualities. The alphabet is firmly fixed in the shapes of its letters. Three-year-olds recognize letterforms. Yet there are on the order of 50,000 typefaces in existence, each different. Subtle and not-

10 point type, 11 point linespace

The alphabet is firmly fixed in the shapes of its letters. Three-year-olds recognize letterforms. Yet there are on the order of 50,000 typefaces in existence, each different. Subtle and not-so-subtle variations in the thickness of the lines, the curves and angles, the shapes of the serifs, the relative sizes of the parts of the letters, and other design features, all add up to individualities. The alphabet is firmly fixed in the shapes of its letters. Three-year-olds recognize letterforms. Yet there are on the order of 50,000 typefaces in existence, each different. Subtle and not-so-subtle variations in the thickness of the lines, the curves and angles, the shapes of the serifs, the relative sizes of the parts of the letters, and other design features, all add up to individualities. The alphabet is firmly fixed in the shapes of its letters. Three-year-olds recognize letterforms. Yet there are on the order

12 point type, 13 point linespace

The alphabet is firmly fixed in the shapes of its letters. Three-year-olds recognize letterforms. Yet there are on the order of 50,000 typefaces in existence, each different. Subtle and not-so-subtle variations in the thickness of the lines, the curves and angles, the shapes of the serifs, the relative sizes of the parts of the letters, and other design features, all add up to individualities. The alphabet is firmly fixed in the shapes of its letters. Three-year-olds recognize letterforms. Yet there are on the order of 50,000 typefaces in existence, each different. Subtle and not-so-subtle variations in the thickness of the lines, the curves and angles,

The capitals work much better than lower-case in this design. As a whole it does add some elan to, if not the sterility, at least the pristineness of the roman. It shows the rich can grow more than roses.

ABCDEFGHIJKLMNOPQRSTUVWXYZ
abcdefghijklmnopqrstuvwxyz
0123456789&?!$%“”.,/;()

8 point type, 9 point linespace

The alphabet is firmly fixed in the shapes of its letters. Three-year-olds recognize letterforms. Yet there are on the order of 50,000 typefaces in existence, each different. Subtle and not-so-subtle variations in the thickness of the lines, the curves and angles, the shapes of the serifs, the relative sizes of the parts of the letters, and other design features, all add up to individualities. The alphabet is firmly fixed in the shapes of its letters. Three-year-olds recognize letterforms. Yet there are on the order of 50,000 typefaces in existence, each different. Subtle and not-so-subtle variations in the thickness of the lines, the curves and angles, the shapes of the serifs, the relative sizes of the parts of the letters, and other design features, all add up to individualities. The alphabet is firmly fixed in the shapes of its letters. Three-year-olds recognize letterforms. Yet there are on the order of 50,000 typefaces in existence, each different. Subtle and not-so-subtle variations in the thickness of the lines, the curves and angles, the shapes of the serifs, the relative sizes of the parts of the letters, and other design features, all add up to individualities. The alphabet is firmly fixed in the shapes of its letters. Three-year-olds recognize letterforms. Yet there are on the order of 50,000 typefaces in existence, each

10 point type, 11 point linespace

The alphabet is firmly fixed in the shapes of its letters. Three-year-olds recognize letterforms. Yet there are on the order of 50,000 typefaces in existence, each different. Subtle and not-so-subtle variations in the thickness of the lines, the curves and angles, the shapes of the serifs, the relative sizes of the parts of the letters, and other design features, all add up to individualities. The alphabet is firmly fixed in the shapes of its letters. Three-year-olds recognize letterforms. Yet there are on the order of 50,000 typefaces in existence, each different. Subtle and not-so-subtle variations in the thickness of the lines, the curves and angles, the shapes of the serifs, the relative sizes of the parts of the letters, and other design features, all add up to individualities. The alphabet is firmly fixed in the shapes of its letters. Three-year-olds

12 point type, 13 point linespace

The alphabet is firmly fixed in the shapes of its letters. Three-year-olds recognize letterforms. Yet there are on the order of 50,000 typefaces in existence, each different. Subtle and not-so-subtle variations in the thickness of the lines, the curves and angles, the shapes of the serifs, the relative sizes of the parts of the letters, and other design features, all add up to individualities. The alphabet is firmly fixed in the shapes of its letters. Three-year-olds recognize letterforms. Yet there are on the order of 50,000 typefaces in existence, each different. Subtle and not-so-subtle variations in the thick-

Adding force—showing some steel hand in the silk glove—this is the face of the financier, the baron who will not be taken lightly, but seldom has to threaten. It's a rich face, quite filling, so serve in small portions.

ABCDEFGHIJKLMNOPQRSTUVWXYZ
abcdefghijklmnopqrstuvwxyz
0123456789&?!$%“”.,/;()

8 point type, 9 point linespace

The alphabet is firmly fixed in the shapes of its letters. Three-year-olds recognize letterforms. Yet there are on the order of 50,000 typefaces in existence, each different. Subtle and not-so-subtle variations in the thickness of the lines, the curves and angles, the shapes of the serifs, the relative sizes of the parts of the letters, and other design features, all add up to individualities. The alphabet is firmly fixed in the shapes of its letters. Three-year-olds recognize letterforms. Yet there are on the order of 50,000 typefaces in existence, each different. Subtle and not-so-subtle variations in the thickness of the lines, the curves and angles, the shapes of the serifs, the relative sizes of the parts of the letters, and other design features, all add up to individualities. The alphabet is firmly fixed in the shapes of its letters. Three-year-olds recognize letterforms. Yet there are on the order of 50,000 typefaces in existence, each different. Subtle and not-so-subtle variations in the thickness of the lines, the curves and angles, the shapes of the serifs, the relative sizes of the parts of the letters, and other design features, all add up to individualities. The alphabet is firmly fixed in the shapes of its letters. Three-year-olds recognize letterforms. Yet there

10 point type, 11 point linespace

The alphabet is firmly fixed in the shapes of its letters. Three-year-olds recognize letterforms. Yet there are on the order of 50,000 typefaces in existence, each different. Subtle and not-so-subtle variations in the thickness of the lines, the curves and angles, the shapes of the serifs, the relative sizes of the parts of the letters, and other design features, all add up to individualities. The alphabet is firmly fixed in the shapes of its letters. Three-year-olds recognize letterforms. Yet there are on the order of 50,000 typefaces in existence, each different. Subtle and not-so-subtle variations in the thickness of the lines, the curves and angles, the shapes of the serifs, the relative sizes of the parts of the letters, and other design features, all add up to individualities. The alphabet is firmly fixed in the

12 point type, 13 point linespace

The alphabet is firmly fixed in the shapes of its letters. Three-year-olds recognize letterforms. Yet there are on the order of 50,000 typefaces in existence, each different. Subtle and not-so-subtle variations in the thickness of the lines, the curves and angles, the shapes of the serifs, the relative sizes of the parts of the letters, and other design features, all add up to individualities. The alphabet is firmly fixed in the shapes of its letters. Three-year-olds recognize letterforms. Yet there are on the order of 50,000 typefaces in existence, each different. Subtle and not-so-subtle variations in the

The gloves are off, but Marquis of Queensberry rules prevail. This face definitely casts the gauntlet, and should be saved for appeals to high-rollers from their peers. Perfect for the word PROSPECTUS.

ABCDEFGHIJKLMNOPQRSTUVWXYZ
abcdefghijklmnopqrstuvwxyz
0123456789&?!$%"".,/;()

8 point type, 9 point linespace

The alphabet is firmly fixed in the shapes of its letters. Three-year-olds recognize letterforms. Yet there are on the order of 50,000 typefaces in existence, each different. Subtle and not-so-subtle variations in the thickness of the lines, the curves and angles, the shapes of the serifs, the relative sizes of the parts of the letters, and other design features, all add up to individualities. The alphabet is firmly fixed in the shapes of its letters. Three-year-olds recognize letterforms. Yet there are on the order of 50,000 typefaces in existence, each different. Subtle and not-so-subtle variations in the thickness of the lines, the curves and angles, the shapes of the serifs, the relative sizes of the parts of the letters, and other design features, all add up to individualities. The alphabet is firmly fixed in the shapes of its letters. Three-year-olds recognize letterforms. Yet there are on the order of 50,000 typefaces in existence, each different. Subtle and not-so-subtle variations in the thickness of the lines, the curves and angles, the shapes of the serifs, the relative sizes of the parts of the letters, and other design features, all add up to individualities. The alphabet is firmly fixed in the shapes of its letters. Three-year-olds recognize letterforms. Yet there are on the order of 50,000 typefaces in existence, each different. Subtle and not-so-subtle variations in the thickness of the lines, the curves and angles, the

10 point type, 11 point linespace

The alphabet is firmly fixed in the shapes of its letters. Three-year-olds recognize letterforms. Yet there are on the order of 50,000 typefaces in existence, each different. Subtle and not-so-subtle variations in the thickness of the lines, the curves and angles, the shapes of the serifs, the relative sizes of the parts of the letters, and other design features, all add up to individualities. The alphabet is firmly fixed in the shapes of its letters. Three-year-olds recognize letterforms. Yet there are on the order of 50,000 typefaces in existence, each different. Subtle and not-so-subtle variations in the thickness of the lines, the curves and angles, the shapes of the serifs, the relative sizes of the parts of the letters, and other design features, all add up to individualities. The alphabet is firmly fixed in the shapes of its letters. Three-year-olds recognize letterforms. Yet there are on the order of 50,000 typefaces in existence, each different. Subtle and

12 point type, 13 point linespace

The alphabet is firmly fixed in the shapes of its letters. Three-year-olds recognize letterforms. Yet there are on the order of 50,000 typefaces in existence, each different. Subtle and not-so-subtle variations in the thickness of the lines, the curves and angles, the shapes of the serifs, the relative sizes of the parts of the letters, and other design features, all add up to individualities. The alphabet is firmly fixed in the shapes of its letters. Three-year-olds recognize letterforms. Yet there are on the order of 50,000 typefaces in existence, each different. Subtle and not-so-subtle variations in the thickness of the lines, the curves and angles, the shapes of the serifs, the relative sizes of

Never, ever set any of the Avant Gardes in blocks of text. They are fine for a line or two, for headlines with serif text, advertising work, and stationery. En masse, Avant Garde is very hard to read.

ABCDEFGHIJKLMNOPQRSTUVWXYZ
abcdefghijklmnopqrstuvwxyz
0123456789&?!$%"".,/;()

8 point type, 9 point linespace

The alphabet is firmly fixed in the shapes of its letters. Three-year-olds recognize letterforms. Yet there are on the order of 50,000 typefaces in existence, each different. Subtle and not-so-subtle variations in the thickness of the lines, the curves and angles, the shapes of the serifs, the relative sizes of the parts of the letters, and other design features, all add up to individualities. The alphabet is firmly fixed in the shapes of its letters. Three-year-olds recognize letterforms. Yet there are on the order of 50,000 typefaces in existence, each different. Subtle and not-so-subtle variations in the thickness of the lines, the curves and angles, the shapes of the serifs, the relative sizes of the parts of the letters, and other design features, all add up to individualities. The alphabet is firmly fixed in the shapes of its letters. Three-year-olds recognize letterforms. Yet there are on the order of 50,000 typefaces in existence, each different. Subtle and not-so-subtle variations in the thickness of the lines, the curves and angles, the shapes of the serifs, the relative sizes of the parts of the letters, and other design features, all add up to individualities. The alphabet is firmly fixed in the shapes of its letters. Three-year-olds recognize letterforms. Yet there are on the order of 50,000 typefaces in existence, each different. Subtle and not-so-subtle variations in the shapes of the serifs, the the relative sizes of the

10 point type, 11 point linespace

The alphabet is firmly fixed in the shapes of its letters. Three-year-olds recognize letterforms. Yet there are on the order of 50,000 typefaces in existence, each different. Subtle and not-so-subtle variations in the thickness of the lines, the curves and angles, the shapes of the serifs, the relative sizes of the parts of the letters, and other design features, all add up to individualities. The alphabet is firmly fixed in the shapes of its letters. Three-year-olds recognize letterforms. Yet there are on the order of 50,000 typefaces in existence, each different. Subtle and not-so-subtle variations in the thickness of the lines, the curves and angles, the shapes of the serifs, the relative sizes of the parts of the letters, and other design features, all add up to individualities. The alphabet is firmly fixed in the shapes of its letters. Three-year-olds recognize letterforms. Yet there are on the order of 50,000 typefaces in existence, each different. Subtle and

12 point type, 13 point linespace

The alphabet is firmly fixed in the shapes of its letters. Three-year-olds recognize letterforms. Yet there are on the order of 50,000 typefaces in existence, each different. Subtle and not-so-subtle variations in the thickness of the lines, the curves and angles, the shapes of the serifs, the relative sizes of the parts of the letters, and other design features, all add up to individualities. The alphabet is firmly fixed in the shapes of its letters. Three-year-olds recognize letterforms. Yet there are on the order of 50,000 typefaces in existence, each different. Subtle and not-so-subtle variations in the thickness of the lines, the curves and angles, the shapes of the serifs, the relative sizes of

Little more than a slanted version of the roman, it is somewhat lighter in appearance so should be set tightly. It does convey a dynamic motion to its message, and urgency, so it does have valid uses.

ABCDEFGHIJKLMNOPQRSTUVWXYZ
abcdefghijklmnopqrstuvwxyz
0123456789&?!$%“”.,/;()

8 point type, 9 point linespace

The alphabet is firmly fixed in the shapes of its letters. Three-year-olds recognize letterforms. Yet there are on the order of 50,000 typefaces in existence, each different. Subtle and not-so-subtle variations in the thickness of the lines, the curves and angles, the shapes of the serifs, the relative sizes of the parts of the letters, and other design features, all add up to individualities. The alphabet is firmly fixed in the shapes of its letters. Three-year-olds recognize letterforms. Yet there are on the order of 50,000 typefaces in existence, each different. Subtle and not-so-subtle variations in the thickness of the lines, the curves and angles, the shapes of the serifs, the relative sizes of the parts of the letters, and other design features, all add up to individualities. The alphabet is firmly fixed in the shapes of its letters. Three-year-olds recognize letterforms. Yet there are on the order of 50,000 typefaces in existence, each different. Subtle and not-so-subtle variations in the thickness of the lines, the curves and angles, the shapes of the serifs, the relative sizes of the parts of the letters, and other design features, all add up to individualities. The alphabet is firmly fixed in the shapes of its letters. Three-year-olds recognize letterforms. Yet there are on the order of 50,000 typefaces in existence, each different. Subtle and not-so-subtle variations in the thickness of the lines, the curves and angles, the

10 point type, 11 point linespace

The alphabet is firmly fixed in the shapes of its letters. Three-year-olds recognize letterforms. Yet there are on the order of 50,000 typefaces in existence, each different. Subtle and not-so-subtle variations in the thickness of the lines, the curves and angles, the shapes of the serifs, the relative sizes of the parts of the letters, and other design features, all add up to individualities. The alphabet is firmly fixed in the shapes of its letters. Three-year-olds recognize letterforms. Yet there are on the order of 50,000 typefaces in existence, each different. Subtle and not-so-subtle variations in the thickness of the lines, the curves and angles, the shapes of the serifs, the relative sizes of the parts of the letters, and other design features, all add up to individualities. The alphabet is firmly fixed in the shapes of its letters. Three-year-olds recognize letterforms. Yet there are on the order of 50,000 typefaces in existence,

12 point type, 13 point linespace

The alphabet is firmly fixed in the shapes of its letters. Three-year-olds recognize letterforms. Yet there are on the order of 50,000 typefaces in existence, each different. Subtle and not-so-subtle variations in the thickness of the lines, the curves and angles, the shapes of the serifs, the relative sizes of the parts of the letters, and other design features, all add up to individualities. The alphabet is firmly fixed in the shapes of its letters. Three-year-olds recognize letterforms. Yet there are on the order of 50,000 typefaces in existence, each different. Subtle and not-so-subtle variations in the thickness of the lines, the curves and angles, the shapes of the serifs, the

This is surprisingly effective as a headline face and works well with artwork, especially of a modern nature. The roundness and angles of the characters reflect well on most design-oriented graphics.

ABCDEFGHIJKLMNOPQRSTUVWXYZ
abcdefghijklmnopqrstuvwxyz
0123456789&?!$%“”.,/;()

8 point type, 9 point linespace

The alphabet is firmly fixed in the shapes of its letters. Three-year-olds recognize letterforms. Yet there are on the order of 50,000 typefaces in existence, each different. Subtle and not-so-subtle variations in the thickness of the lines, the curves and angles, the shapes of the serifs, the relative sizes of the parts of the letters, and other design features, all add up to individualities. The alphabet is firmly fixed in the shapes of its letters. Three-year-olds recognize letterforms. Yet there are on the order of 50,000 typefaces in existence, each different. Subtle and not-so-subtle variations in the thickness of the lines, the curves and angles, the shapes of the serifs, the relative sizes of the parts of the letters, and other design features, all add up to individualities. The alphabet is firmly fixed in the shapes of its letters. Three-year-olds recognize letterforms. Yet there are on the order of 50,000 typefaces in existence, each different. Subtle and not-so-subtle variations in the thickness of the lines, the curves and angles, the shapes of the serifs, the relative sizes of the parts of the letters, and other design features, all add up to individualities. The alphabet is firmly fixed in the shapes of its letters. Three-year-olds recognize letterforms. Yet there are on the order of 50,000 typefaces in existence, each different. Subtle and not-so-subtle variations in the thickness of the lines, the curves and angles, the

10 point type, 11 point linespace

The alphabet is firmly fixed in the shapes of its letters. Three-year-olds recognize letterforms. Yet there are on the order of 50,000 typefaces in existence, each different. Subtle and not-so-subtle variations in the thickness of the lines, the curves and angles, the shapes of the serifs, the relative sizes of the parts of the letters, and other design features, all add up to individualities. The alphabet is firmly fixed in the shapes of its letters. Three-year-olds recognize letterforms. Yet there are on the order of 50,000 typefaces in existence, each different. Subtle and not-so-subtle variations in the thickness of the lines, the curves and angles, the shapes of the serifs, the relative sizes of the parts of the letters, and other design features, all add up to individualities. The alphabet is firmly fixed in the shapes of its letters. Three-year-olds recognize letterforms. Yet there are on the order of 50,000 typefaces in existence,

12 point type, 13 point linespace

The alphabet is firmly fixed in the shapes of its letters. Three-year-olds recognize letterforms. Yet there are on the order of 50,000 typefaces in existence, each different. Subtle and not-so-subtle variations in the thickness of the lines, the curves and angles, the shapes of the serifs, the relative sizes of the parts of the letters, and other design features, all add up to individualities. The alphabet is firmly fixed in the shapes of its letters. Three-year-olds recognize letterforms. Yet there are on the order of 50,000 typefaces in existence, each different. Subtle and not-so-subtle variations in the thickness of the lines, the curves and angles, the shapes of the serifs, the

Fairly screaming, “Go For It!” this emphatic sister to the roman cut deserves just as much use as her sibling, if not more. Use for a dramatic change of pace, if you dare. Not for the faint of heart.

ABCDEFGHIJKLMNOPQRSTUVWXYZ
abcdefghijklmnopqrstuvwxyz
0123456789&?!$%"".,/;()

8 point type, 9 point linespace

The alphabet is firmly fixed in the shapes of its letters. Three-year-olds recognize letterforms. Yet there are on the order of 50,000 typefaces in existence, each different. Subtle and not-so-subtle variations in the thickness of the lines, the curves and angles, the shapes of the serifs, the relative sizes of the parts of the letters, and other design features, all add up to individualities. The alphabet is firmly fixed in the shapes of its letters. Three-year-olds recognize letterforms. Yet there are on the order of 50,000 typefaces in existence, each different. Subtle and not-so-subtle variations in the thickness of the lines, the curves and angles, the shapes of the serifs, the relative sizes of the parts of the letters, and other design features, all add up to individualities. The alphabet is firmly fixed in the shapes of its letters. Three-year-olds recognize letterforms. Yet there are on the order of 50,000 typefaces in existence, each different. Subtle and not-so-subtle variations in the thickness of the lines, the curves and angles, the shapes of the serifs, the relative sizes of the parts of the letters, and other design features, all add up to individualities. The alphabet is firmly fixed in the shapes of its letters. Three-year-olds recognize letterforms. Yet there are on the order of 50,000 typefaces in existence, each different. Subtle and not-so-subtle variations in the thickness of the lines, the curves and angles, the shapes of the serifs, the relative sizes of the parts of the letters, and other design features, all add up to individualities. The alphabet is firmly fixed in the shapes of its letters. Three-year-olds recognize letterforms. Yet there are on the order of 50,000 typefaces in existence, each different. Subtle and not-so-subtle

10 point type, 11 point linespace

The alphabet is firmly fixed in the shapes of its letters. Three-year-olds recognize letterforms. Yet there are on the order of 50,000 typefaces in existence, each different. Subtle and not-so-subtle variations in the thickness of the lines, the curves and angles, the shapes of the serifs, the relative sizes of the parts of the letters, and other design features, all add up to individualities. The alphabet is firmly fixed in the shapes of its letters. Three-year-olds recognize letterforms. Yet there are on the order of 50,000 typefaces in existence, each different. Subtle and not-so-subtle variations in the thickness of the lines, the curves and angles, the shapes of the serifs, the relative sizes of the parts of the letters, and other design features, all add up to individualities. The alphabet is firmly fixed in the shapes of its letters. Three-year-olds recognize letterforms. Yet there are on the order of 50,000 typefaces in existence, each different. Subtle and not-so-subtle variations in the thickness of the lines, the curves and angles, the shapes of the serifs, the relative sizes of the parts of the letters, and other design features, all add up to

12 point type, 13 point linespace

The alphabet is firmly fixed in the shapes of its letters. Three-year-olds recognize letterforms. Yet there are on the order of 50,000 typefaces in existence, each different. Subtle and not-so-subtle variations in the thickness of the lines, the curves and angles, the shapes of the serifs, the relative sizes of the parts of the letters, and other design features, all add up to individualities. The alphabet is firmly fixed in the shapes of its letters. Three-year-olds recognize letterforms. Yet there are on the order of 50,000 typefaces in existence, each different. Subtle and not-so-subtle variations in the thickness of the lines, the curves and angles, the shapes of the serifs, the relative sizes of the parts of the letters, and other design features, all add up to individualities. The alphabet is firmly fixed in the shapes of its letters. Three-

Much more readable than the normal Avant Gardes, the condensed versions have some limited applicability in text blocks. Good for catalogue work, or when a more clean-cut sans serif than Helvetica seems appropriate.

ABCDEFGHIJKLMNOPQRSTUVWXYZ
abcdefghijklmnopqrstuvwxyz
0123456789&?!$%"".,/;()

8 point type, 9 point linespace

The alphabet is firmly fixed in the shapes of its letters. Three-year-olds recognize letterforms. Yet there are on the order of 50,000 typefaces in existence, each different. Subtle and not-so-subtle variations in the thickness of the lines, the curves and angles, the shapes of the serifs, the relative sizes of the parts of the letters, and other design features, all add up to individualities. The alphabet is firmly fixed in the shapes of its letters. Three-year-olds recognize letterforms. Yet there are on the order of 50,000 typefaces in existence, each different. Subtle and not-so-subtle variations in the thickness of the lines, the curves and angles, the shapes of the serifs, the relative sizes of the parts of the letters, and other design features, all add up to individualities. The alphabet is firmly fixed in the shapes of its letters. Three-year-olds recognize letterforms. Yet there are on the order of 50,000 typefaces in existence, each different. Subtle and not-so-subtle variations in the thickness of the lines, the curves and angles, the shapes of the serifs, the relative sizes of the parts of the letters, and other design features, all add up to individualities. The alphabet is firmly fixed in the shapes of its letters. Three-year-olds recognize letterforms. Yet there are on the order of 50,000 typefaces in existence, each different. Subtle and not-so-subtle variations in the shapes of the serifs, the relative sizes of the parts of the letters, and other design features, all add up to individualities. The alphabet is firmly fixed in the shapes of its letters. Three-year-olds recognize letterforms. Yet there are on the order of 50,000 typefaces in existence, each different. Subtle and not-so-subtle variations in the shapes of the serifs, the relative sizes

10 point type, 11 point linespace

The alphabet is firmly fixed in the shapes of its letters. Three-year-olds recognize letterforms. Yet there are on the order of 50,000 typefaces in existence, each different. Subtle and not-so-subtle variations in the thickness of the lines, the curves and angles, the shapes of the serifs, the relative sizes of the parts of the letters, and other design features, all add up to individualities. The alphabet is firmly fixed in the shapes of its letters. Three-year-olds recognize letterforms. Yet there are on the order of 50,000 typefaces in existence, each different. Subtle and not-so-subtle variations in the thickness of the lines, the curves and angles, the shapes of the serifs, the relative sizes of the parts of the letters, and other design features, all add up to individualities. The alphabet is firmly fixed in the shapes of its letters. Three-year-olds recognize letterforms. Yet there are on the order of 50,000 typefaces in existence, each different. Subtle and not-so-subtle variations in the thickness of the lines, the curves and angles, the shapes of the serifs, the relative sizes of the parts of the letters, and other design features, all add up to individualities.

12 point type, 13 point linespace

The alphabet is firmly fixed in the shapes of its letters. Three-year-olds recognize letterforms. Yet there are on the order of 50,000 typefaces in existence, each different. Subtle and not-so-subtle variations in the thickness of the lines, the curves and angles, the shapes of the serifs, the relative sizes of the parts of the letters, and other design features, all add up to individualities. The alphabet is firmly fixed in the shapes of its letters. Three-year-olds recognize letterforms. Yet there are on the order of 50,000 typefaces in existence, each different. Subtle and not-so-subtle variations in the thickness of the lines, the curves and angles, the shapes of the serifs, the relative sizes of the parts of the letters, and other design features, all add up to individualities. The alphabet is firmly fixed in the shapes of its letters. Three-year-olds recognize letterforms. Yet there are on the order

Better to use this weight in smaller sizes (under 10 point) than the Book weight. Otherwise very similar in feel and use to the Book weight, with the same caveats.

ABCDEFGHIJKLMNOPQRSTUVWXYZ
abcdefghijklmnopqrstuvwxyz
0123456789&?!$%“”.,/;()

8 point type, 9 point linespace

The alphabet is firmly fixed in the shapes of its letters. Three-year-olds recognize letterforms. Yet there are on the order of 50,000 typefaces in existence, each different. Subtle and not-so-subtle variations in the thickness of the lines, the curves and angles, the shapes of the serifs, the relative sizes of the parts of the letters, and other design features, all add up to individualities. The alphabet is firmly fixed in the shapes of its letters. Three-year-olds recognize letterforms. Yet there are on the order of 50,000 typefaces in existence, each different. Subtle and not-so-subtle variations in the thickness of the lines, the curves and angles, the shapes of the serifs, the relative sizes of the parts of the letters, and other design features, all add up to individualities. The alphabet is firmly fixed in the shapes of its letters. Three-year-olds recognize letterforms. Yet there are on the order of 50,000 typefaces in existence, each different. Subtle and not-so-subtle variations in the thickness of the lines, the curves and angles, the shapes of the serifs, the relative sizes of the parts of the letters, and other design features, all add up to individualities. The alphabet is firmly fixed in the shapes of its letters. Three-year-olds recognize letterforms. Yet there are on the order of 50,000 typefaces in existence, each different. Subtle and not-so-subtle variations in the thickness of the lines, the curves and angles, the shapes of the serifs, the relative sizes of the parts of the letters, and other design features, all add up to individualities. The alphabet is firmly fixed in the shapes of its letters. Three-year-olds recognize letterforms. Yet there are on the order of

10 point type, 11 point linespace

The alphabet is firmly fixed in the shapes of its letters. Three-year-olds recognize letterforms. Yet there are on the order of 50,000 typefaces in existence, each different. Subtle and not-so-subtle variations in the thickness of the lines, the curves and angles, the shapes of the serifs, the relative sizes of the parts of the letters, and other design features, all add up to individualities. The alphabet is firmly fixed in the shapes of its letters. Three-year-olds recognize letterforms. Yet there are on the order of 50,000 typefaces in existence, each different. Subtle and not-so-subtle variations in the thickness of the lines, the curves and angles, the shapes of the serifs, the relative sizes of the parts of the letters, and other design features, all add up to individualities. The alphabet is firmly fixed in the shapes of its letters. Three-year-olds recognize letterforms. Yet there are on the order of 50,000 typefaces in existence, each different. Subtle and not-so-subtle variations in the thickness of the lines, the curves and angles, the shapes of the serifs, the relative sizes of the parts of

12 point type, 13 point linespace

The alphabet is firmly fixed in the shapes of its letters. Three-year-olds recognize letterforms. Yet there are on the order of 50,000 typefaces in existence, each different. Subtle and not-so-subtle variations in the thickness of the lines, the curves and angles, the shapes of the serifs, the relative sizes of the parts of the letters, and other design features, all add up to individualities. The alphabet is firmly fixed in the shapes of its letters. Three-year-olds recognize letterforms. Yet there are on the order of 50,000 typefaces in existence, each different. Subtle and not-so-subtle variations in the thickness of the lines, the curves and angles, the shapes of the serifs, the relative sizes of the parts of the letters, and other design features, all add up to individualities. The alphabet is firmly

Too heavy for text and too light for most headlines, the best use for this weight is as an accent face, to highlight words in text, to introduce list items, or wherever italic would normally be used.

ABCDEFGHIJKLMNOPQRSTUVWXYZ
abcdefghijklmnopqrstuvwxyz
0123456789&?!$%“”.,/;()

8 point type, 9 point linespace

The alphabet is firmly fixed in the shapes of its letters. Three-year-olds recognize letterforms. Yet there are on the order of 50,000 typefaces in existence, each different. Subtle and not-so-subtle variations in the thickness of the lines, the curves and angles, the shapes of the serifs, the relative sizes of the parts of the letters, and other design features, all add up to individualities. The alphabet is firmly fixed in the shapes of its letters. Three-year-olds recognize letterforms. Yet there are on the order of 50,000 typefaces in existence, each different. Subtle and not-so-subtle variations in the thickness of the lines, the curves and angles, the shapes of the serifs, the relative sizes of the parts of the letters, and other design features, all add up to individualities. The alphabet is firmly fixed in the shapes of its letters. Three-year-olds recognize letterforms. Yet there are on the order of 50,000 typefaces in existence, each different. Subtle and not-so-subtle variations in the thickness of the lines, the curves and angles, the shapes of the serifs, the relative sizes of the parts of the letters, and other design features, all add up to individualities. The alphabet is firmly fixed in the shapes of its letters. Three-year-olds recognize letterforms. Yet there are on the order of 50,000 typefaces in existence, each different. Subtle and not-so-subtle variations in the shapes of the serifs, the relative sizes of the parts of the letters, and other design features, all add up to individualities. The alphabet is firmly fixed in the shapes of its letters. Three-year-olds recognize letterforms. Yet there are on the order of 50,000

10 point type, 11 point linespace

The alphabet is firmly fixed in the shapes of its letters. Three-year-olds recognize letterforms. Yet there are on the order of 50,000 typefaces in existence, each different. Subtle and not-so-subtle variations in the thickness of the lines, the curves and angles, the shapes of the serifs, the relative sizes of the parts of the letters, and other design features, all add up to individualities. The alphabet is firmly fixed in the shapes of its letters. Three-year-olds recognize letterforms. Yet there are on the order of 50,000 typefaces in existence, each different. Subtle and not-so-subtle variations in the thickness of the lines, the curves and angles, the shapes of the serifs, the relative sizes of the parts of the letters, and other design features, all add up to individualities. The alphabet is firmly fixed in the shapes of its letters. Three-year-olds recognize letterforms. Yet there are on the order of 50,000 typefaces in existence, each different. Subtle and not-so-subtle variations in the thickness of the lines, the curves and angles, the shapes of the serifs, the relative

12 point type, 13 point linespace

The alphabet is firmly fixed in the shapes of its letters. Three-year-olds recognize letterforms. Yet there are on the order of 50,000 typefaces in existence, each different. Subtle and not-so-subtle variations in the thickness of the lines, the curves and angles, the shapes of the serifs, the relative sizes of the parts of the letters, and other design features, all add up to individualities. The alphabet is firmly fixed in the shapes of its letters. Three-year-olds recognize letterforms. Yet there are on the order of 50,000 typefaces in existence, each different. Subtle and not-so-subtle variations in the thickness of the lines, the curves and angles, the shapes of the serifs, the relative sizes of the parts of the letters, and other design features, all add up to individualities.

This face works in headlines. Set it very tightly, with as much size to it as the space will afford. It reads just as well in all capitals or in upper and lower case, which gives you unusual flexibility.

ABCDEFGHIJKLMNOPQRSTUVWXYZ
abcdefghijklmnopqrstuvwxyz
0123456789&?!$%“”.,/;()

8 point type, 9 point linespace

The alphabet is firmly fixed in the shapes of its letters. Three-year-olds recognize letterforms. Yet there are on the order of 50,000 typefaces in existence, each different. Subtle and not-so-subtle variations in the thickness of the lines, the curves and angles, the shapes of the serifs, the relative sizes of the parts of the letters, and other design features, all add up to individualities. The alphabet is firmly fixed in the shapes of its letters. Three-year-olds recognize letterforms. Yet there are on the order of 50,000 typefaces in existence, each different. Subtle and not-so-subtle variations in the thickness of the lines, the curves and angles, the shapes of the serifs, the relative sizes of the parts of the letters, and other design features, all add up to individualities. The alphabet is firmly fixed in the shapes of its letters. Three-year-olds recognize letterforms. Yet there are on the order of 50,000 typefaces in existence, each different. Subtle and not-so-subtle variations in the thickness of the lines, the curves and angles, the shapes of the serifs, the relative sizes of the parts of the letters, and other design features, all add up to individualities. The alphabet is firmly fixed in the shapes of its letters. Three-year-olds recognize letterforms. Yet there are on the order of 50,000 typefaces in existence, each different. Subtle and not-so-subtle variations in the thickness of the lines, the curves and angles, the shapes of the serifs, the relative sizes of the parts of the letters, and other design features, all add up to individualities. The alphabet is firmly

10 point type, 11 point linespace

The alphabet is firmly fixed in the shapes of its letters. Three-year-olds recognize letterforms. Yet there are on the order of 50,000 typefaces in existence, each different. Subtle and not-so-subtle variations in the thickness of the lines, the curves and angles, the shapes of the serifs, the relative sizes of the parts of the letters, and other design features, all add up to individualities. The alphabet is firmly fixed in the shapes of its letters. Three-year-olds recognize letterforms. Yet there are on the order of 50,000 typefaces in existence, each different. Subtle and not-so-subtle variations in the thickness of the lines, the curves and angles, the shapes of the serifs, the relative sizes of the parts of the letters, and other design features, all add up to individualities. The alphabet is firmly fixed in the shapes of its letters. Three-year-olds recognize letterforms. Yet there are on the order of 50,000 typefaces in existence, each different. Subtle and not-so-subtle variations in the thickness of the lines, the curves and angles, the shapes

12 point type, 13 point linespace

The alphabet is firmly fixed in the shapes of its letters. Three-year-olds recognize letterforms. Yet there are on the order of 50,000 typefaces in existence, each different. Subtle and not-so-subtle variations in the thickness of the lines, the curves and angles, the shapes of the serifs, the relative sizes of the parts of the letters, and other design features, all add up to individualities. The alphabet is firmly fixed in the shapes of its letters. Three-year-olds recognize letterforms. Yet there are on the order of 50,000 typefaces in existence, each different. Subtle and not-so-subtle variations in the thickness of the lines, the curves and angles, the shapes of the serifs, the relative sizes of the parts of the letters, and other design features, all add up to

Extremely popular as a text face, especially for books, this recent redesign of a venerable typeface captures the essence of art in type. It is a very “alive” face, easy to read, which doesn’t get boring.

ABCDEFGHIJKLMNOPQRSTUVWXYZ
abcdefghijklmnopqrstuvwxyz
0123456789&?!$%“”.,/;()

8 point type, 9 point linespace

The alphabet is firmly fixed in the shapes of its letters. Three-year-olds recognize letterforms. Yet there are on the order of 50,000 typefaces in existence, each different. Subtle and not-so-subtle variations in the thickness of the lines, the curves and angles, the shapes of the serifs, the relative sizes of the parts of the letters, and other design features, all add up to individualities. The alphabet is firmly fixed in the shapes of its letters. Three-year-olds recognize letterforms. Yet there are on the order of 50,000 typefaces in existence, each different. Subtle and not-so-subtle variations in the thickness of the lines, the curves and angles, the shapes of the serifs, the relative sizes of the parts of the letters, and other design features, all add up to individualities. The alphabet is firmly fixed in the shapes of its letters. Three-year-olds recognize letterforms. Yet there are on the order of 50,000 typefaces in existence, each different. Subtle and not-so-subtle variations in the thickness of the lines, the curves and angles, the shapes of the serifs, the relative sizes of the parts of the letters, and other design features, all add up to individualities. The alphabet is firmly fixed in the shapes of its letters. Three-year-olds recognize letterforms. Yet there are on the order of 50,000 typefaces in existence, each different. Subtle and not-so-subtle variations in the thickness of the lines, the curves and angles, the shapes of the serifs, the relative sizes of the parts of the letters, and other design features, all add up to individualities. The alphabet is firmly fixed in the shapes of its letters. Three-year-olds recognize letterforms. Yet there are on the order of 50,000 typefaces in existence, each different. Subtle and not-so-subtle variations in the thickness of the lines, the curves and angles, the shapes of the serifs,

10 point type, 11 point linespace

The alphabet is firmly fixed in the shapes of its letters. Three-year-olds recognize letterforms. Yet there are on the order of 50,000 typefaces in existence, each different. Subtle and not-so-subtle variations in the thickness of the lines, the curves and angles, the shapes of the serifs, the relative sizes of the parts of the letters, and other design features, all add up to individualities. The alphabet is firmly fixed in the shapes of its letters. Three-year-olds recognize letterforms. Yet there are on the order of 50,000 typefaces in existence, each different. Subtle and not-so-subtle variations in the thickness of the lines, the curves and angles, the shapes of the serifs, the relative sizes of the parts of the letters, and other design features, all add up to individualities. The alphabet is firmly fixed in the shapes of its letters. Three-year-olds recognize letterforms. Yet there are on the order of 50,000 typefaces in existence, each different. Subtle and not-so-subtle variations in the thickness of the lines, the curves and angles, the shapes of the serifs, the relative sizes of the parts of the letters, and other design features, all add up to individualities. The alphabet is firmly fixed in the shapes of its letters.

12 point type, 13 point linespace

The alphabet is firmly fixed in the shapes of its letters. Three-year-olds recognize letterforms. Yet there are on the order of 50,000 typefaces in existence, each different. Subtle and not-so-subtle variations in the thickness of the lines, the curves and angles, the shapes of the serifs, the relative sizes of the parts of the letters, and other design features, all add up to individualities. The alphabet is firmly fixed in the shapes of its letters. Three-year-olds recognize letterforms. Yet there are on the order of 50,000 typefaces in existence, each different. Subtle and not-so-subtle variations in the thickness of the lines, the curves and angles, the shapes of the serifs, the relative sizes of the parts of the letters, and other design features, all add up to individualities. The alphabet is firmly fixed in the shapes of its letters. Three-year-olds recognize letterforms. Yet

Flourish with a purpose—to accentuate and reinforce the aesthetics of the roman cut. This italic does what an italic should do—it assists the roman to fully and easily convey a message.

ABCDEFGHIJKLMNOPQRSTUVWXYZ
abcdefghijklmnopqrstuvwxyz
0123456789&?!$%“”.,/;()

8 point type, 9 point linespace

The alphabet is firmly fixed in the shapes of its letters. Three-year-olds recognize letterforms. Yet there are on the order of 50,000 typefaces in existence, each different. Subtle and not-so-subtle variations in the thickness of the lines, the curves and angles, the shapes of the serifs, the relative sizes of the parts of the letters, and other design features, all add up to individualities. The alphabet is firmly fixed in the shapes of its letters. Three-year-olds recognize letterforms. Yet there are on the order of 50,000 typefaces in existence, each different. Subtle and not-so-subtle variations in the thickness of the lines, the curves and angles, the shapes of the serifs, the relative sizes of the parts of the letters, and other design features, all add up to individualities. The alphabet is firmly fixed in the shapes of its letters. Three-year-olds recognize letterforms. Yet there are on the order of 50,000 typefaces in existence, each different. Subtle and not-so-subtle variations in the thickness of the lines, the curves and angles, the shapes of the serifs, the relative sizes of the parts of the letters, and other design features, all add up to individualities. The alphabet is firmly fixed in the shapes of its letters. Three-year-olds recognize letterforms. Yet there are on the order of 50,000 typefaces in existence, each different. Subtle and not-so-subtle variations in the thickness of the lines, the curves and angles, the shapes of the serifs, the relative sizes of the parts of the letters, and other design features, all add up to individualities. The alphabet is firmly

10 point type, 11 point linespace

The alphabet is firmly fixed in the shapes of its letters. Three-year-olds recognize letterforms. Yet there are on the order of 50,000 typefaces in existence, each different. Subtle and not-so-subtle variations in the thickness of the lines, the curves and angles, the shapes of the serifs, the relative sizes of the parts of the letters, and other design features, all add up to individualities. The alphabet is firmly fixed in the shapes of its letters. Three-year-olds recognize letterforms. Yet there are on the order of 50,000 typefaces in existence, each different. Subtle and not-so-subtle variations in the thickness of the lines, the curves and angles, the shapes of the serifs, the relative sizes of the parts of the letters, and other design features, all add up to individualities. The alphabet is firmly fixed in the shapes of its letters. Three-year-olds recognize letterforms. Yet there are on the order of 50,000 typefaces in existence, each different. Subtle and not-so-subtle variations in the thickness of the lines, the curves and

12 point type, 13 point linespace

The alphabet is firmly fixed in the shapes of its letters. Three-year-olds recognize letterforms. Yet there are on the order of 50,000 typefaces in existence, each different. Subtle and not-so-subtle variations in the thickness of the lines, the curves and angles, the shapes of the serifs, the relative sizes of the parts of the letters, and other design features, all add up to individualities. The alphabet is firmly fixed in the shapes of its letters. Three-year-olds recognize letterforms. Yet there are on the order of 50,000 typefaces in existence, each different. Subtle and not-so-subtle variations in the thickness of the lines, the curves and angles, the shapes of the serifs, the relative sizes of the parts of the letters, and other design features, all add up to

Vividly contrasting with the regular roman weight, but not fighting with it, this is your classic bold cut for titles, subheads, and other attention-getting applications. It has a natural feel.

ABCDEFGHIJKLMNOPQRSTUVWXYZ
abcdefghijklmnopqrstuvwxyz
0123456789&?!$%“”.,/;()

8 point type, 9 point linespace

The alphabet is firmly fixed in the shapes of its letters. Three-year-olds recognize letterforms. Yet there are on the order of 50,000 typefaces in existence, each different. Subtle and not-so-subtle variations in the thickness of the lines, the curves and angles, the shapes of the serifs, the relative sizes of the parts of the letters, and other design features, all add up to individualities. The alphabet is firmly fixed in the shapes of its letters. Three-year-olds recognize letterforms. Yet there are on the order of 50,000 typefaces in existence, each different. Subtle and not-so-subtle variations in the thickness of the lines, the curves and angles, the shapes of the serifs, the relative sizes of the parts of the letters, and other design features, all add up to individualities. The alphabet is firmly fixed in the shapes of its letters. Three-year-olds recognize letterforms. Yet there are on the order of 50,000 typefaces in existence, each different. Subtle and not-so-subtle variations in the thickness of the lines, the curves and angles, the shapes of the serifs, the relative sizes of the parts of the letters, and other design features, all add up to individualities. The alphabet is firmly fixed in the shapes of its letters. Three-year-olds recognize letterforms. Yet there are on the order of 50,000 typefaces in existence, each different. Subtle and not-so-subtle variations in the thickness of the lines, the curves and angles, the shapes of the serifs, the relative sizes of the parts of the letters, and other design features, all add up to individualities. The alphabet is firmly fixed in the shapes of its letters. Three-year-olds recognize letterforms. Yet there are on the order of 50,000 typefaces in existence, each different. Subtle and not-so-subtle variations in

10 point type, 11 point linespace

The alphabet is firmly fixed in the shapes of its letters. Three-year-olds recognize letterforms. Yet there are on the order of 50,000 typefaces in existence, each different. Subtle and not-so-subtle variations in the thickness of the lines, the curves and angles, the shapes of the serifs, the relative sizes of the parts of the letters, and other design features, all add up to individualities. The alphabet is firmly fixed in the shapes of its letters. Three-year-olds recognize letterforms. Yet there are on the order of 50,000 typefaces in existence, each different. Subtle and not-so-subtle variations in the thickness of the lines, the curves and angles, the shapes of the serifs, the relative sizes of the parts of the letters, and other design features, all add up to individualities. The alphabet is firmly fixed in the shapes of its letters. Three-year-olds recognize letterforms. Yet there are on the order of 50,000 typefaces in existence, each different. Subtle and not-so-subtle variations in the thickness of the lines, the curves and angles, the shapes of the serifs, the relative sizes of the parts of the letters, and other design features, all add up to individuali-

12 point type, 13 point linespace

The alphabet is firmly fixed in the shapes of its letters. Three-year-olds recognize letterforms. Yet there are on the order of 50,000 typefaces in existence, each different. Subtle and not-so-subtle variations in the thickness of the lines, the curves and angles, the shapes of the serifs, the relative sizes of the parts of the letters, and other design features, all add up to individualities. The alphabet is firmly fixed in the shapes of its letters. Three-year-olds recognize letterforms. Yet there are on the order of 50,000 typefaces in existence, each different. Subtle and not-so-subtle variations in the thickness of the lines, the curves and angles, the shapes of the serifs, the relative sizes of the parts of the letters, and other design features, all add up to individualities. The alphabet is firmly fixed in the shapes of its letters. Three-

Fine for subheads, etc., this is an auxiliary face that can be used to good effect with any other Baskerville. Easy to read and pleasant to the eye, it can stand a lot of exposure.

ABCDEFGHIJKLMNOPQRSTUVWXYZ
abcdefghijklmnopqrstuvwxyz
0123456789&?!$%“”.,/;()

8 point type, 9 point linespace

The alphabet is firmly fixed in the shapes of its letters. Three-year-olds recognize letterforms. Yet there are on the order of 50,000 typefaces in existence, each different. Subtle and not-so-subtle variations in the thickness of the lines, the curves and angles, the shapes of the serifs, the relative sizes of the parts of the letters, and other design features, all add up to individualities. The alphabet is firmly fixed in the shapes of its letters. Three-year-olds recognize letterforms. Yet there are on the order of 50,000 typefaces in existence, each different. Subtle and not-so-subtle variations in the thickness of the lines, the curves and angles, the shapes of the serifs, the relative sizes of the parts of the letters, and other design features, all add up to individualities. The alphabet is firmly fixed in the shapes of its letters. Three-year-olds recognize letterforms. Yet there are on the order of 50,000 typefaces in existence, each different. Subtle and not-so-subtle variations in the thickness of the lines, the curves and angles, the shapes of the serifs, the relative sizes of the parts of the letters, and other design features, all add up to individualities. The alphabet is firmly fixed in the shapes of its letters. Three-year-olds recognize letterforms. Yet there are on the order of 50,000 typefaces in existence, each different. Subtle and not-so-subtle variations in the thickness of the lines, the curves and angles, the shapes of the serifs, the relative sizes of the parts of the letters, and other design features, all add up to individualities. The alphabet is firmly fixed in the shapes of its letters. Three-year-olds recognize letterforms. Yet there are on the order of 50,000 typefaces in existence, each different. Subtle and not-so-subtle variations in

10 point type, 11 point linespace

The alphabet is firmly fixed in the shapes of its letters. Three-year-olds recognize letterforms. Yet there are on the order of 50,000 typefaces in existence, each different. Subtle and not-so-subtle variations in the thickness of the lines, the curves and angles, the shapes of the serifs, the relative sizes of the parts of the letters, and other design features, all add up to individualities. The alphabet is firmly fixed in the shapes of its letters. Three-year-olds recognize letterforms. Yet there are on the order of 50,000 typefaces in existence, each different. Subtle and not-so-subtle variations in the thickness of the lines, the curves and angles, the shapes of the serifs, the relative sizes of the parts of the letters, and other design features, all add up to individualities. The alphabet is firmly fixed in the shapes of its letters. Three-year-olds recognize letterforms. Yet there are on the order of 50,000 typefaces in existence, each different. Subtle and not-so-subtle variations in the thickness of the lines, the curves and angles, the shapes of the serifs, the relative sizes of the parts of the letters, and other design features, all add up to individualities.

12 point type, 13 point linespace

The alphabet is firmly fixed in the shapes of its letters. Three-year-olds recognize letterforms. Yet there are on the order of 50,000 typefaces in existence, each different. Subtle and not-so-subtle variations in the thickness of the lines, the curves and angles, the shapes of the serifs, the relative sizes of the parts of the letters, and other design features, all add up to individualities. The alphabet is firmly fixed in the shapes of its letters. Three-year-olds recognize letterforms. Yet there are on the order of 50,000 typefaces in existence, each different. Subtle and not-so-subtle variations in the thickness of the lines, the curves and angles, the shapes of its letters. Three-year-olds recognize letterforms. Yet there are on the order of 50,000 typefaces in existence, each different. Subtle and not-so-subtle variations in

The lines of this face are thin, so it doesn’t stand up well below ten-point. Other than that, it is very readable, though only appropriate to certain subject matter: “old school” moralism, or ultra conservative types.

ABCDEFGHIJKLMNOPQRSTUVWXYZ
abcdefghijklmnopqrstuvwxyz
0123456789&?!$%“”.,/;()

8 point type, 9 point linespace

The alphabet is firmly fixed in the shapes of its letters. Three-year-olds recognize letterforms. Yet there are on the order of 50,000 typefaces in existence, each different. Subtle and not-so-subtle variations in the thickness of the lines, the curves and angles, the shapes of the serifs, the relative sizes of the parts of the letters, and other design features, all add up to individualities. The alphabet is firmly fixed in the shapes of its letters. Three-year-olds recognize letterforms. Yet there are on the order of 50,000 typefaces in existence, each different. Subtle and not-so-subtle variations in the thickness of the lines, the curves and angles, the shapes of the serifs, the relative sizes of the parts of the letters, and other design features, all add up to individualities. The alphabet is firmly fixed in the shapes of its letters. Three-year-olds recognize letterforms. Yet there are on the order of 50,000 typefaces in existence, each different. Subtle and not-so-subtle variations in the thickness of the lines, the curves and angles, the shapes of the serifs, the relative sizes of the parts of the letters, and other design features, all add up to individualities. The alphabet is firmly fixed in the shapes of its letters. Three-year-olds recognize letterforms. Yet there are on the order of 50,000 typefaces in existence, each different. Subtle and not-so-subtle variations in the thickness of the lines, the curves and angles, the shapes of the serifs, the relative sizes of the parts of the letters, and other design features, all add up to individualities. The alphabet is firmly fixed in the shapes of its letters. Three-year-olds recognize letterforms. Yet there are on the order of 50,000 typefaces in existence, each different. Subtle and not-so-subtle variations in the

10 point type, 11 point linespace

The alphabet is firmly fixed in the shapes of its letters. Three-year-olds recognize letterforms. Yet there are on the order of 50,000 typefaces in existence, each different. Subtle and not-so-subtle variations in the thickness of the lines, the curves and angles, the shapes of the serifs, the relative sizes of the parts of the letters, and other design features, all add up to individualities. The alphabet is firmly fixed in the shapes of its letters. Three-year-olds recognize letterforms. Yet there are on the order of 50,000 typefaces in existence, each different. Subtle and not-so-subtle variations in the thickness of the lines, the curves and angles, the shapes of the serifs, the relative sizes of the parts of the letters, and other design features, all add up to individualities. The alphabet is firmly fixed in the shapes of its letters. Three-year-olds recognize letterforms. Yet there are on the order of 50,000 typefaces in existence, each different. Subtle and not-so-subtle variations in the thickness of the lines, the curves and angles, the shapes of the serifs, the relative sizes of the parts of the letters, and other design features, all add up to individualities. The alphabet is firmly fixed in the shapes of its

12 point type, 13 point linespace

The alphabet is firmly fixed in the shapes of its letters. Three-year-olds recognize letterforms. Yet there are on the order of 50,000 typefaces in existence, each different. Subtle and not-so-subtle variations in the thickness of the lines, the curves and angles, the shapes of the serifs, the relative sizes of the parts of the letters, and other design features, all add up to individualities. The alphabet is firmly fixed in the shapes of its letters. Three-year-olds recognize letterforms. Yet there are on the order of 50,000 typefaces in existence, each different. Subtle and not-so-subtle variations in the thickness of the lines, the curves and angles, the shapes of its letters. Three-year-olds recognize letterforms. Yet there are on the order of 50,000 typefaces in existence, each different. Subtle and not-so-subtle variations in the thickness of the lines, the curves and

An excellent cut, neither overdone nor illegible. It can be used freely, even as a block of text. It actually tends to balance, to soften and offset, some of the rigidity of the roman face, so should be used some.

ABCDEFGHIJKLMNOPQRSTUVWXYZ
abcdefghijklmnopqrstuvwxyz
0123456789&?!$%“”.,/;()

8 point type, 9 point linespace

The alphabet is firmly fixed in the shapes of its letters. Three-year-olds recognize letterforms. Yet there are on the order of 50,000 typefaces in existence, each different. Subtle and not-so-subtle variations in the thickness of the lines, the curves and angles, the shapes of the serifs, the relative sizes of the parts of the letters, and other design features, all add up to individualities. The alphabet is firmly fixed in the shapes of its letters. Three-year-olds recognize letterforms. Yet there are on the order of 50,000 typefaces in existence, each different. Subtle and not-so-subtle variations in the thickness of the lines, the curves and angles, the shapes of the serifs, the relative sizes of the parts of the letters, and other design features, all add up to individualities. The alphabet is firmly fixed in the shapes of its letters. Three-year-olds recognize letterforms. Yet there are on the order of 50,000 typefaces in existence, each different. Subtle and not-so-subtle variations in the thickness of the lines, the curves and angles, the shapes of the serifs, the relative sizes of the parts of the letters, and other design features, all add up to individualities. The alphabet is firmly fixed in the shapes of its letters. Three-year-olds recognize letterforms. Yet there are on the order of 50,000 typefaces in existence, each different. Subtle and not-so-subtle variations in the thickness of the lines, the curves and angles, the shapes of the serifs, the relative sizes of the parts of the letters, and other design features, all add up to individualities. The alphabet is firmly fixed in the shapes of its

10 point type, 11 point linespace

The alphabet is firmly fixed in the shapes of its letters. Three-year-olds recognize letterforms. Yet there are on the order of 50,000 typefaces in existence, each different. Subtle and not-so-subtle variations in the thickness of the lines, the curves and angles, the shapes of the serifs, the relative sizes of the parts of the letters, and other design features, all add up to individualities. The alphabet is firmly fixed in the shapes of its letters. Three-year-olds recognize letterforms. Yet there are on the order of 50,000 typefaces in existence, each different. Subtle and not-so-subtle variations in the thickness of the lines, the curves and angles, the shapes of the serifs, the relative sizes of the parts of the letters, and other design features, all add up to individualities. The alphabet is firmly fixed in the shapes of its letters. Three-year-olds recognize letterforms. Yet there are on the the order of 50,000 typefaces in existence, each different. Subtle and not-so-subtle variations in the thickness of the lines, the curves and angles, the shapes of the

12 point type, 13 point linespace

The alphabet is firmly fixed in the shapes of its letters. Three-year-olds recognize letterforms. Yet there are on the order of 50,000 typefaces in existence, each different. Subtle and not-so-subtle variations in the thickness of the lines, the curves and angles, the shapes of the serifs, the relative sizes of the parts of the letters, and other design features, all add up to individualities. The alphabet is firmly fixed in the shapes of its letters. Three-year-olds recognize letterforms. Yet there are on the order of 50,000 typefaces in existence, each different. Subtle and not-so-subtle variations in the thickness of the lines, the curves and angles, the shapes of its letters. Three-year-olds recognize letterforms. Yet there are on the order of 50,000 typefaces

Highly contrasting stroke thicknesses make this face somewhat difficult to read and very difficult to set well, but when it is used with generous letterspacing in sizes over 11-point, it creates a sophisticated look no other face can.

ABCDEFGHIJKLMNOPQRSTUVWXYZ
abcdefghijklmnopqrstuvwxyz
0123456789&?!$%“”.,/;()

8 point type, 9 point linespace

The alphabet is firmly fixed in the shapes of its letters. Three-year-olds recognize letterforms. Yet there are on the order of 50,000 typefaces in existence, each different. Subtle and not-so-subtle variations in the thickness of the lines, the curves and angles, the shapes of the serifs, the relative sizes of the parts of the letters, and other design features, all add up to individualities. The alphabet is firmly fixed in the shapes of its letters. Three-year-olds recognize letterforms. Yet there are on the order of 50,000 typefaces in existence, each different. Subtle and not-so-subtle variations in the thickness of the lines, the curves and angles, the shapes of the serifs, the relative sizes of the parts of the letters, and other design features, all add up to individualities. The alphabet is firmly fixed in the shapes of its letters. Three-year-olds recognize letterforms. Yet there are on the order of 50,000 typefaces in existence, each different. Subtle and not-so-subtle variations in the thickness of the lines, the curves and angles, the shapes of the serifs, the relative sizes of the parts of the letters, and other design features, all add up to individualities. The alphabet is firmly fixed in the shapes of its letters. Three-year-olds recognize letterforms. Yet there are on the order of 50,000 typefaces in existence, each different. Subtle and not-so-subtle variations in the thickness of the lines, the curves and angles, the shapes of the serifs, the relative sizes of the parts of the letters, and other design features, all add up to individualities. The alphabet is firmly fixed in the shapes of its

10 point type, 11 point linespace

The alphabet is firmly fixed in the shapes of its letters. Three-year-olds recognize letterforms. Yet there are on the order of 50,000 typefaces in existence, each different. Subtle and not-so-subtle variations in the thickness of the lines, the curves and angles, the shapes of the serifs, the relative sizes of the parts of the letters, and other design features, all add up to individualities. The alphabet is firmly fixed in the shapes of its letters. Three-year-olds recognize letterforms. Yet there are on the order of 50,000 typefaces in existence, each different. Subtle and not-so-subtle variations in the thickness of the lines, the curves and angles, the shapes of the serifs, the relative sizes of the parts of the letters, and other design features, all add up to individualities. The alphabet is firmly fixed in the shapes of its letters. Three-year-olds recognize letterforms. Yet there are on the the order of 50,000 typefaces in existence, each different. Subtle and not-so-subtle variations in the thickness of the lines, the curves and angles, the

12 point type, 13 point linespace

The alphabet is firmly fixed in the shapes of its letters. Three-year-olds recognize letterforms. Yet there are on the order of 50,000 typefaces in existence, each different. Subtle and not-so-subtle variations in the thickness of the lines, the curves and angles, the shapes of the serifs, the relative sizes of the parts of the letters, and other design features, all add up to individualities. The alphabet is firmly fixed in the shapes of its letters. Three-year-olds recognize letterforms. Yet there are on the order of 50,000 typefaces in existence, each different. Subtle and not-so-subtle variations in the thickness of the lines, the curves and angles, the shapes of its letters. Three-year-olds recognize letterforms. Yet there are on the order of 50,000 typefaces

Another fine legible cut, but wider than Bodoni Book Italic, thus not as nice a balance to its roman cohort. This doesn't mix terribly well with the roman, in fact, tending to distract more than emphasize. Use sparingly, or by itself.

ABCDEFGHIJKLMNOPQRSTUVWXYZ
abcdefghijklmnopqrstuvwxyz
0123456789&?!$%“”.,/;()

8 point type, 9 point linespace

The alphabet is firmly fixed in the shapes of its letters. Three-year-olds recognize letterforms. Yet there are on the order of 50,000 typefaces in existence, each different. Subtle and not-so-subtle variations in the thickness of the lines, the curves and angles, the shapes of the serifs, the relative sizes of the parts of the letters, and other design features, all add up to individualities. The alphabet is firmly fixed in the shapes of its letters. Three-year-olds recognize letterforms. Yet there are on the order of 50,000 typefaces in existence, each different. Subtle and not-so-subtle variations in the thickness of the lines, the curves and angles, the shapes of the serifs, the relative sizes of the parts of the letters, and other design features, all add up to individualities. The alphabet is firmly fixed in the shapes of its letters. Three-year-olds recognize letterforms. Yet there are on the order of 50,000 typefaces in existence, each different. Subtle and not-so-subtle variations in the thickness of the lines, the curves and angles, the shapes of the serifs, the relative sizes of the parts of the letters, and other design features, all add up to individualities. The alphabet is firmly fixed in the shapes of its letters. Three-year-olds recognize letterforms. Yet there are on the order of 50,000 typefaces in existence, each different. Subtle and not-so-subtle variations in the thickness of the lines, the curves and angles, the shapes of the serifs, the relative sizes of the parts of the letters, and other design features, all add

10 point type, 11 point linespace

The alphabet is firmly fixed in the shapes of its letters. Three-year-olds recognize letterforms. Yet there are on the order of 50,000 typefaces in existence, each different. Subtle and not-so-subtle variations in the thickness of the lines, the curves and angles, the shapes of the serifs, the relative sizes of the parts of the letters, and other design features, all add up to individualities. The alphabet is firmly fixed in the shapes of its letters. Three-year-olds recognize letterforms. Yet there are on the order of 50,000 typefaces in existence, each different. Subtle and not-so-subtle variations in the thickness of the lines, the curves and angles, the shapes of the serifs, the relative sizes of the parts of the letters, and other design features, all add up to individualities. The alphabet is firmly fixed in the shapes of its letters. Three-year-olds recognize letterforms. Yet there are on the the order of 50,000 typefaces in existence, each different. Subtle and not-so-subtle variations in

12 point type, 13 point linespace

The alphabet is firmly fixed in the shapes of its letters. Three-year-olds recognize letterforms. Yet there are on the order of 50,000 typefaces in existence, each different. Subtle and not-so-subtle variations in the thickness of the lines, the curves and angles, the shapes of the serifs, the relative sizes of the parts of the letters, and other design features, all add up to individualities. The alphabet is firmly fixed in the shapes of its letters. Three-year-olds recognize letterforms. Yet there are on the order of 50,000 typefaces in existence, each different. Subtle and not-so-subtle variations in the thickness of the lines, the curves and angles, the shapes of its letters. Three-year-olds recognize letterforms. Yet

Heavy enough to contrast well with either Bodoni or Bodoni Book, this face rounds out the family nicely and can be used for any normal bold application. Do not try to set tightly, as it looks awkward then.

ABCDEFGHIJKLMNOPQRSTUVWXYZ

abcdefghijklmnopqrstuvwxyz

0123456789&?!$%“”.,/;()

8 point type, 9 point linespace

The alphabet is firmly fixed in the shapes of its letters. Three-year-olds recognize letterforms. Yet there are on the order of 50,000 typefaces in existence, each different. Subtle and not-so-subtle variations in the thickness of the lines, the curves and angles, the shapes of the serifs, the relative sizes of the parts of the letters, and other design features, all add up to individualities. The alphabet is firmly fixed in the shapes of its letters. Three-year-olds recognize letterforms. Yet there are on the order of 50,000 typefaces in existence, each different. Subtle and not-so-subtle variations in the thickness of the lines, the curves and angles, the shapes of the serifs, the relative sizes of the parts of the letters, and other design features, all add up to individualities. The alphabet is firmly fixed in the shapes of its letters. Three-year-olds recognize letterforms. Yet there are on the order of 50,000 typefaces in existence, each different. Subtle and not-so-subtle variations in the thickness of the lines, the curves and angles, the shapes of the serifs, the relative sizes of the parts of the letters, and other design features, all add up to individualities. The alphabet is firmly fixed in the shapes of its letters. Three-year-olds recognize letterforms. Yet there are on the order of 50,000 typefaces in existence, each different. Subtle and not-so-subtle variations in the thickness of the lines, the curves and angles, the shapes of the serifs, the relative sizes of the parts of the letters, and other design features, all add

10 point type, 11 point linespace

The alphabet is firmly fixed in the shapes of its letters. Three-year-olds recognize letterforms. Yet there are on the order of 50,000 typefaces in existence, each different. Subtle and not-so-subtle variations in the thickness of the lines, the curves and angles, the shapes of the serifs, the relative sizes of the parts of the letters, and other design features, all add up to individualities. The alphabet is firmly fixed in the shapes of its letters. Three-year-olds recognize letterforms. Yet there are on the order of 50,000 typefaces in existence, each different. Subtle and not-so-subtle variations in the thickness of the lines, the curves and angles, the shapes of the serifs, the relative sizes of the parts of the letters, and other design features, all add up to individualities. The alphabet is firmly fixed in the shapes of its letters. Three-year-olds recognize letterforms. Yet there are on the the order of 50,000 typefaces in existence, each different. Subtle and not-so-subtle variations in the thickness of

12 point type, 13 point linespace

The alphabet is firmly fixed in the shapes of its letters. Three-year-olds recognize letterforms. Yet there are on the order of 50,000 typefaces in existence, each different. Subtle and not-so-subtle variations in the thickness of the lines, the curves and angles, the shapes of the serifs, the relative sizes of the parts of the letters, and other design features, all add up to individualities. The alphabet is firmly fixed in the shapes of its letters. Three-year-olds recognize letterforms. Yet there are on the order of 50,000 typefaces in existence, each different. Subtle and not-so-subtle variations in the thickness of the lines, the curves and angles, the shapes of its letters. Three-year-olds recognize letterforms. Yet there

The least legible of the Bodonis, this face tends to look “choppy” and requires more concentration than is comfortable. It is also hard to print, and should never be used on a screened background.

ABCDEFGHIJKLMNOPQRSTUVWX
YZabcdefghijklmnopqrstuvwxyz
0123456789&?!$%“”.,/;()

8 point type, 9 point linespace

The alphabet is firmly fixed in the shapes of its letters. Three-year-olds recognize letterforms. Yet there are on the order of 50,000 typefaces in existence, each different. Subtle and not-so-subtle variations in the thickness of the lines, the curves and angles, the shapes of the serifs, the relative sizes of the parts of the letters, and other design features, all add up to individualities. The alphabet is firmly fixed in the shapes of its letters. Three-year-olds recognize letterforms. Yet there are on the order of 50,000 typefaces in existence, each different. Subtle and not-so-subtle variations in the thickness of the lines, the curves and angles, the shapes of the serifs, the relative sizes of the parts of the letters, and other design features, all add up to individualities. The alphabet is firmly fixed in the shapes of its letters. Three-year-olds recognize letterforms. Yet there are on the order of 50,000 typefaces in existence, each different. Subtle and not-so-subtle variations in the thickness of the lines, the curves and angles, the shapes of the serifs, the relative sizes of the parts of the letters, and other design features, all add up to individualities. The alphabet is firmly fixed in the shapes of its

10 point type, 11 point linespace

The alphabet is firmly fixed in the shapes of its letters. Three-year-olds recognize letterforms. Yet there are on the order of 50,000 typefaces in existence, each different. Subtle and not-so-subtle variations in the thickness of the lines, the curves and angles, the shapes of the serifs, the relative sizes of the parts of the letters, and other design features, all add up to individualities. The alphabet is firmly fixed in the shapes of its letters. Three-year-olds recognize letterforms. Yet there are on the order of 50,000 typefaces in existence, each different. Subtle and not-so-subtle variations in the thickness of the lines, the curves and angles, the shapes of the serifs, the relative sizes of the parts of the letters, and other design features, all add up to individualities. The alphabet is

12 point type, 13 point linespace

The alphabet is firmly fixed in the shapes of its letters. Three-year-olds recognize letterforms. Yet there are on the order of 50,000 typefaces in existence, each different. Subtle and not-so-subtle variations in the thickness of the lines, the curves and angles, the shapes of the serifs, the relative sizes of the parts of the letters, and other design features, all add up to individualities. The alphabet is firmly fixed in the shapes of its letters. Three-year-olds recognize letterforms. Yet there are on the order of 50,000 typefaces in existence, each different. Subtle

The time to use this face is self-evident. Big, bold, obvious and obviously frivolous, Bodoni Poster is a circus poster face, and occasionally very useful.

ABCDEFGHIJKLMNOPQRSTUVWX YZabcdefghijklmnopqrstuvwxyz 0123456789&?!$%“”.,/;()

8 point type, 9 point linespace

The alphabet is firmly fixed in the shapes of its letters. Three-year-olds recognize letterforms. Yet there are on the order of 50,000 typefaces in existence, each different. Subtle and not-so-subtle variations in the thickness of the lines, the curves and angles, the shapes of the serifs, the relative sizes of the parts of the letters, and other design features, all add up to individualities. The alphabet is firmly fixed in the shapes of its letters. Three-year-olds recognize letterforms. Yet there are on the order of 50,000 typefaces in existence, each different. Subtle and not-so-subtle variations in the thickness of the lines, the curves and angles, the shapes of the serifs, the relative sizes of the parts of the letters, and other design features, all add up to individualities. The alphabet is firmly fixed in the shapes of its letters. Three-year-olds recognize letterforms. Yet there are on the order of 50,000 typefaces in existence, each different. Subtle and not-so-subtle variations in the thickness of the lines, the curves and angles, the shapes of the serifs, the relative sizes of the parts of the letters, and other design features, all add up to individualities. The alphabet is firmly fixed in

10 point type, 11 point linespace

The alphabet is firmly fixed in the shapes of its letters. Three-year-olds recognize letterforms. Yet there are on the order of 50,000 typefaces in existence, each different. Subtle and not-so-subtle variations in the thickness of the lines, the curves and angles, the shapes of the serifs, the relative sizes of the parts of the letters, and other design features, all add up to individualities. The alphabet is firmly fixed in the shapes of its letters. Three-year-olds recognize letterforms. Yet there are on the order of 50,000 typefaces in existence, each different. Subtle and not-so-subtle variations in the thickness of the lines, the curves and angles, the shapes of the serifs, the relative sizes of the parts of the letters, and other design features, all add up to indi-

12 point type, 13 point linespace

The alphabet is firmly fixed in the shapes of its letters. Three-year-olds recognize letterforms. Yet there are on the order of 50,000 typefaces in existence, each different. Subtle and not-so-subtle variations in the thickness of the lines, the curves and angles, the shapes of the serifs, the relative sizes of the parts of the letters, and other design features, all add up to individualities. The alphabet is firmly fixed in the shapes of its letters. Three-year-olds recognize letterforms. Yet there are on the order of 50,000 typefaces in existence, each different. Subtle

A necessary complement to the roman, this italic does not come across well in huge posters, but works at smaller sizes, up to 72 points or so.

ABCDEFGHIJKLMNOPQRSTUVWXYZ
abcdefghijklmnopqrstuvwxyz
0123456789&?!$%“”.,/;()

8 point type, 9 point linespace

The alphabet is firmly fixed in the shapes of its letters. Three-year-olds recognize letterforms. Yet there are on the order of 50,000 typefaces in existence, each different. Subtle and not-so-subtle variations in the thickness of the lines, the curves and angles, the shapes of the serifs, the relative sizes of the parts of the letters, and other design features, all add up to individualities. The alphabet is firmly fixed in the shapes of its letters. Three-year-olds recognize letterforms. Yet there are on the order of 50,000 typefaces in existence, each different. Subtle and not-so-subtle variations in the thickness of the lines, the curves and angles, the shapes of the serifs, the relative sizes of the parts of the letters, and other design features, all add up to individualities. The alphabet is firmly fixed in the shapes of its letters. Three-year-olds recognize letterforms. Yet there are on the order of 50,000 typefaces in existence, each different. Subtle and not-so-subtle variations in the thickness of the lines, the curves and angles, the shapes of the serifs, the relative sizes of the parts of the letters, and other design features, all add up to individualities. The alphabet is firmly fixed in the shapes of its letters. Three-year-olds recognize letterforms. Yet there are on the order of 50,000 typefaces in existence, each different. Subtle and not-so-subtle variations in the thickness of the lines, the curves and angles, the shapes of the serifs, the relative sizes of the parts of the letters, and other design features, all add up to individualities. The alphabet is firmly

10 point type, 11 point linespace

The alphabet is firmly fixed in the shapes of its letters. Three-year-olds recognize letterforms. Yet there are on the order of 50,000 typefaces in existence, each different. Subtle and not-so subtle variations in the thickness of the lines, the curves and angles, the shapes of the serifs, the relative sizes of the parts of the letters, and other design features, all add up to individualities. The alphabet is firmly fixed in the shapes of its letters. Three-year-olds recognize letterforms. Yet there are on the order of 50,000 typefaces in existence, each different. Subtle and not-so-subtle variations in the thickness of the lines, the curves and angles, the shapes of the serifs, the relative sizes of the parts of the letters, and other design features, all add up to individualities. The alphabet is firmly fixed in the shapes of its letters. Three-year-olds recognize letterforms. Yet there are on the order of 50,000 typefaces in existence, each different. Subtle and not-so-subtle variations in the thick-ness of the lines, the curves and angles, the

12 point type, 13 point linespace

The alphabet is firmly fixed in the shapes of its letters. Three-year-olds recognize letterforms. Yet there are on the order of 50,000 typefaces in existence, each differ-ent. Subtle and not-so-subtle variations in the thickness of the lines, the curves and angles, the shapes of the serifs, the relative sizes of the parts of the letters, and other design features, all add up to individuali-ties. The alphabet is firmly fixed in the shapes of its letters. Three-year-olds recognize letterforms. Yet there are on the order of 50,000 typefaces in existence, each different. Subtle and not-so-subtle variations in the thickness of the lines, the curves and angles, the shapes of the serifs, the relative sizes of the parts of the letters, and other design features, all add up to

The main reason for this face to exist is purely a graphic consideration: sometimes a lighter face is needed to work in a design. It is not as legible as the Book weight, or cut as nicely.

ABCDEFGHIJKLMNOPQRSTUVWXYZ
abcdefghijklmnopqrstuvwxyz
0123456789&?!$%“”.,/;()

8 point type, 9 point linespace

The alphabet is firmly fixed in the shapes of its letters. Three-year-olds recognize letterforms. Yet there are on the order of 50,000 typefaces in existence, each different. Subtle and not-so-subtle variations in the thickness of the lines, the curves and angles, the shapes of the serifs, the relative sizes of the parts of the letters, and other design features, all add up to individualities. The alphabet is firmly fixed in the shapes of its letters. Three-year-olds recognize letterforms. Yet there are on the order of 50,000 typefaces in existence, each different. Subtle and not-so-subtle variations in the thickness of the lines, the curves and angles, the shapes of the serifs, the relative sizes of the parts of the letters, and other design features, all add up to individualities. The alphabet is firmly fixed in the shapes of its letters. Three-year-olds recognize letterforms. Yet there are on the order of 50,000 typefaces in existence, each different. Subtle and not-so-subtle variations in the thickness of the lines, the curves and angles, the shapes of the serifs, the relative sizes of the parts of the letters, and other design features, all add up to individualities. The alphabet is firmly fixed in the shapes of its letters. Three-year-olds recognize letterforms. Yet there are on the order of 50,000 typefaces in existence, each different. Subtle and not-so-subtle variations in the thickness of the lines, the curves and angles, the shapes of the serifs, the relative sizes of the parts of the letters, and other design features,

10 point type, 11 point linespace

The alphabet is firmly fixed in the shapes of its letters. Three-year-olds recognize letterforms. Yet there are on the order of 50,000 typefaces in existence, each different. Subtle and not-so-subtle variations in the thickness of the lines, the curves and angles, the shapes of the serifs, the relative sizes of the parts of the letters, and other design features, all add up to individualities. The alphabet is firmly fixed in the shapes of its letters. Three-year-olds recognize letterforms. Yet there are on the order of 50,000 typefaces in existence, each different. Subtle and not-so-subtle variations in the thickness of the lines, the curves and angles, the shapes of the serifs, the relative sizes of the parts of the letters, and other design features, all add up to individualities. The alphabet is firmly fixed in the shapes of its letters. Three-year-olds recognize letterforms. Yet there are on the order of 50,000 typefaces in existence, each different. Subtle and not-so-subtle variations in the

12 point type, 13 point linespace

The alphabet is firmly fixed in the shapes of its letters. Three-year-olds recognize letterforms. Yet there are on the order of 50,000 typefaces in existence, each different. Subtle and not-so-subtle variations in the thickness of the lines, the curves and angles, the shapes of the serifs, the relative sizes of the parts of the letters, and other design features, all add up to individualities. The alphabet is firmly fixed in the shapes of its letters. Three-year-olds recognize letterforms. Yet there are on the order of 50,000 typefaces in existence, each different. Subtle and not-so-subtle variations in the thickness of the lines, the curves and angles, the shapes of the serifs, the relative sizes of the

Very rounded, almost floral characters give this face a somewhat artificial, prettified appearance. It thus does offer a high level of contrast to the roman, but mitigates the mood, so use sparingly when combining with the roman.

ABCDEFGHIJKLMNOPQRSTUVWXYZ
abcdefghijklmnopqrstuvwxyz
0123456789&?!$%“”.,/;()

8 point type, 9 point linespace

The alphabet is firmly fixed in the shapes of its letters. Three-year-olds recognize letterforms. Yet there are on the order of 50,000 typefaces in existence, each different. Subtle and not-so-subtle variations in the thickness of the lines, the curves and angles, the shapes of the serifs, the relative sizes of the parts of the letters, and other design features, all add up to individualities. The alphabet is firmly fixed in the shapes of its letters. Three-year-olds recognize letterforms. Yet there are on the order of 50,000 typefaces in existence, each different. Subtle and not-so-subtle variations in the thickness of the lines, the curves and angles, the shapes of the serifs, the relative sizes of the parts of the letters, and other design features, all add up to individualities. The alphabet is firmly fixed in the shapes of its letters. Three-year-olds recognize letterforms. Yet there are on the order of 50,000 typefaces in existence, each different. Subtle and not-so-subtle variations in the thickness of the lines, the curves and angles, the shapes of the serifs, the relative sizes of the parts of the letters, and other design features, all add up to individualities. The alphabet is firmly fixed in the shapes of its letters. Three-year-olds recognize letterforms. Yet there are on the order of 50,000 typefaces in existence, each different. Subtle and not-so-subtle variations in the thickness of the lines, the curves and angles, the shapes of the serifs, the relative sizes of the parts of the letters, and other design features, all add up to individualities. The alphabet is firmly

10 point type, 11 point linespace

The alphabet is firmly fixed in the shapes of its letters. Three-year-olds recognize letterforms. Yet there are on the order of 50,000 typefaces in existence, each different. Subtle and not-so-subtle variations in the thickness of the lines, the curves and angles, the shapes of the serifs, the relative sizes of the parts of the letters, and other design features, all add up to individualities. The alphabet is firmly fixed in the shapes of its letters. Three-year-olds recognize letterforms. Yet there are on the order of 50,000 typefaces in existence, each different. Subtle and not-so-subtle variations in the thickness of the lines, the curves and angles, the shapes of the serifs, the relative sizes of the parts of the letters, and other design features, all add up to individualities. The alphabet is firmly fixed in the shapes of its letters. Three-year-olds recognize letterforms. Yet there are on the order of 50,000 typefaces in existence, each different. Subtle and not-so-subtle variations in the thickness of the lines, the curves and

12 point type, 13 point linespace

The alphabet is firmly fixed in the shapes of its letters. Three-year-olds recognize letterforms. Yet there are on the order of 50,000 typefaces in existence, each different. Subtle and not-so-subtle variations in the thickness of the lines, the curves and angles, the shapes of the serifs, the relative sizes of the parts of the letters, and other design features, all add up to individualities. The alphabet is firmly fixed in the shapes of its letters. Three-year-olds recognize letterforms. Yet there are on the order of 50,000 typefaces in existence, each different. Subtle and not-so-subtle variations in the thickness of the lines, the curves and angles, the shapes of the serifs, the relative sizes of the parts of the letters, and other design features, all add

Your basic workhorse of the Century family, very legible, this is the preferred face for any piece that needs a sense of life without an overly “artistic” feel. Many business brochures and reports would benefit from this face.

ABCDEFGHIJKLMNOPQRSTUVWXYZ
abcdefghijklmnopqrstuvwxyz
0123456789&?!$%“”.,/;()

8 point type, 9 point linespace

The alphabet is firmly fixed in the shapes of its letters. Three-year-olds recognize letterforms. Yet there are on the order of 50,000 typefaces in existence, each different. Subtle and not-so-subtle variations in the thickness of the lines, the curves and angles, the shapes of the serifs, the relative sizes of the parts of the letters, and other design features, all add up to individualities. The alphabet is firmly fixed in the shapes of its letters. Three-year-olds recognize letterforms. Yet there are on the order of 50,000 typefaces in existence, each different. Subtle and not-so-subtle variations in the thickness of the lines, the curves and angles, the shapes of the serifs, the relative sizes of the parts of the letters, and other design features, all add up to individualities. The alphabet is firmly fixed in the shapes of its letters. Three-year-olds recognize letterforms. Yet there are on the order of 50,000 typefaces in existence, each different. Subtle and not-so-subtle variations in the thickness of the lines, the curves and angles, the shapes of the serifs, the relative sizes of the parts of the letters, and other design features, all add up to individualities. The alphabet is firmly fixed in the shapes of its letters. Three-year-olds recognize letterforms. Yet there are on the order of 50,000 typefaces in existence, each different. Subtle and not-so-subtle variations in the thickness of the lines, the curves and angles, the shapes of the serifs, the relative sizes of the parts of the letters, and other design features,

10 point type, 11 point linespace

The alphabet is firmly fixed in the shapes of its letters. Three-year-olds recognize letterforms. Yet there are on the order of 50,000 typefaces in existence, each different. Subtle and not-so-subtle variations in the thickness of the lines, the curves and angles, the shapes of the serifs, the relative sizes of the parts of the letters, and other design features, all add up to individualities. The alphabet is firmly fixed in the shapes of its letters. Three-year-olds recognize letterforms. Yet there are on the order of 50,000 typefaces in existence, each different. Subtle and not-so-subtle variations in the thickness of the lines, the curves and angles, the shapes of the serifs, the relative sizes of the parts of the letters, and other design features, all add up to individualities. The alphabet is firmly fixed in the shapes of its letters. Three-year-olds recognize letterforms. Yet there are on the order of 50,000 typefaces in existence, each different. Subtle and not-so-subtle variations in the thickness of the

12 point type, 13 point linespace

The alphabet is firmly fixed in the shapes of its letters. Three-year-olds recognize letterforms. Yet there are on the order of 50,000 typefaces in existence, each different. Subtle and not-so-subtle variations in the thickness of the lines, the curves and angles, the shapes of the serifs, the relative sizes of the parts of the letters, and other design features, all add up to individualities. The alphabet is firmly fixed in the shapes of its letters. Three-year-olds recognize letterforms. Yet there are on the order of 50,000 typefaces in existence, each different. Subtle and not-so-subtle variations in the thickness of the lines, the curves and angles, the shapes of the serifs, the relative sizes of the

Nicely done, not so rounded as the Light Italic, this is an excellent partner to its roman. You hardly have to think about when to use this face: it feels natural in almost any situation, almost inserting itself when appropriate.

ABCDEFGHIJKLMNOPQRSTUVWXYZ
abcdefghijklmnopqrstuvwxyz
0123456789&?!$%“”.,/;()

8 point type, 9 point linespace

The alphabet is firmly fixed in the shapes of its letters. Three-year-olds recognize letterforms. Yet there are on the order of 50,000 typefaces in existence, each different. Subtle and not-so-subtle variations in the thickness of the lines, the curves and angles, the shapes of the serifs, the relative sizes of the parts of the letters, and other design features, all add up to individualities. The alphabet is firmly fixed in the shapes of its letters. Three-year-olds recognize letterforms. Yet there are on the order of 50,000 typefaces in existence, each different. Subtle and not-so subtle variations in the thickness of the lines, the curves and angles, the shapes of the serifs, the relative sizes of the parts of the letters, and other design features, all add up to individualities. The alphabet is firmly fixed in the shapes of its letters. Three-year-olds recognize letterforms. Yet there are on the order of 50,000 typefaces in existence, each different. Subtle and not-so-subtle variations in the thickness of the lines, the curves and angles, the shapes of the serifs, the relative sizes of the parts of the letters, and other design features, all add up to individualities. The alphabet is firmly fixed in the shapes of its letters. Three-year-olds recognize letterforms. Yet there are on the order of 50,000 typefaces in existence, each different. Subtle and not-so-subtle variations in the

10 point type, 11 point linespace

The alphabet is firmly fixed in the shapes of its letters. Three-year-olds recognize letterforms. Yet there are on the order of 50,000 typefaces in existence, each different. Subtle and not-so-subtle variations in the thickness of the lines, the curves and angles, the shapes of the serifs, the relative sizes of the parts of the letters, and other design features, all add up to individualities. The alphabet is firmly fixed in the shapes of its letters. Three-year-olds recognize letterforms. Yet there are on the order of 50,000 typefaces in existence, each different. Subtle and not-so-subtle variations in the thickness of the lines, the curves and angles, the shapes of the serifs, the relative sizes of the parts of the letters, and other design features, all add up to individualities. The alphabet is firmly fixed in the shapes of its letters. Three-year-olds recognize letterforms. Yet there are on the order of

12 point type, 13 point linespace

The alphabet is firmly fixed in the shapes of its letters. Three-year-olds recognize letterforms. Yet there are on the order of 50,000 typefaces in existence, each different. Subtle and not-so-subtle variations in the thickness of the lines, the curves and angles, the shapes of the serifs, the relative sizes of the parts of the letters, and other design features, all add up to individualities. The alphabet is firmly fixed in the shapes of its letters. Three-year-olds recognize letterforms. Yet there are on the order of 50,000 typefaces in existence, each different. Subtle and not-so-subtle variations in the thickness of the lines, the curves and angles,

The contrast level between Book and Bold in Century is not as high as in some faces, so a slight increase in size when using Bold in combination with Book is often appropriate to achieve maximum effect.

ABCDEFGHIJKLMNOPQRSTUVWXYZ
abcdefghijklmnopqrstuvwxyz
0123456789&?!$%"".,/;()

8 point type, 9 point linespace

The alphabet is firmly fixed in the shapes of its letters. Three-year-olds recognize letterforms. Yet there are on the order of 50,000 typefaces in existence, each different. Subtle and not-so-subtle variations in the thickness of the lines, the curves and angles, the shapes of the serifs, the relative sizes of the parts of the letters, and other design features, all add up to individualities. The alphabet is firmly fixed in the shapes of its letters. Three-year-olds recognize letterforms. Yet there are on the order of 50,000 typefaces in existence, each different. Subtle and not-so-subtle variations in the thickness of the lines, the curves and angles, the shapes of the serifs, the relative sizes of the parts of the letters, and other design features, all add up to individualities. The alphabet is firmly fixed in the shapes of its letters. Three-year-olds recognize letterforms. Yet there are on the order of 50,000 typefaces in existence, each different. Subtle and not-so-subtle variations in the thickness of the lines, the curves and angles, the shapes of the serifs, the relative sizes of the parts of the letters, and other design features, all add up to individualities. The alphabet is firmly fixed in the shapes of its letters. Three-year-olds recognize letterforms. Yet there are on the order of 50,000 typefaces in existence, each different. Subtle and not-

10 point type, 11 point linespace

The alphabet is firmly fixed in the shapes of its letters. Three-year-olds recognize letterforms. Yet there are on the order of 50,000 typefaces in existence, each different. Subtle and not-so-subtle variations in the thickness of the lines, the curves and angles, the shapes of the serifs, the relative sizes of the parts of the letters, and other design features, all add up to individualities. The alphabet is firmly fixed in the shapes of its letters. Three-year-olds recognize letterforms. Yet there are on the order of 50,000 typefaces in existence, each different. Subtle and not-so-subtle variations in the thickness of the lines, the curves and angles, the shapes of the serifs, the relative sizes of the parts of the letters, and other design features, all add up to individualities. The alphabet is firmly fixed in the shapes of its letters. Three-year-olds recognize letterforms. Yet there are on the

12 point type, 13 point linespace

The alphabet is firmly fixed in the shapes of its letters. Three-year-olds recognize letterforms. Yet there are on the order of 50,000 typefaces in existence, each different. Subtle and not-so-subtle variations in the thickness of the lines, the curves and angles, the shapes of the serifs, the relative sizes of the parts of the letters, and other design features, all add up to individualities. The alphabet is firmly fixed in the shapes of its letters. Three-year-olds recognize letterforms. Yet there are on the order of 50,000 typefaces in existence, each different. Subtle and not-so-subtle variations in the thickness of the lines, the curves and angles,

As well cut and easy to use as the Book Italic. This face also stands well alone, as a headline or introductory line. In fact, it is one of the very few usable bold italic serif faces.

ABCDEFGHIJKLMNOPQRSTUVWX
YZabcdefghijklmnopqrstuvwxyz
0123456789&?!$%“”.,/;()

8 point type, 9 point linespace

The alphabet is firmly fixed in the shapes of its letters. Three-year-olds recognize letterforms. Yet there are on the order of 50,000 typefaces in existence, each different. Subtle and not-so-subtle variations in the thickness of the lines, the curves and angles, the shapes of the serifs, the relative sizes of the parts of the letters, and other design features, all add up to individualities. The alphabet is firmly fixed in the shapes of its letters. Three-year-olds recognize letterforms. Yet there are on the order of 50,000 typefaces in existence, each different. Subtle and not-so-subtle variations in the thickness of the lines, the curves and angles, the shapes of the serifs, the relative sizes of the parts of the letters, and other design features, all add up to individualities. The alphabet is firmly fixed in the shapes of its letters. Three-year-olds recognize letterforms. Yet there are on the order of 50,000 typefaces in existence, each different. Subtle and not-so-subtle variations in the thickness of the lines, the curves and angles, the shapes of the serifs, the relative sizes of the parts of the letters, and other design features, all add up to

10 point type, 11 point linespace

The alphabet is firmly fixed in the shapes of its letters. Three-year-olds recognize letterforms. Yet there are on the order of 50,000 typefaces in existence, each different. Subtle and not-so-subtle variations in the thickness of the lines, the curves and angles, the shapes of the serifs, the relative sizes of the parts of the letters, and other design features, all add up to individualities. The alphabet is firmly fixed in the shapes of its letters. Three-year-olds recognize letterforms. Yet there are on the order of 50,000 typefaces in existence, each different. Subtle and not-so-subtle variations in the thickness of the lines, the curves and angles, the shapes of the serifs, the relative sizes of the parts of the letters, and other design features, all add up to

12 point type, 13 point linespace

The alphabet is firmly fixed in the shapes of its letters. Three-year-olds recognize letterforms. Yet there are on the order of 50,000 typefaces in existence, each different. Subtle and not-so-subtle variations in the thickness of the lines, the curves and angles, the shapes of the serifs, the relative sizes of the parts of the letters, and other design features, all add up to individualities. The alphabet is firmly fixed in the shapes of its letters. Three-year-olds recognize letterforms. Yet there are on the order of 50,000 type-

Ridiculously more heavy than the Bold weight, this face almost loses its Century features. It can be used to accent other Centurys, but is very hard to set well on its own. To be avoided.

ABCDEFGHIJKLMNOPQRSTUVWX YZabcdefghijklmnopqrstuvwxyz 0123456789&?!$%“”.,/;()

8 point type, 9 point linespace

The alphabet is firmly fixed in the shapes of its letters. Three-year-olds recognize letterforms. Yet there are on the order of 50,000 typefaces in existence, each different. Subtle and not-so-subtle variations in the thickness of the lines, the curves and angles, the shapes of the serifs, the relative sizes of the parts of the letters, and other design features, all add up to individualities. The alphabet is firmly fixed in the shapes of its letters. Three-year-olds recognize letterforms. Yet there are on the order of 50,000 typefaces in existence, each different. Subtle and not-so-subtle variations in the thickness of the lines, the curves and angles, the shapes of the serifs, the relative sizes of the parts of the letters, and other design features, all add up to individualities. The alphabet is firmly fixed in the shapes of its letters. Three-year-olds recognize letterforms. Yet there are on the order of 50,000 typefaces in existence, each different. Subtle and not-so-subtle variations in the thickness of the lines, the curves and angles, the shapes of the serifs, the relative sizes of the parts of the letters, and other design features, all add up to

10 point type, 11 point linespace

The alphabet is firmly fixed in the shapes of its letters. Three-year-olds recognize letterforms. Yet there are on the order of 50,000 typefaces in existence, each different. Subtle and not-so-subtle variations in the thickness of the lines, the curves and angles, the shapes of the serifs, the relative sizes of the parts of the letters, and other design features, all add up to individualities. The alphabet is firmly fixed in the shapes of its letters. Three-year-olds recognize letterforms. Yet there are on the order of 50,000 typefaces in existence, each different. Subtle and not-so-subtle variations in the thickness of the lines, the curves and angles, the shapes of the serifs, the relative sizes of the parts of the letters, and other design features, all add up to

12 point type, 13 point linespace

The alphabet is firmly fixed in the shapes of its letters. Three-year-olds recognize letterforms. Yet there are on the order of 50,000 typefaces in existence, each different. Subtle and not-so-subtle variations in the thickness of the lines, the curves and angles, the shapes of the serifs, the relative sizes of the parts of the letters, and other design features, all add up to individualities. The alphabet is firmly fixed in the shapes of its letters. Three-year-olds recognize letterforms. Yet there are on the order of 50,000 typefaces in

This is almost a “toss-off,” created to fill the series. There is no practical application for it that springs to mind, though any face might find a place in a design concept somewhere.

ABCDEFGHIJKLMNOPQRSTUVWXYZ
abcdefghijklmnopqrstuvwxyz
0123456789&?!$%“”.,/;()

8 point type, 9 point linespace

The alphabet is firmly fixed in the shapes of its letters. Three-year-olds recognize letterforms. Yet there are on the order of 50,000 typefaces in existence, each different. Subtle and not-so-subtle variations in the thickness of the lines, the curves and angles, the shapes of the serifs, the relative sizes of the parts of the letters, and other design features, all add up to individualities. The alphabet is firmly fixed in the shapes of its letters. Three-year-olds recognize letterforms. Yet there are on the order of 50,000 typefaces in existence, each different. Subtle and not-so-subtle variations in the thickness of the lines, the curves and angles, the shapes of the serifs, the relative sizes of the parts of the letters, and other design features, all add up to individualities. The alphabet is firmly fixed in the shapes of its letters. Three-year-olds recognize letterforms. Yet there are on the order of 50,000 typefaces in existence, each different. Subtle and not-so-subtle variations in the thickness of the lines, the curves and angles, the shapes of the serifs, the relative sizes of the parts of the letters, and other design features, all add up to individualities. The alphabet is firmly fixed in the shapes of its letters. Three-year-olds recognize letterforms. Yet there are on the order of 50,000 typefaces in existence, each different. Subtle and not-so-subtle variations in the thickness of the lines, the curves and angles, the shapes of the serifs, the relative sizes of the parts of the letters, and other design features, all add up to individualities. The alphabet is firmly fixed in the shapes of its letters. Three-year-olds recognize letterforms. Yet there are on the order

10 point type, 11 point linespace

The alphabet is firmly fixed in the shapes of its letters. Three-year-olds recognize letterforms. Yet there are on the order of 50,000 typefaces in existence, each different. Subtle and not-so-subtle variations in the thickness of the lines, the curves and angles, the shapes of the serifs, the relative sizes of the parts of the letters, and other design features, all add up to individualities. The alphabet is firmly fixed in the shapes of its letters. Three-year-olds recognize letterforms. Yet there are on the order of 50,000 typefaces in existence, each different. Subtle and not-so-subtle variations in the thickness of the lines, the curves and angles, the shapes of the serifs, the relative sizes of the parts of the letters, and other design features, all add up to individualities. The alphabet is firmly fixed in the shapes of its letters. Three-year-olds recognize letterforms. Yet there are on the order of 50,000 typefaces in existence, each different. Subtle and not-so-subtle variations in the thickness of the lines, the curves and angles, the shapes of the serifs, the relative sizes of the parts of

12 point type, 13 point linespace

The alphabet is firmly fixed in the shapes of its letters. Three-year-olds recognize letterforms. Yet there are on the order of 50,000 typefaces in existence, each different. Subtle and not-so-subtle variations in the thickness of the lines, the curves and angles, the shapes of the serifs, the relative sizes of the parts of the letters, and other design features, all add up to individualities. The alphabet is firmly fixed in the shapes of its letters. Three-year-olds recognize letterforms. Yet there are on the order of 50,000 typefaces in existence, each different. Subtle and not-so-subtle variations in the thickness of the lines, the curves and angles, the shapes of the serifs, the relative sizes of the parts of the letters, and other design features, all add up to individualities. The

This face differs from most serif faces by an added artsiness, in this case done effectively. Little bulbs, loops and protrusions make it less formal, rather friendly in fact, without hurting legibility.

ABCDEFGHIJKLMNOPQRSTUVWXYZ
abcdefghijklmnopqrstuvwxyz
0123456789&?!$%“”.,/;()

8 point type, 9 point linespace

The alphabet is firmly fixed in the shapes of its letters. Three-year-olds recognize letterforms. Yet there are on the order of 50,000 typefaces in existence, each different. Subtle and not-so-subtle variations in the thickness of the lines, the curves and angles, the shapes of the serifs, the relative sizes of the parts of the letters, and other design features, all add up to individualities. The alphabet is firmly fixed in the shapes of its letters. Three-year-olds recognize letterforms. Yet there are on the order of 50,000 typefaces in existence, each different. Subtle and not-so-subtle variations in the thickness of the lines, the curves and angles, the shapes of the serifs, the relative sizes of the parts of the letters, and other design features, all add up to individualities. The alphabet is firmly fixed in the shapes of its letters. Three-year-olds recognize letterforms. Yet there are on the order of 50,000 typefaces in existence, each different. Subtle and not-so-subtle variations in the thickness of the lines, the curves and angles, the shapes of the serifs, the relative sizes of the parts of the letters, and other design features, all add up to individualities. The alphabet is firmly fixed in the shapes of its letters. Three-year-olds recognize letterforms. Yet there are on the order of 50,000 typefaces in existence, each different. Subtle and not-so-subtle variations in the thickness of the lines, the curves and angles, the shapes of the serifs, the relative sizes of the parts of the letters, and other design features, all add up to individualities. The alphabet is firmly fixed in the shapes of its letters. Three-year-olds recognize letterforms. Yet there are

10 point type, 11 point linespace

The alphabet is firmly fixed in the shapes of its letters. Three-year-olds recognize letterforms. Yet there are on the order of 50,000 typefaces in existence, each different. Subtle and not-so-subtle variations in the thickness of the lines, the curves and angles, the shapes of the serifs, the relative sizes of the parts of the letters, and other design features, all add up to individualities. The alphabet is firmly fixed in the shapes of its letters. Three-year-olds recognize letterforms. Yet there are on the order of 50,000 typefaces in existence, each different. Subtle and not-so-subtle variations in the thickness of the lines, the curves and angles, the shapes of the serifs, the relative sizes of the parts of the letters, and other design features, all add up to individualities. The alphabet is firmly fixed in the shapes of its letters. Three-year-olds recognize letterforms. Yet there are on the order of 50,000 typefaces in existence, each different. Subtle and not-so-subtle variations in the thickness of the lines, the curves and angles, the shapes of the serifs, the relative sizes of the parts of

12 point type, 13 point linespace

The alphabet is firmly fixed in the shapes of its letters. Three-year-olds recognize letterforms. Yet there are on the order of 50,000 typefaces in existence, each different. Subtle and not-so-subtle variations in the thickness of the lines, the curves and angles, the shapes of the serifs, the relative sizes of the parts of the letters, and other design features, all add up to individualities. The alphabet is firmly fixed in the shapes of its letters. Three-year-olds recognize letterforms. Yet there are on the order of 50,000 typefaces in existence, each different. Subtle and not-so-subtle variations in the thickness of the lines, the curves and angles, the shapes of the serifs, the relative sizes of the parts of the letters, and other design features, all add up to individualities. The

In high contrast to the roman, with a greater slant than most italics and significant changes to serif treatment, this italic both works well with the roman and can stand on its own.

ABCDEFGHIJKLMNOPQRSTUVWXYZ
abcdefghijklmnopqrstuvwxyz
0123456789&?!$%“”.,/;()

8 point type, 9 point linespace

The alphabet is firmly fixed in the shapes of its letters. Three-year-olds recognize letterforms. Yet there are on the order of 50,000 typefaces in existence, each different. Subtle and not-so-subtle variations in the thickness of the lines, the curves and angles, the shapes of the serifs, the relative sizes of the parts of the letters, and other design features, all add up to individualities. The alphabet is firmly fixed in the shapes of its letters. Three-year-olds recognize letterforms. Yet there are on the order of 50,000 typefaces in existence, each different. Subtle and not-so-subtle variations in the thickness of the lines, the curves and angles, the shapes of the serifs, the relative sizes of the parts of the letters, and other design features, all add up to individualities. The alphabet is firmly fixed in the shapes of its letters. Three-year-olds recognize letterforms. Yet there are on the order of 50,000 typefaces in existence, each different. Subtle and not-so-subtle variations in the thickness of the lines, the curves and angles, the shapes of the serifs, the relative sizes of the parts of the letters, and other design features, all add up to individualities. The alphabet is firmly fixed in the shapes of its letters. Three-year-olds recognize letterforms. Yet there are on the order of 50,000 typefaces in existence, each different. Subtle and not-so-subtle variations in the thickness of the lines, the curves and angles, the shapes of the serifs, the relative sizes of the parts of the letters, and other design features, all add up to individualities. The alphabet is firmly fixed in the shapes of its letters. Three-year-olds recognize letterforms. Yet there are on

10 point type, 11 point linespace

The alphabet is firmly fixed in the shapes of its letters. Three-year-olds recognize letterforms. Yet there are on the order of 50,000 typefaces in existence, each different. Subtle and not-so-subtle variations in the thickness of the lines, the curves and angles, the shapes of the serifs, the relative sizes of the parts of the letters, and other design features, all add up to individualities. The alphabet is firmly fixed in the shapes of its letters. Three-year-olds recognize letterforms. Yet there are on the order of 50,000 typefaces in existence, each different. Subtle and not-so-subtle variations in the thickness of the lines, the curves and angles, the shapes of the serifs, the relative sizes of the parts of the letters, and other design features, all add up to individualities. The alphabet is firmly fixed in the shapes of its letters. Three-year-olds recognize letterforms. Yet there are on the order of 50,000 typefaces in existence, each different. Subtle and not-so-subtle variations in the thickness of the lines, the curves and angles, the shapes of the serifs, the relative sizes of the parts of

12 point type, 13 point linespace

The alphabet is firmly fixed in the shapes of its letters. Three-year-olds recognize letterforms. Yet there are on the order of 50,000 typefaces in existence, each different. Subtle and not-so-subtle variations in the thickness of the lines, the curves and angles, the shapes of the serifs, the relative sizes of the parts of the letters, and other design features, all add up to individualities. The alphabet is firmly fixed in the shapes of its letters. Three-year-olds recognize letterforms. Yet there are on the order of 50,000 typefaces in existence, each different. Subtle and not-so-subtle variations in the thickness of the lines, the curves and angles, the shapes of the serifs, the relative sizes of the parts of the letters, and other design features, all add up to individualities. The

The difference in weight between this and the Regular is not terribly pronounced, which means it can be used for emphasizing against the Regular just as well as a Regular Italic can. This doubles the flexibility of this family automatically.

ABCDEFGHIJKLMNOPQRSTUVWXYZ
abcdefghijklmnopqrstuvwxyz
0123456789&?!$%“”.,/;()

8 point type, 9 point linespace

The alphabet is firmly fixed in the shapes of its letters. Three-year-olds recognize letterforms. Yet there are on the order of 50,000 typefaces in existence, each different. Subtle and not-so-subtle variations in the thickness of the lines, the curves and angles, the shapes of the serifs, the relative sizes of the parts of the letters, and other design features, all add up to individualities. The alphabet is firmly fixed in the shapes of its letters. Three-year-olds recognize letterforms. Yet there are on the order of 50,000 typefaces in existence, each different. Subtle and not-so-subtle variations in the thickness of the lines, the curves and angles, the shapes of the serifs, the relative sizes of the parts of the letters, and other design features, all add up to individualities. The alphabet is firmly fixed in the shapes of its letters. Three-year-olds recognize letterforms. Yet there are on the order of 50,000 typefaces in existence, each different. Subtle and not-so-subtle variations in the thickness of the lines, the curves and angles, the shapes of the serifs, the relative sizes of the parts of the letters, and other design features, all add up to individualities. The alphabet is firmly fixed in the shapes of its letters. Three-year-olds recognize letterforms. Yet there are on the order of 50,000 typefaces in existence, each different. Subtle and not-so-subtle variations in the shapes of the serifs, the relative sizes of the parts of the letters, and other design features, all add up to individualities. The alphabet is firmly fixed in the shapes of its letters. Three-year-olds recognize letterforms. Yet there are on the order of 50,000 typefaces in

10 point type, 11 point linespace

The alphabet is firmly fixed in the shapes of its letters. Three-year-olds recognize letterforms. Yet there are on the order of 50,000 typefaces in existence, each different. Subtle and not-so-subtle variations in the thickness of the lines, the curves and angles, the shapes of the serifs, the relative sizes of the parts of the letters, and other design features, all add up to individualities. The alphabet is firmly fixed in the shapes of its letters. Three-year-olds recognize letterforms. Yet there are on the order of 50,000 typefaces in existence, each different. Subtle and not-so-subtle variations in the thickness of the lines, the curves and angles, the shapes of the serifs, the relative sizes of the parts of the letters, and other design features, all add up to individualities. The alphabet is firmly fixed in the shapes of its letters. Three-year-olds recognize letterforms. Yet there are on the order of 50,000 typefaces in existence, each different. Subtle and not-so-subtle variations in the thickness of the lines, the curves and angles, the shapes of the serifs, the relative sizes of the parts of

12 point type, 13 point linespace

The alphabet is firmly fixed in the shapes of its letters. Three-year-olds recognize letterforms. Yet there are on the order of 50,000 typefaces in existence, each different. Subtle and not-so-subtle variations in the thickness of the lines, the curves and angles, the shapes of the serifs, the relative sizes of the parts of the letters, and other design features, all add up to individualities. The alphabet is firmly fixed in the shapes of its letters. Three-year-olds recognize letterforms. Yet there are on the order of 50,000 typefaces in existence, each different. Subtle and not-so-subtle variations in the thickness of the lines, the curves and angles, the shapes of the serifs, the relative sizes of the parts of the letters, and other design features, all add up to individualities. The

The designer never falters in this family: the Bold Italic mixes with all its siblings of equal or lighter weight without acrimony. This principle applies to each of the italics in the family—mix down, not up.

ABCDEFGHIJKLMNOPQRSTUVWXYZ
abcdefghijklmnopqrstuvwxyz
0123456789&?!$%“”.,/;()

8 point type, 9 point linespace

The alphabet is firmly fixed in the shapes of its letters. Three-year-olds recognize letterforms. Yet there are on the order of 50,000 typefaces in existence, each different. Subtle and not-so-subtle variations in the thickness of the lines, the curves and angles, the shapes of the serifs, the relative sizes of the parts of the letters, and other design features, all add up to individualities. The alphabet is firmly fixed in the shapes of its letters. Three-year-olds recognize letterforms. Yet there are on the order of 50,000 typefaces in existence, each different. Subtle and not-so-subtle variations in the thickness of the lines, the curves and angles, the shapes of the serifs, the relative sizes of the parts of the letters, and other design features, all add up to individualities. The alphabet is firmly fixed in the shapes of its letters. Three-year-olds recognize letterforms. Yet there are on the order of 50,000 typefaces in existence, each different. Subtle and not-so-subtle variations in the thickness of the lines, the curves and angles, the shapes of the serifs, the relative sizes of the parts of the letters, and other design features, all add up to individualities. The alphabet is firmly fixed in the shapes of its letters. Three-year-olds recognize letterforms. Yet there are on the order of 50,000 typefaces in existence, each different. Subtle and not-so-subtle variations in the thickness of the lines, the curves and angles, the shapes of the serifs, the relative sizes of the parts of the letters, and other design features, all add up to individualities. The alphabet is firmly fixed in the shapes of its

10 point type, 11 point linespace

The alphabet is firmly fixed in the shapes of its letters. Three-year-olds recognize letterforms. Yet there are on the order of 50,000 typefaces in existence, each different. Subtle and not-so-subtle variations in the thickness of the lines, the curves and angles, the shapes of the serifs, the relative sizes of the parts of the letters, and other design features, all add up to individualities. The alphabet is firmly fixed in the shapes of its letters. Three-year-olds recognize letterforms. Yet there are on the order of 50,000 typefaces in existence, each different. Subtle and not-so-subtle variations in the thickness of the lines, the curves and angles, the shapes of the serifs, the relative sizes of the parts of the letters, and other design features, all add up to individualities. The alphabet is firmly fixed in the shapes of its letters. Three-year-olds recognize letterforms. Yet there are on the order of 50,000 typefaces in existence, each different. Subtle and not-so-subtle variations in the thickness of the lines, the curves and angles, the shapes of the

12 point type, 13 point linespace

The alphabet is firmly fixed in the shapes of its letters. Three-year-olds recognize letterforms. Yet there are on the order of 50,000 typefaces in existence, each different. Subtle and not-so-subtle variations in the thickness of the lines, the curves and angles, the shapes of the serifs, the relative sizes of the parts of the letters, and other design features, all add up to individualities. The alphabet is firmly fixed in the shapes of its letters. Three-year-olds recognize letterforms. Yet there are on the order of 50,000 typefaces in existence, each different. Subtle and not-so-subtle variations in the thickness of the lines, the curves and angles, the shapes of the serifs, the relative sizes of the parts of the letters, and other design features, all add up to individualities.

One of the better serif headline faces, balancing light and dark in its design so it flows well. The overall narrowness of the Clearface family allows an economy of white space in the heavier weights, and the design invites close letterspacing.

ABCDEFGHIJKLMNOPQRSTUVWXYZ
abcdefghijklmnopqrstuvwxyz
0123456789&?!$%“”.,/;()

8 point type, 9 point linespace

The alphabet is firmly fixed in the shapes of its letters. Three-year-olds recognize letterforms. Yet there are on the order of 50,000 typefaces in existence, each different. Subtle and not-so-subtle variations in the thickness of the lines, the curves and angles, the shapes of the serifs, the relative sizes of the parts of the letters, and other design features, all add up to individualities. The alphabet is firmly fixed in the shapes of its letters. Three-year-olds recognize letterforms. Yet there are on the order of 50,000 typefaces in existence, each different. Subtle and not-so-subtle variations in the thickness of the lines, the curves and angles, the shapes of the serifs, the relative sizes of the parts of the letters, and other design features, all add up to individualities. The alphabet is firmly fixed in the shapes of its letters. Three-year-olds recognize letterforms. Yet there are on the order of 50,000 typefaces in existence, each different. Subtle and not-so-subtle variations in the thickness of the lines, the curves and angles, the shapes of the serifs, the relative sizes of the parts of the letters, and other design features, all add up to individualities. The alphabet is firmly fixed in the shapes of its letters. Three-year-olds recognize letterforms. Yet there are on the order of 50,000 typefaces in existence, each different. Subtle and not-so-subtle variations in the thickness of the lines, the curves and angles, the shapes of the serifs, the relative sizes of the parts of the letters, and other design features, all add up to individualities. The alphabet is firmly fixed in the

10 point type, 11 point linespace

The alphabet is firmly fixed in the shapes of its letters. Three-year-olds recognize letterforms. Yet there are on the order of 50,000 typefaces in existence, each different. Subtle and not-so-subtle variations in the thickness of the lines, the curves and angles, the shapes of the serifs, the relative sizes of the parts of the letters, and other design features, all add up to individualities. The alphabet is firmly fixed in the shapes of its letters. Three-year-olds recognize letterforms. Yet there are on the order of 50,000 typefaces in existence, each different. Subtle and not-so-subtle variations in the thickness of the lines, the curves and angles, the shapes of the serifs, the relative sizes of the parts of the letters, and other design features, all add up to individualities. The alphabet is firmly fixed in the shapes of its letters. Three-year-olds recognize letterforms. Yet there are on the order of 50,000 typefaces in existence, each different. Subtle and not-so-subtle variations in the thickness of the lines, the curves and angles, the shapes

12 point type, 13 point linespace

The alphabet is firmly fixed in the shapes of its letters. Three-year-olds recognize letterforms. Yet there are on the order of 50,000 typefaces in existence, each different. Subtle and not-so-subtle variations in the thickness of the lines, the curves and angles, the shapes of the serifs, the relative sizes of the parts of the letters, and other design features, all add up to individualities. The alphabet is firmly fixed in the shapes of its letters. Three-year-olds recognize letterforms. Yet there are on the order of 50,000 typefaces in existence, each different. Subtle and not-so-subtle variations in the thickness of the lines, the curves and angles, the shapes of the serifs, the relative sizes of the parts of the letters, and other design features, all add up to

You can make a dramatic entrance with this face! What is especially nice about this and Clearface Heavy is that they can both be used in a wide size range, from 8-point on up.

ABCDEFGHIJKLMNOPQRSTUVWXYZ
abcdefghijklmnopqrstuvwxyz
0123456789&?!$%“”.,/;()

8 point type, 9 point linespace

The alphabet is firmly fixed in the shapes of its letters. Three-year-olds recognize letterforms. Yet there are on the order of 50,000 typefaces in existence, each different. Subtle and not-so-subtle variations in the thickness of the lines, the curves and angles, the shapes of the serifs, the relative sizes of the parts of the letters, and other design features, all add up to individualities. The alphabet is firmly fixed in the shapes of its letters. Three-year-olds recognize letterforms. Yet there are on the order of 50,000 typefaces in existence, each different. Subtle and not-so-subtle variations in the thickness of the lines, the curves and angles, the shapes of the serifs, the relative sizes of the parts of the letters, and other design features, all add up to individualities. The alphabet is firmly fixed in the shapes of its letters. Three-year-olds recognize letterforms. Yet there are on the order of 50,000 typefaces in existence, each different. Subtle and not-so-subtle variations in the thickness of the lines, the curves and angles, the shapes of the serifs, the relative sizes of the parts of the letters, and other design features, all add up to individualities. The alphabet is firmly fixed in the shapes of its letters. Three-year-olds recognize letterforms. Yet there are on the order of 50,000 typefaces in existence, each different. Subtle and not-so-subtle variations in the thickness of the lines, the curves and angles, the shapes

10 point type, 11 point linespace

The alphabet is firmly fixed in the shapes of its letters. Three-year-olds recognize letterforms. Yet there are on the order of 50,000 typefaces in existence, each different. Subtle and not-so-subtle variations in the thickness of the lines, the curves and angles, the shapes of the serifs, the relative sizes of the parts of the letters, and other design features, all add up to individualities. The alphabet is firmly fixed in the shapes of its letters. Three-year-olds recognize letterforms. Yet there are on the order of 50,000 typefaces in existence, each different. Subtle and not-so-subtle variations in the thickness of the lines, the curves and angles, the shapes of the serifs, the relative sizes of the parts of the letters, and other design features, all add up to individualities. The alphabet is firmly fixed in the shapes of its letters. Three-year-olds recognize letterforms. Yet there are on the order of 50,000 typefaces in existence, each

12 point type, 13 point linespace

The alphabet is firmly fixed in the shapes of its letters. Three-year-olds recognize letterforms. Yet there are on the order of 50,000 typefaces in exist-ence, each different. Subtle and not-so-subtle variations in the thickness of the lines, the curves and angles, the shapes of the serifs, the relative sizes of the parts of the letters, and other design features, all add up to individu-alities. The alphabet is firmly fixed in the shapes of its letters. Three-year-olds recognize letterforms. Yet there are on the order of 50,000 typefaces in existence, each different. Subtle and not-so-subtle variations in the thick-ness of the lines, the curves and angles, the shapes of the serifs, the

Getting a bit carried away here: a bit too much of a good thing. In head-lines, it needs to crash its characters together to give an even “color,” which means lower legibility. Use sparingly, but not never.

ABCDEFGHIJKLMNOPQRSTUVWXYZ
abcdefghijklmnopqrstuvwxyz
0123456789&?!$%“”.,/;()

8 point type, 9 point linespace

The alphabet is firmly fixed in the shapes of its letters. Three-year-olds recognize letterforms. Yet there are on the order of 50,000 typefaces in existence, each different. Subtle and not-so-subtle variations in the thickness of the lines, the curves and angles, the shapes of the serifs, the relative sizes of the parts of the letters, and other design features, all add up to individualities. The alphabet is firmly fixed in the shapes of its letters. Three-year-olds recognize letterforms. Yet there are on the order of 50,000 typefaces in existence, each different. Subtle and not-so-subtle variations in the thickness of the lines, the curves and angles, the shapes of the serifs, the relative sizes of the parts of the letters, and other design features, all add up to individualities. The alphabet is firmly fixed in the shapes of its letters. Three-year-olds recognize letterforms. Yet there are on the order of 50,000 typefaces in existence, each different. Subtle and not-so-subtle variations in the thickness of the lines, the curves and angles, the shapes of the serifs, the relative sizes of the parts of the letters, and other design features, all add up to individualities. The alphabet is firmly fixed in the shapes of its letters. Three-year-olds recognize letterforms. Yet there are on the order of 50,000 typefaces in existence, each different. Subtle and not-so-subtle variations in the shapes of the serifs, the the relative sizes of the parts of

10 point type, 11 point linespace

The alphabet is firmly fixed in the shapes of its letters. Three-year-olds recognize letterforms. Yet there are on the order of 50,000 typefaces in existence, each different. Subtle and not-so-subtle variations in the thickness of the lines, the curves and angles, the shapes of the serifs, the relative sizes of the parts of the letters, and other design features, all add up to individualities. The alphabet is firmly fixed in the shapes of its letters. Three-year-olds recognize letterforms. Yet there are on the order of 50,000 typefaces in existence, each different. Subtle and not-so-subtle variations in the thickness of the lines, the curves and angles, the shapes of the serifs, the relative sizes of the parts of the letters, and other design features, all add up to individualities. The alphabet is firmly fixed in the shapes of its letters. Three-year-olds recognize letterforms. Yet there are on the order of 50,000 typefaces in existence, each

12 point type, 13 point linespace

The alphabet is firmly fixed in the shapes of its letters. Three-year-olds recognize letterforms. Yet there are on the order of 50,000 typefaces in exist-ence, each different. Subtle and not-so-subtle variations in the thickness of the lines, the curves and angles, the shapes of the serifs, the relative sizes of the parts of the letters, and other design features, all add up to individu-alities. The alphabet is firmly fixed in the shapes of its letters. Three-year-olds recognize letterforms. Yet there are on the order of 50,000 typefaces in existence, each different. Subtle and not-so-subtle variations in the thick-ness of the lines, the curves and angles, the shapes of the serifs, the

An appropriate complement to other Clearfaces, perhaps, occasionally, if you think so, or want to drive a point home with a pile driver. The letters fill in when set below 14-point. Handle with care.

ABCDEFGHIJKLMNOPQRSTUVWXYZ

ABCDEFGHIJKLMNOPQRSTUVWXYZ

0123456789&?!$%“”.,/;()

8 point type, 9 point linespace

THE ALPHABET IS FIRMLY FIXED IN THE SHAPES OF ITS LETTERS. THREE-YEAR-OLDS RECOGNIZE LETTERFORMS. YET THERE ARE ON THE ORDER OF 50,000 TYPEFACES IN EXISTENCE, EACH DIFFERENT. SUBTLE AND NOT-SO-SUBTLE VARIATIONS IN THE THICKNESS OF THE LINES, THE CURVES AND ANGLES, THE SHAPES OF THE SERIFS, THE RELATIVE SIZES OF THE PARTS OF THE LETTERS, AND OTHER DESIGN FEATURES, ALL ADD UP TO INDIVIDUALITIES. THE ALPHABET IS FIRMLY FIXED IN THE SHAPES OF ITS LETTERS. THREE-YEAR-OLDS RECOGNIZE LETTERFORMS. YET THERE ARE ON THE ORDER OF 50,000 TYPEFACES IN EXISTENCE, EACH DIFFERENT. SUBTLE AND NOT-SO-SUBTLE VARIATIONS IN THE THICKNESS OF THE LINES, THE CURVES AND ANGLES, THE SHAPES OF THE SERIFS, THE RELATIVE SIZES OF THE PARTS OF THE LETTERS, AND OTHER DESIGN FEATURES, ALL ADD UP TO INDIVIDUALITIES. THE ALPHABET IS FIRMLY FIXED IN THE SHAPES OF ITS LETTERS. THREE-YEAR-OLDS RECOGNIZE LETTERFORMS. YET THERE ARE ON THE ORDER OF 50,000 TYPEFACES IN EXISTENCE, EACH DIFFERENT. SUBTLE AND NOT-SO-SUBTLE VARIATIONS IN THE THICKNESS OF THE LINES, THE CURVES AND ANGLES, THE SHAPES OF THE SERIFS, THE RELATIVE SIZES OF THE PARTS OF THE LETTERS, AND OTHER DESIGN FEATURES, ALL ADD UP TO INDIVIDUALITIES. THE ALPHABET IS FIRMLY FIXED IN THE SHAPES OF ITS LETTERS. THREE-YEAR-OLDS RECOGNIZE LETTERFORMS. YET THERE ARE ON THE ORDER OF 50,000 TYPEFACES IN EXISTENCE, EACH DIFFERENT. SUBTLE AND NOT-SO-SUBTLE VARIATIONS IN THE THICKNESS OF THE LINES, THE CURVES AND ANGLES, THE SHAPES OF THE SERIFS, THE RELATIVE SIZES OF THE PARTS OF THE OF THE LETTERS, AND OTHER DESIGN FEATURES, ALL ADD UP TO INDIVIDUALITIES. THE ALPHABET IS FIRMLY FIXED IN THE SHAPES

10 point type, 11 point linespace

THE ALPHABET IS FIRMLY FIXED IN THE SHAPES OF ITS LETTERS. THREE-YEAR-OLDS RECOGNIZE LETTERFORMS. YET THERE ARE ON THE ORDER OF 50,000 TYPEFACES IN EXISTENCE, EACH DIFFERENT. SUBTLE AND NOT-SO-SUBTLE VARIATIONS IN THE THICKNESS OF THE LINES, THE CURVES AND ANGLES, THE SHAPES OF THE SERIFS, THE RELATIVE SIZES OF THE PARTS OF THE LETTERS, AND OTHER DESIGN FEATURES, ALL ADD UP TO INDIVIDUALITIES. THE ALPHABET IS FIRMLY FIXED IN THE SHAPES OF ITS LETTERS. THREE-YEAR-OLDS RECOGNIZE LETTERFORMS. YET THERE ARE ON THE ORDER OF 50,000 TYPEFACES IN EXISTENCE, EACH DIFFERENT. SUBTLE AND NOT-SO-SUBTLE VARIATIONS IN THE THICKNESS OF THE LINES, THE CURVES AND ANGLES, THE SHAPES OF THE SERIFS, THE RELATIVE SIZES OF THE PARTS OF THE LETTERS, AND OTHER DESIGN FEATURES, ALL ADD UP TO INDIVIDUALITIES. THE ALPHABET IS FIRMLY FIXED IN THE SHAPES OF ITS LETTERS. THREE-YEAR-OLDS RECOGNIZE LETTERFORMS. YET THERE ARE ON THE ORDER OF 50,000 TYPEFACES IN EXISTENCE, EACH DIFFERENT. SUBTLE AND NOT-SO-SUBTLE VARIATIONS IN THE THICKNESS OF THE LINES, THE CURVES AND ANGLES, THE SHAPES OF THE

12 point type, 13 point linespace

THE ALPHABET IS FIRMLY FIXED IN THE SHAPES OF ITS LETTERS. THREE-YEAR-OLDS RECOGNIZE LETTERFORMS. YET THERE ARE ON THE ORDER OF 50,000 TYPEFACES IN EXISTENCE, EACH DIFFER-ENT. SUBTLE AND NOT-SO-SUBTLE VARIATIONS IN THE THICKNESS OF THE LINES, THE CURVES AND ANGLES, THE SHAPES OF THE SERIFS, THE RELATIVE SIZES OF THE PARTS OF THE LETTERS, AND OTHER DESIGN FEATURES, ALL ADD UP TO INDIVIDUALI-TIES. THE ALPHABET IS FIRMLY FIXED IN THE SHAPES OF ITS LETTERS. THREE-YEAR-OLDS RECOGNIZE LETTERFORMS. YET THERE ARE ON THE ORDER OF 50,000 TYPEFACES IN EXISTENCE, EACH DIFFERENT. SUBTLE AND NOT-SO-SUBTLE VARIA-TIONS IN THE THICKNESS OF THE LINES, THE CURVES AND ANGLES, THE SHAPES OF THE SERIFS, THE RELATIVE SIZES OF THE PARTS OF THE LETTERS, AND OTHER DESIGN FEATURES, ALL ADD UP TO

THE “BC” SERIES OF COPPERPLATES ARE VERY SHORT COMPARED TO MOST TYPEFACES, SO ARE SET WITH NO EXTRA LINESPACE, OR EVEN MINUS LINESPACE. THEY ARE INTENDED TO BE SET WITH LOOSE LETTERSPACING AND LITTLE OR NO KERNING.

ABCDEFGHIJKLMNOPQRSTUVWXYZ

ABCDEFGHIJKLMNOPQRSTUVWXYZ

0123456789&?!$%“”.,/;()

8 point type, 9 point linespace

The alphabet is firmly fixed in the shapes of its letters. Three-year-olds recognize letterforms. Yet there are on the order of 50,000 typefaces in existence, each different. Subtle and not-so-subtle variations in the thickness of the lines, the curves and angles, the shapes of the serifs, the relative sizes of the parts of the letters, and other design features, all add up to individualities. The alphabet is firmly fixed in the shapes of its letters. Three-year-olds recognize letterforms. Yet there are on the order of 50,000 typefaces in existence, each different. Subtle and not-so-subtle variations in the thickness of the lines, the curves and angles, the shapes of the serifs, the relative sizes of the parts of the letters, and other design features, all add up to individualities. The alphabet is firmly fixed in the shapes of its letters. Three-year-olds recognize letterforms. Yet there are on the order of 50,000 typefaces in existence, each different. Subtle and not-so-subtle variations in the thickness of the lines, the curves and angles, the shapes of the serifs, the relative sizes of the parts of the letters, and other design features, all add up to individualities. The alphabet is firmly fixed in the shapes of its letters. Three-year-olds recognize letterforms. Yet there are on the order of 50,000 typefaces in existence, each different. Subtle and not-so-subtle variations in the thickness of the lines, the curves and angles, the shapes of the serifs, the relative sizes of the parts of the letters, and other design features, all add up to individualities. The alphabet is firmly fixed in the shapes of its

10 point type, 11 point linespace

The alphabet is firmly fixed in the shapes of its letters. Three-year-olds recognize letterforms. Yet there are on the order of 50,000 typefaces in existence, each different. Subtle and not-so-subtle variations in the thickness of the lines, the curves and angles, the shapes of the serifs, the relative sizes of the parts of the letters, and other design features, all add up to individualities. The alphabet is firmly fixed in the shapes of its letters. Three-year-olds recognize letterforms. Yet there are on the order of 50,000 typefaces in existence, each different. Subtle and not-so-subtle variations in the thickness of the lines, the curves and angles, the shapes of the serifs, the relative sizes of the parts of the letters, and other design features, all add up to individualities. The alphabet is firmly fixed in the shapes of its letters. Three-year-olds recognize letterforms. Yet there are on the order of 50,000 typefaces in existence, each different. Subtle and not-so-subtle variations in the thickness of the lines, the curves and angles, the shapes of the

12 point type, 13 point linespace

The alphabet is firmly fixed in the shapes of its letters. Three-year-olds recognize letterforms. Yet there are on the order of 50,000 typefaces in existence, each different. Subtle and not-so-subtle variations in the thickness of the lines, the curves and angles, the shapes of the serifs, the relative sizes of the parts of the letters, and other design features, all add up to individualities. The alphabet is firmly fixed in the shapes of its letters. Three-year-olds recognize letterforms. Yet there are on the order of 50,000 typefaces in existence, each different. Subtle and not-so-subtle variations in the thickness of the lines, the curves and angles, the shapes of the serifs, the relative sizes of the parts of the letters, and other design features, all add up to

Copperplates emulate engraved type, with almost unnoticeable serifs and no embellishments. These are staid faces, distinguished-looking, used for stationery especially. Very conservative applications.

ABCDEFGHIJKLMNOPQRSTUVWXYZ

ABCDEFGHIJKLMNOPQRSTUVWXYZ

0123456789&?!$%“”.,/;()

8 point type, 9 point linespace

THE ALPHABET IS FIRMLY FIXED IN THE SHAPES OF ITS LETTERS. THREE-YEAR-OLDS RECOGNIZE LETTERFORMS. YET THERE ARE ON THE ORDER OF 50,000 TYPEFACES IN EXISTENCE, EACH DIFFERENT. SUBTLE AND NOT-SO-SUBTLE VARIATIONS IN THE THICKNESS OF THE LINES, THE CURVES AND ANGLES, THE SHAPES OF THE SERIFS, THE RELATIVE SIZES OF THE PARTS OF THE LETTERS, AND OTHER DESIGN FEATURES, ALL ADD UP TO INDIVIDUALITIES. THE ALPHABET IS FIRMLY FIXED IN THE SHAPES OF ITS LETTERS. THREE-YEAR-OLDS RECOGNIZE LETTERFORMS. YET THERE ARE ON THE ORDER OF 50,000 TYPEFACES IN EXISTENCE, EACH DIFFERENT. SUBTLE AND NOT-SO-SUBTLE VARIATIONS IN THE THICKNESS OF THE LINES, THE CURVES AND ANGLES, THE SHAPES OF THE SERIFS, THE RELATIVE SIZES OF THE PARTS OF THE LETTERS, AND OTHER DESIGN FEATURES, ALL ADD UP TO INDIVIDUALITIES. THE ALPHABET IS FIRMLY FIXED IN THE SHAPES OF ITS LETTERS. THREE-YEAR-OLDS RECOGNIZE LETTERFORMS. YET THERE ARE ON THE ORDER OF 50,000 TYPEFACES IN EXISTENCE, EACH DIFFERENT. SUBTLE AND NOT-SO-SUBTLE VARIATIONS IN THE THICKNESS OF THE LINES, THE CURVES AND ANGLES, THE SHAPES OF THE SERIFS, THE RELATIVE SIZES OF THE PARTS OF THE LETTERS, AND OTHER DESIGN FEATURES, ALL ADD UP TO INDIVIDUALITIES. THE ALPHABET IS FIRMLY FIXED IN THE SHAPES OF ITS LETTERS. THREE-YEAR-OLDS RECOGNIZE

10 point type, 11 point linespace

THE ALPHABET IS FIRMLY FIXED IN THE SHAPES OF ITS LETTERS. THREE-YEAR-OLDS RECOGNIZE LETTERFORMS. YET THERE ARE ON THE ORDER OF 50,000 TYPEFACES IN EXISTENCE, EACH DIFFERENT. SUBTLE AND NOT-SO-SUBTLE VARIATIONS IN THE THICKNESS OF THE LINES, THE CURVES AND ANGLES, THE SHAPES OF THE SERIFS, THE RELATIVE SIZES OF THE PARTS OF THE LETTERS, AND OTHER DESIGN FEATURES, ALL ADD UP TO INDIVIDUALITIES. THE ALPHABET IS FIRMLY FIXED IN THE SHAPES OF ITS LETTERS. THREE-YEAR-OLDS RECOGNIZE LETTERFORMS. YET THERE ARE ON THE ORDER OF 50,000 TYPEFACES IN EXISTENCE, EACH DIFFERENT. SUBTLE AND NOT-SO-SUBTLE VARIATIONS IN THE THICKNESS OF THE LINES, THE CURVES AND ANGLES, THE SHAPES OF THE SERIFS, THE RELATIVE SIZES OF THE PARTS OF THE LETTERS, AND OTHER DESIGN FEATURES, ALL ADD UP TO INDIVIDUALITIES. THE ALPHABET IS FIRMLY FIXED IN THE SHAPES OF ITS

12 point type, 13 point linespace

THE ALPHABET IS FIRMLY FIXED IN THE SHAPES OF ITS LETTERS. THREE-YEAR-OLDS RECOGNIZE LETTERFORMS. YET THERE ARE ON THE ORDER OF 50,000 TYPEFACES IN EXISTENCE, EACH DIFFERENT. SUBTLE AND NOT-SO-SUBTLE VARIATIONS IN THE THICKNESS OF THE LINES, THE CURVES AND ANGLES, THE SHAPES OF THE SERIFS, THE RELATIVE SIZES OF THE PARTS OF THE LETTERS, AND OTHER DESIGN FEATURES, ALL ADD UP TO INDIVIDUALITIES. THE ALPHABET IS FIRMLY FIXED IN THE SHAPES OF ITS LETTERS. THREE-YEAR-OLDS RECOGNIZE LETTERFORMS. YET THERE ARE ON THE ORDER OF 50,000 TYPEFACES IN EXISTENCE, EACH DIFFERENT. SUBTLE AND NOT-SO-SUBTLE VARIATIONS IN THE

THE GREATER WIDTH OF THESE CHARACTERS ALLOWS EVEN MORE LETTER-SPACING, AND INCREASES THE APPLICATIONS FOR WHICH IT IS USEFUL. WHILE COPPERPLATE WILL NEVER BE ELEGANT, IT CAN WORK WITH ELEGANT CONCEPTS OR ART.

ABCDEFGHIJKLMNOPQRSTUVWXYZ

ABCDEFGHIJKLMNOPQRSTUVWXYZ

0123456789&?!$% “” .,/;()

8 point type, 9 point linespace

The alphabet is firmly fixed in the shapes of its letters. Three-year-olds recognize letterforms. Yet there are on the order of 50,000 typefaces in existence, each different. Subtle and not-so-subtle variations in the thickness of the lines, the curves and angles, the shapes of the serifs, the relative sizes of the parts of the letters, and other design features, all add up to individualities. The alphabet is firmly fixed in the shapes of its letters. Three-year-olds recognize letterforms. Yet there are on the order of 50,000 typefaces in existence, each different. Subtle and not-so-subtle variations in the thickness of the lines, the curves and angles, the shapes of the serifs, the relative sizes of the parts of the letters, and other design features, all add up to individualities. The alphabet is firmly fixed in the shapes of its letters. Three-year-olds recognize letterforms. Yet there are on the order of 50,000 typefaces in existence, each different. Subtle and not-so-subtle variations in the thickness of the lines, the curves and angles, the shapes of the serifs, the relative sizes of the parts of the letters, and other design features, all add up to individualities. The alphabet is firmly fixed in the shapes of its letters. Three-year-olds recognize

10 point type, 11 point linespace

The alphabet is firmly fixed in the shapes of its letters. Three-year-olds recognize letterforms. Yet there are on the order of 50,000 typefaces in existence, each different. Subtle and not-so-subtle variations in the thickness of the lines, the curves and angles, the shapes of the serifs, the relative sizes of the parts of the letters, and other design features, all add up to individualities. The alphabet is firmly fixed in the shapes of its letters. Three-year-olds recognize letterforms. Yet there are on the order of 50,000 typefaces in existence, each different. Subtle and not-so-subtle variations in the thickness of the lines, the curves and angles, the shapes of the serifs, the relative sizes of the parts of the letters, and other design features, all add up to individualities. The alphabet is firmly fixed in the shapes of its

12 point type, 13 point linespace

The alphabet is firmly fixed in the shapes of its letters. Three-year-olds recognize letterforms. Yet there are on the order of 50,000 typefaces in existence, each different. Subtle and not-so-subtle variations in the thickness of the lines, the curves and angles, the shapes of the serifs, the relative sizes of the parts of the letters, and other design features, all add up to individualities. The alphabet is firmly fixed in the shapes of its letters. Three-year-olds recognize letterforms. Yet there are on the order of 50,000 typefaces in existence, each different. Subtle and not-so-subtle variations in the

Lighter than 31BC, this is as close to elegance as Copperplate ever gets. Copperplate is an understated face—in fact, it works best low on a page, as a footline rather than a headline.

ABCDEFGHIJKLMNOPQRSTUVWXYZ

ABCDEFGHIJKLMNOPQRSTUVWXYZ

0123456789&?!$%“”.,/;()

8 point type, 9 point linespace

THE ALPHABET IS FIRMLY FIXED IN THE SHAPES OF ITS LETTERS. THREE-YEAR-OLDS RECOGNIZE LETTERFORMS. YET THERE ARE ON THE ORDER OF 50,000 TYPEFACES IN EXISTENCE, EACH DIFFERENT. SUBTLE AND NOT-SO-SUBTLE VARIATIONS IN THE THICKNESS OF THE LINES, THE CURVES AND ANGLES, THE SHAPES OF THE SERIFS, THE RELATIVE SIZES OF THE PARTS OF THE LETTERS, AND OTHER DESIGN FEATURES, ALL ADD UP TO INDIVIDUALITIES. THE ALPHABET IS FIRMLY FIXED IN THE SHAPES OF ITS LETTERS. THREE-YEAR-OLDS RECOGNIZE LETTERFORMS. YET THERE ARE ON THE ORDER OF 50,000 TYPEFACES IN EXISTENCE, EACH DIFFERENT. SUBTLE AND NOT-SO-SUBTLE VARIATIONS IN THE THICKNESS OF THE LINES, THE CURVES AND ANGLES, THE SHAPES OF THE SERIFS, THE RELATIVE SIZES OF THE PARTS OF THE LETTERS, AND OTHER DESIGN FEATURES, ALL ADD UP TO INDIVIDUALITIES. THE ALPHABET IS FIRMLY FIXED IN THE SHAPES OF ITS LETTERS. THREE-YEAR-OLDS RECOGNIZE LETTERFORMS. YET THERE ARE ON THE ORDER OF 50,000 TYPEFACES IN EXISTENCE, EACH DIFFERENT. SUBTLE AND NOT-SO-SUBTLE VARIATIONS IN THE THICKNESS OF THE LINES, THE CURVES AND ANGLES, THE SHAPES OF THE SERIFS, THE RELATIVE SIZES OF THE PARTS OF THE LETTERS, AND OTHER DESIGN FEATURES, ALL ADD UP TO INDIVIDUALITIES. THE ALPHABET IS FIRMLY FIXED IN THE SHAPES

10 point type, 11 point linespace

THE ALPHABET IS FIRMLY FIXED IN THE SHAPES OF ITS LETTERS. THREE-YEAR-OLDS RECOGNIZE LETTERFORMS. YET THERE ARE ON THE ORDER OF 50,000 TYPEFACES IN EXISTENCE, EACH DIFFERENT. SUBTLE AND NOT-SO-SUBTLE VARIATIONS IN THE THICKNESS OF THE LINES, THE CURVES AND ANGLES, THE SHAPES OF THE SERIFS, THE RELATIVE SIZES OF THE PARTS OF THE LETTERS, AND OTHER DESIGN FEATURES, ALL ADD UP TO INDIVIDUALITIES. THE ALPHABET IS FIRMLY FIXED IN THE SHAPES OF ITS LETTERS. THREE-YEAR-OLDS RECOGNIZE LETTERFORMS. YET THERE ARE ON THE ORDER OF 50,000 TYPEFACES IN EXISTENCE, EACH DIFFERENT. SUBTLE AND NOT-SO-SUBTLE VARIATIONS IN THE THICKNESS OF THE LINES, THE CURVES AND ANGLES, THE SHAPES OF THE SERIFS, THE RELATIVE SIZES OF THE PARTS OF THE LETTERS, AND OTHER DESIGN FEATURES, ALL ADD UP TO INDIVIDUALITIES. THE ALPHABET

12 point type, 13 point linespace

THE ALPHABET IS FIRMLY FIXED IN THE SHAPES OF ITS LETTERS. THREE-YEAR-OLDS RECOGNIZE LETTERFORMS. YET THERE ARE ON THE ORDER OF 50,000 TYPEFACES IN EXISTENCE, EACH DIFFERENT. SUBTLE AND NOT-SO-SUBTLE VARIATIONS IN THE THICKNESS OF THE LINES, THE CURVES AND ANGLES, THE SHAPES OF THE SERIFS, THE RELATIVE SIZES OF THE PARTS OF THE LETTERS, AND OTHER DESIGN FEATURES, ALL ADD UP TO INDIVIDUALITIES. THE ALPHABET IS FIRMLY FIXED IN THE SHAPES OF ITS LETTERS. THREE-YEAR-OLDS RECOGNIZE LETTERFORMS. YET THERE ARE ON THE ORDER OF 50,000 TYPEFACES IN EXISTENCE, EACH DIFFERENT. SUBTLE

THE ONLY JUSTIFICATION FOR THIS FACE IS THAT IT STANDS UP TO REVERSAL (WHITE ON BLACK) OR PRINTING IN A LIGHT COLOR OR WITH A SCREEN. EVEN IN THOSE CASES, HOWEVER, IT LOOKS UNGAINLY AND ARTIFICIAL.

ABCDEFGHIJKLMNOPQRSTUVWXYZ
abcdefghijklmnopqrstuvwxyz
0123456789&?!$%“”.,/;()

8 point type, 9 point linespace

The alphabet is firmly fixed in the shapes of its letters. Three-year-olds recognize letterforms. Yet there are on the order of 50,000 typefaces in existence, each different. Subtle and not-so-subtle variations in the thickness of the lines, the curves and angles, the shapes of the serifs, the relative sizes of the parts of the letters, and other design features, all add up to individualities. The alphabet is firmly fixed in the shapes of its letters. Three-year-olds recognize letterforms. Yet there are on the order of 50,000 typefaces in existence, each different. Subtle and not-so-subtle variations in the thickness of the lines, the curves and angles, the shapes of the serifs, the relative sizes of the parts of the letters, and other design features, all add up to individualities. The alphabet is firmly fixed in the shapes of its letters. Three-year-olds recognize letterforms. Yet there are on the order of 50,000 typefaces in existence, each different. Subtle and not-so-subtle variations in the thickness of the lines, the curves and angles, the shapes of the serifs, the relative sizes of the parts of the letters, and other design features, all add up to individualities. The alphabet is firmly fixed in the shapes of its letters. Three-year-olds recognize letterforms. Yet there are on the order of 50,000 typefaces in existence, each different. Subtle and not-so-subtle variations in the shapes of the serifs,

10 point type, 11 point linespace

The alphabet is firmly fixed in the shapes of its letters. Three-year-olds recognize letterforms. Yet there are on the order of 50,000 typefaces in existence, each different. Subtle and not-so-subtle variations in the thickness of the lines, the curves and angles, the shapes of the serifs, the relative sizes of the parts of the letters, and other design features, all add up to individualities. The alphabet is firmly fixed in the shapes of its letters. Three-year-olds recognize letterforms. Yet there are on the order of 50,000 typefaces in existence, each different. Subtle and not-so-subtle variations in the thickness of the lines, the curves and angles, the shapes of the serifs, the relative sizes of the parts of the letters, and other design features, all add up to individualities. The alphabet is firmly fixed in the shapes of its letters. Three-year-olds recognize letterforms. Yet there are on the order of 50,000 typefaces in existence,

12 point type, 13 point linespace

The alphabet is firmly fixed in the shapes of its letters. Three-year-olds recognize letterforms. Yet there are on the order of 50,000 typefaces in existence, each different. Subtle and not-so-subtle variations in the thickness of the lines, the curves and angles, the shapes of the serifs, the relative sizes of the parts of the letters, and other design features, all add up to individualities. The alphabet is firmly fixed in the shapes of its letters. Three-year-olds recognize letterforms. Yet there are on the order of 50,000 typefaces in existence, each different. Subtle and not-so-subtle variations in the thickness of the lines, the curves and angles, the

The squareness of these characters give an impression of stability and a sense of mathematical precision. Not particularly easy to read, but important when conveying a message of dependability, as in engineering or architecture.

ABCDEFGHIJKLMNOPQRSTUVWXYZ
abcdefghijklmnopqrstuvwxyz
0123456789&?!$%“”.,/;()

8 point type, 9 point linespace

The alphabet is firmly fixed in the shapes of its letters. Three-year-olds recognize letterforms. Yet there are on the order of 50,000 typefaces in existence, each different. Subtle and not-so-subtle variations in the thickness of the lines, the curves and angles, the shapes of the serifs, the relative sizes of the parts of the letters, and other design features, all add up to individualities. The alphabet is firmly fixed in the shapes of its letters. Three-year-olds recognize letterforms. Yet there are on the order of 50,000 typefaces in existence, each different. Subtle and not-so-subtle variations in the thickness of the lines, the curves and angles, the shapes of the serifs, the relative sizes of the parts of the letters, and other design features, all add up to individualities. The alphabet is firmly fixed in the shapes of its letters. Three-year-olds recognize letterforms. Yet there are on the order of 50,000 typefaces in existence, each different. Subtle and not-so-subtle variations in the thickness of the lines, the curves and angles, the shapes of the serifs, the relative sizes of the parts of the letters, and other design features, all add up to individualities. The alphabet is firmly fixed in the shapes of its letters. Three-year-olds recognize letterforms. Yet there are on the order of 50,000 typefaces in

10 point type, 11 point linespace

The alphabet is firmly fixed in the shapes of its letters. Three-year-olds recognize letterforms. Yet there are on the order of 50,000 typefaces in existence, each different. Subtle and not-so-subtle variations in the thickness of the lines, the curves and angles, the shapes of the serifs, the relative sizes of the parts of the letters, and other design features, all add up to individualities. The alphabet is firmly fixed in the shapes of its letters. Three-year-olds recognize letterforms. Yet there are on the order of 50,000 typefaces in existence, each different. Subtle and not-so-subtle variations in the thickness of the lines, the curves and angles, the shapes of the serifs, the relative sizes of the parts of the letters, and other design features, all add up to individualities. The alphabet is firmly fixed in the shapes of its letters. Three-year-olds

12 point type, 13 point linespace

The alphabet is firmly fixed in the shapes of its letters. Three-year-olds recognize letterforms. Yet there are on the order of 50,000 typefaces in existence, each different. Subtle and not-so-subtle variations in the thickness of the lines, the curves and angles, the shapes of the serifs, the relative sizes of the parts of the letters, and other design features, all add up to individualities. The alphabet is firmly fixed in the shapes of its letters. Three-year-olds recognize letterforms. Yet there are on the order of 50,000 typefaces in existence, each different. Subtle and not-so-subtle variations in the

This can and should be set tightly, as any letterspace dilutes the *very* strong impression this face makes. There is also a semibold weight, but it doesn’t serve much purpose. The whole point of Eurostile is strength.

ABCDEFGHIJKLMNOPQRST UVWXYZabcdefghijklmnopqrs tuvwxyz0123456789&?!$%

8 point type, 9 point linespace

The alphabet is firmly fixed in the shapes of its letters. Three-year-olds recognize letterforms. Yet there are on the order of 50,000 typefaces in existence, each different. Subtle and not-so-subtle variations in the thickness of the lines, the curves and angles, the shapes of the serifs, the relative sizes of the parts of the letters, and other design features, all add up to individualities. The alphabet is firmly fixed in the shapes of its letters. Three-year-olds recognize letterforms. Yet there are on the order of 50,000 typefaces in existence, each different. Subtle and not-so-subtle variations in the thickness of the lines, the curves and angles, the shapes of the serifs, the relative sizes of the parts of the letters, and other design features, all add up to individualities. The alphabet is firmly fixed in the shapes of its letters. Three-year-olds recognize letterforms. Yet there are on the order of 50,000 typefaces in existence, each different. Subtle and not-so-subtle variations in the thickness

10 point type, 11 point linespace

The alphabet is firmly fixed in the shapes of its letters. Three-year-olds recognize letterforms. Yet there are on the order of 50,000 typefaces in existence, each different. Subtle and not-so-subtle variations in the thickness of the lines, the curves and angles, the shapes of the serifs, the relative sizes of the parts of the letters, and other design features, all add up to individualities. The alphabet is firmly fixed in the shapes of its letters. Three-year-olds recognize letterforms. Yet there are on the order of 50,000 typefaces in existence, each different. Subtle and not-so-subtle variations in the thickness of the lines, the curves and angles,

12 point type, 13 point linespace

The alphabet is firmly fixed in the shapes of its letters. Three-year-olds recognize letterforms. Yet there are on the order of 50,000 typefaces in existence, each different. Subtle and not-so-subtle variations in the thickness of the lines, the curves and angles, the shapes of the serifs, the relative sizes of the parts of the letters, and other design features, all add up to individualities. The alphabet is firmly fixed in the shapes of its letters. Three-year-olds recognize

More than just stable, this face could serve as a foundation for a skyscraper. Very hard to read, so useful in small quantities only, but very very useful in a horizontal design format.

ABCDEFGHIJKLMNOPQRST
UVWXYZabcdefghijklmnopqr
stuvwxyz0123456789&?!$

8 point type, 9 point linespace

The alphabet is firmly fixed in the shapes of its letters. Three-year-olds recognize letterforms. Yet there are on the order of 50,000 typefaces in existence, each different. Subtle and not-so-subtle variations in the thickness of the lines, the curves and angles, the shapes of the serifs, the relative sizes of the parts of the letters, and other design features, all add up to individualities. The alphabet is firmly fixed in the shapes of its letters. Three-year-olds recognize letterforms. Yet there are on the order of 50,000 typefaces in existence, each different. Subtle and not-so-subtle variations in the thickness of the lines, the curves and angles, the shapes of the serifs, the relative sizes of the parts of the letters, and other design features, all add up to individualities. The alphabet is firmly fixed in the shapes of its letters. Three-year-olds recognize letterforms. Yet there are on the order of 50,000 typefaces in existence, each different.

10 point type, 11 point linespace

The alphabet is firmly fixed in the shapes of its letters. Three-year-olds recognize letterforms. Yet there are on the order of 50,000 typefaces in existence, each different. Subtle and not-so-subtle variations in the thickness of the lines, the curves and angles, the shapes of the serifs, the relative sizes of the parts of the letters, and other design features, all add up to individualities. The alphabet is firmly fixed in the shapes of its letters. Three-year-olds recognize letterforms. Yet there are on the order of 50,000 typefaces in existence, each different. Subtle and not-so-subtle variations in the thickness of the

12 point type, 13 point linespace

The alphabet is firmly fixed in the shapes of its letters. Three-year-olds recognize letterforms. Yet there are on the order of 50,000 typefaces in existence, each different. Subtle and not-so-subtle variations in the thickness of the lines, the curves and angles, the shapes of the serifs, the relative sizes of the parts of the letters, and other design features, all add up to individualities. The alphabet is firmly fixed in the shapes of its letters.

The strength of this face translates into flexibility—not solid pillars, but steel I-beams. It's a "tough" face, able to take punishment and still get a message across.

ABCDEFGHIJKLMNOPQRSTUVWXYZ
abcdefghijklmnopqrstuvwxyz
0123456789&?!$%“”.,/;()

8 point type, 9 point linespace

The alphabet is firmly fixed in the shapes of its letters. Three-year-olds recognize letterforms. Yet there are on the order of 50,000 typefaces in existence, each different. Subtle and not-so-subtle variations in the thickness of the lines, the curves and angles, the shapes of the serifs, the relative sizes of the parts of the letters, and other design features, all add up to individualities. The alphabet is firmly fixed in the shapes of its letters. Three-year-olds recognize letterforms. Yet there are on the order of 50,000 typefaces in existence, each different. Subtle and not-so-subtle variations in the thickness of the lines, the curves and angles, the shapes of the serifs, the relative sizes of the parts of the letters, and other design features, all add up to individualities. The alphabet is firmly fixed in the shapes of its letters. Three-year-olds recognize letterforms. Yet there are on the order of 50,000 typefaces in existence, each different. Subtle and not-so-subtle variations in the thickness of the lines, the curves and angles, the shapes of the serifs, the relative sizes of the parts of the letters, and other design features, all add up to individualities. The alphabet is firmly fixed in the shapes of its letters. Three-year-olds recognize letterforms. Yet there are on the order of 50,000 typefaces in existence, each different. Subtle and not-so-subtle variations in the thickness of the lines, the curves and angles, the shapes of the serifs, the relative sizes of the parts of the letters, and other design features, all add up to individualities. The alphabet is firmly fixed in the shapes

10 point type, 11 point linespace

The alphabet is firmly fixed in the shapes of its letters. Three-year-olds recognize letterforms. Yet there are on the order of 50,000 typefaces in existence, each different. Subtle and not-so-subtle variations in the thickness of the lines, the curves and angles, the shapes of the serifs, the relative sizes of the parts of the letters, and other design features, all add up to individualities. The alphabet is firmly fixed in the shapes of its letters. Three-year-olds recognize letterforms. Yet there are on the order of 50,000 typefaces in existence, each different. Subtle and not-so-subtle variations in the thickness of the lines, the curves and angles, the shapes of the serifs, the relative sizes of the parts of the letters, and other design features, all add up to individualities. The alphabet is firmly fixed in the shapes of its letters. Three-year-olds recognize letterforms. Yet there are on the order of 50,000 typefaces in existence, each different. Subtle and not-so-subtle variations in the thickness of the lines, the curves and angles, the shapes of the

12 point type, 13 point linespace

The alphabet is firmly fixed in the shapes of its letters. Three-year-olds recognize letterforms. Yet there are on the order of 50,000 typefaces in existence, each different. Subtle and not-so-subtle variations in the thickness of the lines, the curves and angles, the shapes of the serifs, the relative sizes of the parts of the letters, and other design features, all add up to individualities. The alphabet is firmly fixed in the shapes of its letters. Three-year-olds recognize letterforms. Yet there are on the order of 50,000 typefaces in existence, each different. Subtle and not-so-subtle variations in the thickness of the lines, the curves and angles, the shapes of the serifs, the relative sizes of the parts of the letters, and other design features, all add up to

This is for the art of it, a show-off kind of face that provides a free-swinging feel to any graphic piece. Anything but conservative, Friz (pronounced “Fritz”) Quadrata is for fun pieces.

ABCDEFGHIJKLMNOPQRSTUVWXYZ
abcdefghijklmnopqrstuvwxyz
0123456789&?!$%“”.,/;()

8 point type, 9 point linespace

The alphabet is firmly fixed in the shapes of its letters. Three-year-olds recognize letterforms. Yet there are on the order of 50,000 typefaces in existence, each different. Subtle and not-so-subtle variations in the thickness of the lines, the curves and angles, the shapes of the serifs, the relative sizes of the parts of the letters, and other design features, all add up to individualities. The alphabet is firmly fixed in the shapes of its letters. Three-year-olds recognize letterforms. Yet there are on the order of 50,000 typefaces in existence, each different. Subtle and not-so-subtle variations in the thickness of the lines, the curves and angles, the shapes of the serifs, the relative sizes of the parts of the letters, and other design features, all add up to individualities. The alphabet is firmly fixed in the shapes of its letters. Three-year-olds recognize letterforms. Yet there are on the order of 50,000 typefaces in existence, each different. Subtle and not-so-subtle variations in the thickness of the lines, the curves and angles, the shapes of the serifs, the relative sizes of the parts of the letters, and other design features, all add up to individualities. The alphabet is firmly fixed in the shapes of its letters. Three-year-olds recognize letterforms. Yet there are on the order of 50,000 typefaces in existence, each different. Subtle and not-so-subtle variations in the thickness of the lines, the curves and angles, the shapes of the serifs, the relative sizes of the

10 point type, 11 point linespace

The alphabet is firmly fixed in the shapes of its letters. Three-year-olds recognize letterforms. Yet there are on the order of 50,000 typefaces in existence, each different. Subtle and not-so-subtle variations in the thickness of the lines, the curves and angles, the shapes of the serifs, the relative sizes of the parts of the letters, and other design features, all add up to individualities. The alphabet is firmly fixed in the shapes of its letters. Three-year-olds recognize letterforms. Yet there are on the order of 50,000 typefaces in existence, each different. Subtle and not-so-subtle variations in the thickness of the lines, the curves and angles, the shapes of the serifs, the relative sizes of the parts of the letters, and other design features, all add up to individualities. The alphabet is firmly fixed in the shapes of its letters. Three-year-olds recognize letterforms. Yet there are on the order of 50,000 typefaces in existence, each different. Subtle and not-so-subtle

12 point type, 13 point linespace

The alphabet is firmly fixed in the shapes of its letters. Three-year-olds recognize letterforms. Yet there are on the order of 50,000 typefaces in existence, each different. Subtle and not-so-subtle variations in the thickness of the lines, the curves and angles, the shapes of the serifs, the relative sizes of the parts of the letters, and other design features, all add up to individualities. The alphabet is firmly fixed in the shapes of its letters. Three-year-olds recognize letterforms. Yet there are on the order of 50,000 typefaces in existence, each different. Subtle and not-so-subtle variations in the thickness of the lines, the curves and angles, the shapes of its letters. Three-year-olds recognize

Makes for striking heads, interesting callout lines, spirited contrast to more conservative faces, and a forceful complement to normal Friz Quadrata. This is a family to play with, for playful people.

ABCDEFGHIJKLMNOPQRSTUVWXYZ
abcdefghijklmnopqrstuvwxyz
0123456789&?!$%“”.,/;()

8 point type, 9 point linespace

The alphabet is firmly fixed in the shapes of its letters. Three-year-olds recognize letterforms. Yet there are on the order of 50,000 typefaces in existence, each different. Subtle and not-so-subtle variations in the thickness of the lines, the curves and angles, the shapes of the serifs, the relative sizes of the parts of the letters, and other design features, all add up to individualities. The alphabet is firmly fixed in the shapes of its letters. Three-year-olds recognize letterforms. Yet there are on the order of 50,000 typefaces in existence, each different. Subtle and not-so-subtle variations in the thickness of the lines, the curves and angles, the shapes of the serifs, the relative sizes of the parts of the letters, and other design features, all add up to individualities. The alphabet is firmly fixed in the shapes of its letters. Three-year-olds recognize letterforms. Yet there are on the order of 50,000 typefaces in existence, each different. Subtle and not-so-subtle variations in the thickness of the lines, the curves and angles, the shapes of the serifs, the relative sizes of the parts of the letters, and other design features, all add up to individualities. The alphabet is firmly fixed in the shapes of its letters. Three-year-olds recognize letterforms. Yet there are on the order of 50,000 typefaces in existence, each different. Subtle and not-so-subtle variations in the thickness of the lines, the curves and angles, the shapes of the serifs, the relative sizes of the parts of the letters, and other design features, all add up to individualities. The alphabet is firmly fixed in the shapes of its

10 point type, 11 point linespace

The alphabet is firmly fixed in the shapes of its letters. Three-year-olds recognize letterforms. Yet there are on the order of 50,000 typefaces in existence, each different. Subtle and not-so-subtle variations in the thickness of the lines, the curves and angles, the shapes of the serifs, the relative sizes of the parts of the letters, and other design features, all add up to individualities. The alphabet is firmly fixed in the shapes of its letters. Three-year-olds recognize letterforms. Yet there are on the order of 50,000 typefaces in existence, each different. Subtle and not-so-subtle variations in the thickness of the lines, the curves and angles, the shapes of the serifs, the relative sizes of the parts of the letters, and other design features, all add up to individualities. The alphabet is firmly fixed in the shapes of its letters. Three-year-olds recognize letterforms. Yet there are on the order of 50,000 typefaces in existence, each different. Subtle and not-so-subtle variations in the thickness of the lines, the curves and angles, the shapes of the

12 point type, 13 point linespace

The alphabet is firmly fixed in the shapes of its letters. Three-year-olds recognize letterforms. Yet there are on the order of 50,000 typefaces in existence, each different. Subtle and not-so-subtle variations in the thickness of the lines, the curves and angles, the shapes of the serifs, the relative sizes of the parts of the letters, and other design features, all add up to individualities. The alphabet is firmly fixed in the shapes of its letters. Three-year-olds recognize letterforms. Yet there are on the order of 50,000 typefaces in existence, each different. Subtle and not-so-subtle variations in the thickness of the lines, the curves and angles, the shapes of its letters. Three-year-olds recognize letterforms. Yet there are on the order of 50,000 typefaces

No frills, no ornamentation, just a very clean sans serif face to use in pieces of sparse design. Frutiger does not compete well with busy artwork. The light face especially needs plenty of air.

ABCDEFGHIJKLMNOPQRSTUVWXYZ
abcdefghijklmnopqrstuvwxyz
0123456789&?!$%"".,/;()

8 point type, 9 point linespace

The alphabet is firmly fixed in the shapes of its letters. Three-year-olds recognize letterforms. Yet there are on the order of 50,000 typefaces in existence, each different. Subtle and not-so-subtle variations in the thickness of the lines, the curves and angles, the shapes of the serifs, the relative sizes of the parts of the letters, and other design features, all add up to individualities. The alphabet is firmly fixed in the shapes of its letters. Three-year-olds recognize letterforms. Yet there are on the order of 50,000 typefaces in existence, each different. Subtle and not-so-subtle variations in the thickness of the lines, the curves and angles, the shapes of the serifs, the relative sizes of the parts of the letters, and other design features, all add up to individualities. The alphabet is firmly fixed in the shapes of its letters. Three-year-olds recognize letterforms. Yet there are on the order of 50,000 typefaces in existence, each different. Subtle and not-so-subtle variations in the thickness of the lines, the curves and angles, the shapes of the serifs, the relative sizes of the parts of the letters, and other design features, all add up to individualities. The alphabet is firmly fixed in the shapes of its letters. Three-year-olds recognize letterforms. Yet there are on the order of 50,000 typefaces in existence, each different. Subtle and not-so-subtle variations in the thickness of the lines, the curves and angles, the shapes of the serifs, the relative sizes of the parts of the letters, and other design features, all add up to individualities. The alphabet is firmly fixed in the shapes of its

10 point type, 11 point linespace

The alphabet is firmly fixed in the shapes of its letters. Three-year-olds recognize letterforms. Yet there are on the order of 50,000 typefaces in existence, each different. Subtle and not-so-subtle variations in the thickness of the lines, the curves and angles, the shapes of the serifs, the relative sizes of the parts of the letters, and other design features, all add up to individualities. The alphabet is firmly fixed in the shapes of its letters. Three-year-olds recognize letterforms. Yet there are on the order of 50,000 typefaces in existence, each different. Subtle and not-so-subtle variations in the thickness of the lines, the curves and angles, the shapes of the serifs, the relative sizes of the parts of the letters, and other design features, all add up to individualities. The alphabet is firmly fixed in the shapes of its letters. Three-year-olds recognize letterforms. Yet there are on the the order of 50,000 typefaces in existence, each different. Subtle and not-so-subtle variations in the thickness of the lines, the curves and angles, the shapes of

12 point type, 13 point linespace

The alphabet is firmly fixed in the shapes of its letters. Three-year-olds recognize letterforms. Yet there are on the order of 50,000 typefaces in existence, each different. Subtle and not-so-subtle variations in the thickness of the lines, the curves and angles, the shapes of the serifs, the relative sizes of the parts of the letters, and other design features, all add up to individualities. The alphabet is firmly fixed in the shapes of its letters. Three-year-olds recognize letterforms. Yet there are on the order of 50,000 typefaces in existence, each different. Subtle and not-so-subtle variations in the thickness of the lines, the curves and angles, the shapes of its letters. Three-year-olds recognize letterforms. Yet there are on the order of 50,000 typefaces

This face does exactly and only what an italic is supposed to do: add emphasis and motion. Therefore it should be used only and exactly where italic is needed, not willy-nilly.

ABCDEFGHIJKLMNOPQRSTUVWXYZ
abcdefghijklmnopqrstuvwxyz
0123456789&?!$%“”.,/;()

8 point type, 9 point linespace

The alphabet is firmly fixed in the shapes of its letters. Three-year-olds recognize letterforms. Yet there are on the order of 50,000 typefaces in existence, each different. Subtle and not-so-subtle variations in the thickness of the lines, the curves and angles, the shapes of the serifs, the relative sizes of the parts of the letters, and other design features, all add up to individualities. The alphabet is firmly fixed in the shapes of its letters. Three-year-olds recognize letterforms. Yet there are on the order of 50,000 typefaces in existence, each different. Subtle and not-so-subtle variations in the thickness of the lines, the curves and angles, the shapes of the serifs, the relative sizes of the parts of the letters, and other design features, all add up to individualities. The alphabet is firmly fixed in the shapes of its letters. Three-year-olds recognize letterforms. Yet there are on the order of 50,000 typefaces in existence, each different. Subtle and not-so-subtle variations in the thickness of the lines, the curves and angles, the shapes of the serifs, the relative sizes of the parts of the letters, and other design features, all add up to individualities. The alphabet is firmly fixed in the shapes of its letters. Three-year-olds recognize letterforms. Yet there are on the order of 50,000 typefaces in existence, each different. Subtle and not-so-subtle variations in the thickness of the lines, the curves and angles, the shapes

10 point type, 11 point linespace

The alphabet is firmly fixed in the shapes of its letters. Three-year-olds recognize letterforms. Yet there are on the order of 50,000 typefaces in existence, each different. Subtle and not-so-subtle variations in the thickness of the lines, the curves and angles, the shapes of the serifs, the relative sizes of the parts of the letters, and other design features, all add up to individualities. The alphabet is firmly fixed in the shapes of its letters. Three-year-olds recognize letterforms. Yet there are on the order of 50,000 typefaces in existence, each different. Subtle and not-so-subtle variations in the thickness of the lines, the curves and angles, the shapes of the serifs, the relative sizes of the parts of the letters, and other design features, all add up to individualities. The alphabet is firmly fixed in the shapes of its letters. Three-year-olds recognize letterforms. Yet there are on the the order of 50,000 typefaces in existence, each different. Subtle

12 point type, 13 point linespace

The alphabet is firmly fixed in the shapes of its letters. Three-year-olds recognize letterforms. Yet there are on the order of 50,000 typefaces in exist-ence, each different. Subtle and not-so-subtle variations in the thickness of the lines, the curves and angles, the shapes of the serifs, the relative sizes of the parts of the letters, and other design features, all add up to individu-alities. The alphabet is firmly fixed in the shapes of its letters. Three-year-olds recognize letterforms. Yet there are on the order of 50,000 typefaces in existence, each different. Subtle and not-so-subtle variations in the thickness of the lines, the curves and angles, the shapes of its letters. Three-year-olds

Part of Frutiger’s appeal is its airiness, so setting it tightly defeats its pur-pose. Its even strokes permit this weight to be set in small sizes without harm. Especially good for art-oriented publications.

ABCDEFGHIJKLMNOPQRSTUVWXYZ abcdefghijklmnopqrstuvwxyz 0123456789&?!$% “ ” .,/;()

8 point type, 9 point linespace

The alphabet is firmly fixed in the shapes of its letters. Three-year-olds recognize letterforms. Yet there are on the order of 50,000 typefaces in existence, each different. Subtle and not-so-subtle variations in the thickness of the lines, the curves and angles, the shapes of the serifs, the relative sizes of the parts of the letters, and other design features, all add up to individualities. The alphabet is firmly fixed in the shapes of its letters. Three-year-olds recognize letterforms. Yet there are on the order of 50,000 typefaces in existence, each different. Subtle and not-so-subtle variations in the thickness of the lines, the curves and angles, the shapes of the serifs, the relative sizes of the parts of the letters, and other design features, all add up to individualities. The alphabet is firmly fixed in the shapes of its letters. Three-year-olds recognize letterforms. Yet there are on the order of 50,000 typefaces in existence, each different. Subtle and not-so-subtle variations in the thickness of the lines, the curves and angles, the shapes of the serifs, the relative sizes of the parts of the letters, and other design features, all add up to individualities. The alphabet is firmly fixed in the shapes of its letters. Three-year-olds recognize letterforms. Yet there are on the order of 50,000 typefaces in existence, each different. Subtle and not-so-subtle variations in the thickness of the lines, the curves and angles, the shapes

10 point type, 11 point linespace

The alphabet is firmly fixed in the shapes of its letters. Three-year-olds recognize letterforms. Yet there are on the order of 50,000 typefaces in existence, each different. Subtle and not-so-subtle variations in the thickness of the lines, the curves and angles, the shapes of the serifs, the relative sizes of the parts of the letters, and other design features, all add up to individualities. The alphabet is firmly fixed in the shapes of its letters. Three-year-olds recognize letterforms. Yet there are on the order of 50,000 typefaces in existence, each different. Subtle and not-so-subtle variations in the thickness of the lines, the curves and angles, the shapes of the serifs, the relative sizes of the parts of the letters, and other design features, all add up to individualities. The alphabet is firmly fixed in the shapes of its letters. Three-year-olds recognize letterforms. Yet there are on the the order of 50,000 typefaces in existence, each different. Subtle

12 point type, 13 point linespace

The alphabet is firmly fixed in the shapes of its letters. Three-year-olds recognize letterforms. Yet there are on the order of 50,000 typefaces in exist-ence, each different. Subtle and not-so-subtle variations in the thickness of the lines, the curves and angles, the shapes of the serifs, the relative sizes of the parts of the letters, and other design features, all add up to individu-alities. The alphabet is firmly fixed in the shapes of its letters. Three-year-olds recognize letterforms. Yet there are on the order of 50,000 typefaces in existence, each different. Subtle and not-so-subtle variations in the thickness of the lines, the curves and angles, the shapes of its letters. Three-year-olds

Actually rather nondescript as italics go, it doesn’t add much to any printed piece. Slanting it another couple of degrees makes a huge difference in the impact it can have. Or set it tighter.

ABCDEFGHIJKLMNOPQRSTUVWXYZ
abcdefghijklmnopqrstuvwxyz
0123456789&?!$%“”.,/;()

8 point type, 9 point linespace

The alphabet is firmly fixed in the shapes of its letters. Three-year-olds recognize letterforms. Yet there are on the order of 50,000 typefaces in existence, each different. Subtle and not-so-subtle variations in the thickness of the lines, the curves and angles, the shapes of the serifs, the relative sizes of the parts of the letters, and other design features, all add up to individualities. The alphabet is firmly fixed in the shapes of its letters. Three-year-olds recognize letterforms. Yet there are on the order of 50,000 typefaces in existence, each different. Subtle and not-so-subtle variations in the thickness of the lines, the curves and angles, the shapes of the serifs, the relative sizes of the parts of the letters, and other design features, all add up to individualities. The alphabet is firmly fixed in the shapes of its letters. Three-year-olds recognize letterforms. Yet there are on the order of 50,000 typefaces in existence, each different. Subtle and not-so-subtle variations in the thickness of the lines, the curves and angles, the shapes of the serifs, the relative sizes of the parts of the letters, and other design features, all add up to individualities. The alphabet is firmly fixed in the shapes of its letters. Three-year-olds recognize letterforms. Yet there are on the order of 50,000 typefaces in existence, each different. Subtle and not-so-subtle variations in the thickness of the lines, the curves and angles, the shapes

10 point type, 11 point linespace

The alphabet is firmly fixed in the shapes of its letters. Three-year-olds recognize letterforms. Yet there are on the order of 50,000 typefaces in existence, each different. Subtle and not-so-subtle variations in the thickness of the lines, the curves and angles, the shapes of the serifs, the relative sizes of the parts of the letters, and other design features, all add up to individualities. The alphabet is firmly fixed in the shapes of its letters. Three-year-olds recognize letterforms. Yet there are on the order of 50,000 typefaces in existence, each different. Subtle and not-so-subtle variations in the thickness of the lines, the curves and angles, the shapes of the serifs, the relative sizes of the parts of the letters, and other design features, all add up to individualities. The alphabet is firmly fixed in the shapes of its letters. Three-year-olds recognize letterforms. Yet there are on the the order of 50,000 typefaces in existence,

12 point type, 13 point linespace

The alphabet is firmly fixed in the shapes of its letters. Three-year-olds recognize letterforms. Yet there are on the order of 50,000 typefaces in exist-ence, each different. Subtle and not-so-subtle variations in the thickness of the lines, the curves and angles, the shapes of the serifs, the relative sizes of the parts of the letters, and other design features, all add up to individu-alities. The alphabet is firmly fixed in the shapes of its letters. Three-year-olds recognize letterforms. Yet there are on the order of 50,000 typefaces in existence, each different. Subtle and not-so-subtle variations in the thick-ness of the lines, the curves and angles, the shapes of its letters. Three-

This bold face isn’t a very dark bold face and shouldn’t be used as if it were. It is a more diffident face, unprepossessing, for use to point out something, but not demand it be appreciated.

ABCDEFGHIJKLMNOPQRSTUVWXYZ
abcdefghijklmnopqrstuvwxyz
0123456789&?!$%"".,/;()

8 point type, 9 point linespace

The alphabet is firmly fixed in the shapes of its letters. Three-year-olds recognize letterforms. Yet there are on the order of 50,000 typefaces in existence, each different. Subtle and not-so-subtle variations in the thickness of the lines, the curves and angles, the shapes of the serifs, the relative sizes of the parts of the letters, and other design features, all add up to individualities. The alphabet is firmly fixed in the shapes of its letters. Three-year-olds recognize letterforms. Yet there are on the order of 50,000 typefaces in existence, each different. Subtle and not-so-subtle variations in the thickness of the lines, the curves and angles, the shapes of the serifs, the relative sizes of the parts of the letters, and other design features, all add up to individualities. The alphabet is firmly fixed in the shapes of its letters. Three-year-olds recognize letterforms. Yet there are on the order of 50,000 typefaces in existence, each different. Subtle and not-so-subtle variations in the thickness of the lines, the curves and angles, the shapes of the serifs, the relative sizes of the parts of the letters, and other design features, all add up to individualities. The alphabet is firmly fixed in the shapes of its letters. Three-year-olds recognize letterforms.Yet there are on the order of 50,000 typefaces in existence, each different. Subtle and not-so-subtle variations in the thickness of the lines, the curves and angles, the shapes

10 point type, 11 point linespace

The alphabet is firmly fixed in the shapes of its letters. Three-year-olds recognize letterforms. Yet there are on the order of 50,000 typefaces in existence, each different. Subtle and not-so-subtle variations in the thickness of the lines, the curves and angles, the shapes of the serifs, the relative sizes of the parts of the letters, and other design features, all add up to individualities. The alphabet is firmly fixed in the shapes of its letters. Three-year-olds recognize letterforms. Yet there are on the order of 50,000 typefaces in existence, each different. Subtle and not-so-subtle variations in the thickness of the lines, the curves and angles, the shapes of the serifs, the relative sizes of the parts of the letters, and other design features, all add up to individualities. The alphabet is firmly fixed in the shapes of its letters. Three-year-olds recognize letterforms. Yet there are on the order of 50,000 typefaces in existence, each

12 point type, 13 point linespace

The alphabet is firmly fixed in the shapes of its letters. Three-year-olds recognize letterforms. Yet there are on the order of 50,000 typefaces in existence, each different. Subtle and not-so-subtle variations in the thickness of the lines, the curves and angles, the shapes of the serifs, the relative sizes of the parts of the letters, and other design features, all add up to individualities. The alphabet is firmly fixed in the shapes of its letters. Three-year-olds recognize letterforms. Yet there are on the order of 50,000 typefaces in existence, each different. Subtle and not-so-subtle variations in the thickness of the lines, the curves and angles, the shapes of the serifs, the

This one has some life to it and is preferable to the plain bold when importance is an issue. Here is one of the very few cases when italic can be used more than roman to best make the point.

ABCDEFGHIJKLMNOPQRSTUVWXYZ
abcdefghijklmnopqrstuvwxyz
0123456789&?!$%“”.,/;()

8 point type, 9 point linespace

The alphabet is firmly fixed in the shapes of its letters. Three-year-olds recognize letterforms. Yet there are on the order of 50,000 typefaces in existence, each different. Subtle and not-so-subtle variations in the thickness of the lines, the curves and angles, the shapes of the serifs, the relative sizes of the parts of the letters, and other design features, all add up to individualities. The alphabet is firmly fixed in the shapes of its letters. Three-year-olds recognize letterforms. Yet there are on the order of 50,000 typefaces in existence, each different. Subtle and not-so-subtle variations in the thickness of the lines, the curves and angles, the shapes of the serifs, the relative sizes of the parts of the letters, and other design features, all add up to individualities. The alphabet is firmly fixed in the shapes of its letters. Three-year-olds recognize letterforms. Yet there are on the order of 50,000 typefaces in existence, each different. Subtle and not-so-subtle variations in the thickness of the lines, the curves and angles, the shapes of the serifs, the relative sizes of the parts of the letters, and other design features, all add up to individualities. The alphabet is firmly fixed in the shapes of its letters. Three-year-olds recognize letterforms. Yet there

10 point type, 11 point linespace

The alphabet is firmly fixed in the shapes of its letters. Three-year-olds recognize letterforms. Yet there are on the order of 50,000 typefaces in existence, each different. Subtle and not-so-subtle variations in the thickness of the lines, the curves and angles, the shapes of the serifs, the relative sizes of the parts of the letters, and other design features, all add up to individualities. The alphabet is firmly fixed in the shapes of its letters. Three-year-olds recognize letterforms. Yet there are on the order of 50,000 typefaces in existence, each different. Subtle and not-so-subtle variations in the thickness of the lines, the curves and angles, the shapes of the serifs, the relative sizes of the parts of the letters, and other design features, all add up to individualities. The alphabet is firmly fixed in the shapes of its letters. Three-

12 point type, 13 point linespace

The alphabet is firmly fixed in the shapes of its letters. Three-year-olds recognize letterforms. Yet there are on the order of 50,000 typefaces in existence, each different. Subtle and not-so-subtle variations in the thickness of the lines, the curves and angles, the shapes of the serifs, the relative sizes of the parts of the letters, and other design features, all add up to individualities. The alphabet is firmly fixed in the shapes of its letters. Three-year-olds recognize letterforms. Yet there are on the order of 50,000 typefaces in existence, each different. Subtle and not-so-subtle variations in the

Now we get into a headline face, and a very good one. Clean, easy to read instantly, and attractive in its own right, it works both with Frutiger body copy and with all but the most conservative serif faces. Set tightly.

ABCDEFGHIJKLMNOPQRSTUVWXYZ
abcdefghijklmnopqrstuvwxyz
0123456789&?!$%“”.,/;()

8 point type, 9 point linespace

The alphabet is firmly fixed in the shapes of its letters. Three-year-olds recognize letterforms. Yet there are on the order of 50,000 typefaces in existence, each different. Subtle and not-so-subtle variations in the thickness of the lines, the curves and angles, the shapes of the serifs, the relative sizes of the parts of the letters, and other design features, all add up to individualities. The alphabet is firmly fixed in the shapes of its letters. Three-year-olds recognize letterforms. Yet there are on the order of 50,000 typefaces in existence, each different. Subtle and not-so-subtle variations in the thickness of the lines, the curves and angles, the shapes of the serifs, the relative sizes of the parts of the letters, and other design features, all add up to individualities. The alphabet is firmly fixed in the shapes of its letters. Three-year-olds recognize letterforms. Yet there are on the order of 50,000 typefaces in existence, each different. Subtle and not-so-subtle variations in the thickness of the lines, the curves and angles, the shapes of the serifs, the relative sizes of the parts of the letters, and other design features, all add up to individualities. The alphabet is firmly fixed in the shapes of its letters. Three-year-olds recognize letterforms. Yet there

10 point type, 11 point linespace

The alphabet is firmly fixed in the shapes of its letters. Three-year-olds recognize letterforms. Yet there are on the order of 50,000 typefaces in existence, each different. Subtle and not-so-subtle variations in the thickness of the lines, the curves and angles, the shapes of the serifs, the relative sizes of the parts of the letters, and other design features, all add up to individualities. The alphabet is firmly fixed in the shapes of its letters. Three-year-olds recognize letterforms. Yet there are on the order of 50,000 typefaces in existence, each different. Subtle and not-so-subtle variations in the thickness of the lines, the curves and angles, the shapes of the serifs, the relative sizes of the parts of the letters, and other design features, all add up to individualities. The alphabet is firmly fixed in the shapes of its letters. Three-year-olds

12 point type, 13 point linespace

The alphabet is firmly fixed in the shapes of its letters. Three-year-olds recognize letterforms. Yet there are on the order of 50,000 typefaces in existence, each different. Subtle and not-so-subtle variations in the thickness of the lines, the curves and angles, the shapes of the serifs, the relative sizes of the parts of the letters, and other design features, all add up to individualities. The alphabet is firmly fixed in the shapes of its letters. Three-year-olds recognize letterforms. Yet there are on the order of 50,000 typefaces in existence, each different. Subtle and not-so-subtle variations in the

This face starts a piece off with a bang, so whatever follows it has to be pretty high-powered to avoid a letdown in energy level. Save this face for the most intense design and copy combos.

ABCDEFGHIJKLMNOPQRSTUVWXYZ
abcdefghijklmnopqrstuvwxyz
0123456789&?!$%“”.,/;()

8 point type, 9 point linespace

The alphabet is firmly fixed in the shapes of its letters. Three-year-olds recognize letterforms. Yet there are on the order of 50,000 typefaces in existence, each different. Subtle and not-so-subtle variations in the thickness of the lines, the curves and angles, the shapes of the serifs, the relative sizes of the parts of the letters, and other design features, all add up to individualities. The alphabet is firmly fixed in the shapes of its letters. Three-year-olds recognize letterforms. Yet there are on the order of 50,000 typefaces in existence, each different. Subtle and not-so-subtle variations in the thickness of the lines, the curves and angles, the shapes of the serifs, the relative sizes of the parts of the letters, and other design features, all add up to individualities. The alphabet is firmly fixed in the shapes of its letters. Three-year-olds recognize letterforms. Yet there are on the order of 50,000 typefaces in existence, each different. Subtle and not-so-subtle variations in the thickness of the lines, the curves and angles, the shapes of the serifs, the relative sizes of the parts of the letters, and other design features, all add up to individualities. The alphabet is firmly fixed in

10 point type, 11 point linespace

The alphabet is firmly fixed in the shapes of its letters. Three-year-olds recognize letterforms. Yet there are on the order of 50,000 typefaces in existence, each different. Subtle and not-so-subtle variations in the thickness of the lines, the curves and angles, the shapes of the serifs, the relative sizes of the parts of the letters, and other design features, all add up to individualities. The alphabet is firmly fixed in the shapes of its letters. Three-year-olds recognize letterforms. Yet there are on the order of 50,000 typefaces in existence, each different. Subtle and not-so-subtle variations in the thickness of the lines, the curves and angles, the shapes of the serifs, the relative sizes of the parts of the letters, and other design features, all add up to individualities.

12 point type, 13 point linespace

The alphabet is firmly fixed in the shapes of its letters. Three-year-olds recognize letterforms. Yet there are on the order of 50,000 typefaces in existence, each different. Subtle and not-so-subtle variations in the thickness of the lines, the curves and angles, the shapes of the serifs, the relative sizes of the parts of the letters, and other design features, all add up to individualities. The alphabet is firmly fixed in the shapes of its letters. Three-year-olds recognize letterforms. Yet there are on the order of 50,000 typefaces in existence, each different. Subtle

This face is almost silly. It is heavy, unwieldy, and overblown. May be okay for a single word headline, or an individual character thrown in here and there, but not for general use.

ABCDEFGHIJKLMNOPQRSTUVWXYZ
abcdefghijklmnopqrstuvwxyz
0123456789&?!$%“”.,/;()

8 point type, 9 point linespace

The alphabet is firmly fixed in the shapes of its letters. Three-year-olds recognize letterforms. Yet there are on the order of 50,000 typefaces in existence, each different. Subtle and not-so-subtle variations in the thickness of the lines, the curves and angles, the shapes of the serifs, the relative sizes of the parts of the letters, and other design features, all add up to individualities. The alphabet is firmly fixed in the shapes of its letters. Three-year-olds recognize letterforms. Yet there are on the order of 50,000 typefaces in existence, each different. Subtle and not-so-subtle variations in the thickness of the lines, the curves and angles, the shapes of the serifs, the relative sizes of the parts of the letters, and other design features, all add up to individualities. The alphabet is firmly fixed in the shapes of its letters. Three-year-olds recognize letterforms. Yet there are on the order of 50,000 typefaces in existence, each different. Subtle and not-so-subtle variations in the thickness of the lines, the curves and angles, the shapes of the serifs, the relative sizes of the parts of the letters, and other design features, all add up to individualities. The alphabet is firmly fixed in the shapes of its letters. Three-year-olds recognize letterforms. Yet there are on the order of 50,000 typefaces in existence, each different. Subtle and not-so-subtle variations in the thickness of the lines, the curves and angles, the shapes of the serifs, the relative sizes of the parts of the letters, and other design features, all add up to individualities. The

10 point type, 11 point linespace

The alphabet is firmly fixed in the shapes of its letters. Three-year-olds recognize letterforms. Yet there are on the order of 50,000 typefaces in existence, each different. Subtle and not-so-subtle variations in the thickness of the lines, the curves and angles, the shapes of the serifs, the relative sizes of the parts of the letters, and other design features, all add up to individualities. The alphabet is firmly fixed in the shapes of its letters. Three-year-olds recognize letterforms. Yet there are on the order of 50,000 typefaces in existence, each different. Subtle and not-so-subtle variations in the thickness of the lines, the curves and angles, the shapes of the serifs, the relative sizes of the parts of the letters, and other design features, all add up to individualities. The alphabet is firmly fixed in the shapes of its letters. Three-year-olds recognize letterforms. Yet there are on the order of 50,000 typefaces in existence, each different. Subtle and not-so-subtle variations in the thickness of the lines, the

12 point type, 13 point linespace

The alphabet is firmly fixed in the shapes of its letters. Three-year-olds recognize letterforms. Yet there are on the order of 50,000 typefaces in existence, each different. Subtle and not-so-subtle variations in the thickness of the lines, the curves and angles, the shapes of the serifs, the relative sizes of the parts of the letters, and other design features, all add up to individualities. The alphabet is firmly fixed in the shapes of its letters. Three-year-olds recognize letterforms. Yet there are on the order of 50,000 typefaces in existence, each different. Subtle and not-so-subtle variations in the thickness of the lines, the curves and angles, the shapes of the serifs, the relative sizes of the parts of the letters, and other design features,

Some letters have *very* thin strokes, so this face should never be used under 10-point, and 12 or above is safer. Set loosely, as squeezing the letters defeats its purpose of being airy and graceful.

ABCDEFGHIJKLMNOPQRSTUVWXYZ
abcdefghijklmnopqrstuvwxyz
0123456789&?!$%“”.,/;()

8 point type, 9 point linespace

The alphabet is firmly fixed in the shapes of its letters. Three-year-olds recognize letterforms. Yet there are on the order of 50,000 typefaces in existence, each different. Subtle and not-so-subtle variations in the thickness of the lines, the curves and angles, the shapes of the serifs, the relative sizes of the parts of the letters, and other design features, all add up to individualities. The alphabet is firmly fixed in the shapes of its letters. Three-year-olds recognize letterforms. Yet there are on the order of 50,000 typefaces in existence, each different. Subtle and not-so-subtle variations in the thickness of the lines, the curves and angles, the shapes of the serifs, the relative sizes of the parts of the letters, and other design features, all add up to individualities. The alphabet is firmly fixed in the shapes of its letters. Three-year-olds recognize letterforms. Yet there are on the order of 50,000 typefaces in existence, each different. Subtle and not-so-subtle variations in the thickness of the lines, the curves and angles, the shapes of the serifs, the relative sizes of the parts of the letters, and other design features, all add up to individualities. The alphabet is firmly fixed in the shapes of its letters. Three-year-olds recognize letterforms. Yet there are on the order of 50,000 typefaces in existence, each different. Subtle and not-so-subtle variations in the thickness of the lines, the curves and angles, the shapes of the serifs, the relative sizes of the parts of the letters, and other design features, all add up to individualities. The alphabet is firmly fixed in the

10 point type, 11 point linespace

The alphabet is firmly fixed in the shapes of its letters. Three-year-olds recognize letterforms. Yet there are on the order of 50,000 typefaces in existence, each different. Subtle and not-so-subtle variations in the thickness of the lines, the curves and angles, the shapes of the serifs, the relative sizes of the parts of the letters, and other design features, all add up to individualities. The alphabet is firmly fixed in the shapes of its letters. Three-year-olds recognize letterforms. Yet there are on the order of 50,000 typefaces in existence, each different. Subtle and not-so-subtle variations in the thickness of the lines, the curves and angles, the shapes of the serifs, the relative sizes of the parts of the letters, and other design features, all add up to individualities. The alphabet is firmly fixed in the shapes of its letters. Three-year-olds recognize letterforms. Yet there are on the order of 50,000 typefaces in existence, each different. Subtle and not-so-subtle variations in the thickness of the lines, the curves and angles,

12 point type, 13 point linespace

The alphabet is firmly fixed in the shapes of its letters. Three-year-olds recognize letterforms. Yet there are on the order of 50,000 typefaces in existence, each different. Subtle and not-so-subtle variations in the thickness of the lines, the curves and angles, the shapes of the serifs, the relative sizes of the parts of the letters, and other design features, all add up to individualities. The alphabet is firmly fixed in the shapes of its letters. Three-year-olds recognize letterforms. Yet there are on the order of 50,000 typefaces in existence, each different. Subtle and not-so-subtle variations in the thickness of the lines, the curves and angles, the shapes of the serifs, the relative sizes of the parts of the letters, and other design features, all add up to

Overall a bit darker than the roman, this can create a jarring note if used indiscriminately within roman text. Some characters not easy to read (h, u, v). Use with caution and in small quantities.

ABCDEFGHIJKLMNOPQRSTUVWXYZ
abcdefghijklmnopqrstuvwxyz
0123456789&?!$%“”.,/;()

8 point type, 9 point linespace

The alphabet is firmly fixed in the shapes of its letters. Three-year-olds recognize letterforms. Yet there are on the order of 50,000 typefaces in existence, each different. Subtle and not-so-subtle variations in the thickness of the lines, the curves and angles, the shapes of the serifs, the relative sizes of the parts of the letters, and other design features, all add up to individualities. The alphabet is firmly fixed in the shapes of its letters. Three-year-olds recognize letterforms. Yet there are on the order of 50,000 typefaces in existence, each different. Subtle and not-so-subtle variations in the thickness of the lines, the curves and angles, the shapes of the serifs, the relative sizes of the parts of the letters, and other design features, all add up to individualities. The alphabet is firmly fixed in the shapes of its letters. Three-year-olds recognize letterforms. Yet there are on the order of 50,000 typefaces in existence, each different. Subtle and not-so-subtle variations in the thickness of the lines, the curves and angles, the shapes of the serifs, the relative sizes of the parts of the letters, and other design features, all add up to individualities. The alphabet is firmly fixed in the shapes of its letters. Three-year-olds recognize letterforms. Yet there are on the order of 50,000 typefaces in existence, each different. Subtle and not-so-subtle variations in the thickness of the lines, the curves and angles, the shapes of the serifs, the relative sizes of the parts of the letters, and other design features, all add up to individualities. The alphabet is firmly fixed in the shapes of its letters. Three-year-

10 point type, 11 point linespace

The alphabet is firmly fixed in the shapes of its letters. Three-year-olds recognize letterforms. Yet there are on the order of 50,000 typefaces in existence, each different. Subtle and not-so-subtle variations in the thickness of the lines, the curves and angles, the shapes of the serifs, the relative sizes of the parts of the letters, and other design features, all add up to individualities. The alphabet is firmly fixed in the shapes of its letters. Three-year-olds recognize letterforms. Yet there are on the order of 50,000 typefaces in existence, each different. Subtle and not-so-subtle variations in the thickness of the lines, the curves and angles, the shapes of the serifs, the relative sizes of the parts of the letters, and other design features, all add up to individualities. The alphabet is firmly fixed in the shapes of its letters. Three-year-olds recognize letterforms. Yet there are on the order of 50,000 typefaces in existence, each different. Subtle and not-so-subtle variations in the thickness of the lines, the curves and angles, the shapes of the serifs, the

12 point type, 13 point linespace

The alphabet is firmly fixed in the shapes of its letters. Three-year-olds recognize letterforms. Yet there are on the order of 50,000 typefaces in existence, each different. Subtle and not-so-subtle variations in the thickness of the lines, the curves and angles, the shapes of the serifs, the relative sizes of the parts of the letters, and other design features, all add up to individualities. The alphabet is firmly fixed in the shapes of its letters. Three-year-olds recognize letterforms. Yet there are on the order of 50,000 typefaces in existence, each different. Subtle and not-so-subtle variations in the thickness of the lines, the curves and angles, the shapes of the serifs, the relative sizes of the parts of the letters, and other design features, all add up to

Much more useful than Light, can be used from 8 to 30 point effectively, but best from 12 to 18. Often used in children’s books, because is easy to read. Demonstrates an awareness of aesthetics and consideration for the reader.

ABCDEFGHIJKLMNOPQRSTUVWXYZ
abcdefghijklmnopqrstuvwxyz
0123456789&?!$%“”.,/;()

8 point type, 9 point linespace

The alphabet is firmly fixed in the shapes of its letters. Three-year-olds recognize letterforms. Yet there are on the order of 50,000 typefaces in existence, each different. Subtle and not-so-subtle variations in the thickness of the lines, the curves and angles, the shapes of the serifs, the relative sizes of the parts of the letters, and other design features, all add up to individualities. The alphabet is firmly fixed in the shapes of its letters. Three-year-olds recognize letterforms. Yet there are on the order of 50,000 typefaces in existence, each different. Subtle and not-so-subtle variations in the thickness of the lines, the curves and angles, the shapes of the serifs, the relative sizes of the parts of the letters, and other design features, all add up to individualities. The alphabet is firmly fixed in the shapes of its letters. Three-year-olds recognize letterforms. Yet there are on the order of 50,000 typefaces in existence, each different. Subtle and not-so-subtle variations in the thickness of the lines, the curves and angles, the shapes of the serifs, the relative sizes of the parts of the letters, and other design features, all add up to individualities. The alphabet is firmly fixed in the shapes of its letters. Three-year-olds recognize letterforms. Yet there are on the order of 50,000 typefaces in existence, each different. Subtle and not-so-subtle variations in the thickness of the lines, the curves and angles, the shapes of the serifs, the relative sizes of the parts of the letters, and other design features, all add up to individualities. The alphabet is firmly fixed in the

10 point type, 11 point linespace

The alphabet is firmly fixed in the shapes of its letters. Three-year-olds recognize letterforms. Yet there are on the order of 50,000 typefaces in existence, each different. Subtle and not-so-subtle variations in the thickness of the lines, the curves and angles, the shapes of the serifs, the relative sizes of the parts of the letters, and other design features, all add up to individualities. The alphabet is firmly fixed in the shapes of its letters. Three-year-olds recognize letterforms. Yet there are on the order of 50,000 typefaces in existence, each different. Subtle and not-so-subtle variations in the thickness of the lines, the curves and angles, the shapes of the serifs, the relative sizes of the parts of the letters, and other design features, all add up to individualities. The alphabet is firmly fixed in the shapes of its letters. Three-year-olds recognize letterforms. Yet there are on the order of 50,000 typefaces in existence, each different. Subtle and not-so-subtle variations in the thickness of the lines, the curves and angles,

12 point type, 13 point linespace

The alphabet is firmly fixed in the shapes of its letters. Three-year-olds recognize letterforms. Yet there are on the order of 50,000 typefaces in existence, each different. Subtle and not-so-subtle variations in the thickness of the lines, the curves and angles, the shapes of the serifs, the relative sizes of the parts of the letters, and other design features, all add up to individualities. The alphabet is firmly fixed in the shapes of its letters. Three-year-olds recognize letterforms. Yet there are on the order of 50,000 typefaces in existence, each different. Subtle and not-so-subtle variations in the thickness of the lines, the curves and angles, the shapes of the serifs, the relative sizes of the parts of the letters, and other design features, all add

Much stronger than the Light Italic, this face may be used less gingerly, though still not splashed hither and yon at random. Use for a specific purpose, not to create contrast for contrast's sake.

ABCDEFGHIJKLMNOPQRSTUVWXYZ
abcdefghijklmnopqrstuvwxyz
0123456789&?!$%“”.,/;()

8 point type, 9 point linespace

The alphabet is firmly fixed in the shapes of its letters. Three-year-olds recognize letterforms. Yet there are on the order of 50,000 typefaces in existence, each different. Subtle and not-so-subtle variations in the thickness of the lines, the curves and angles, the shapes of the serifs, the relative sizes of the parts of the letters, and other design features, all add up to individualities. The alphabet is firmly fixed in the shapes of its letters. Three-year-olds recognize letterforms. Yet there are on the order of 50,000 typefaces in existence, each different. Subtle and not-so-subtle variations in the thickness of the lines, the curves and angles, the shapes of the serifs, the relative sizes of the parts of the letters, and other design features, all add up to individualities. The alphabet is firmly fixed in the shapes of its letters. Three-year-olds recognize letterforms. Yet there are on the order of 50,000 typefaces in existence, each different. Subtle and not-so-subtle variations in the thickness of the lines, the curves and angles, the shapes of the serifs, the relative sizes of the parts of the letters, and other design features, all add up to individualities. The alphabet is firmly fixed in the shapes of its letters. Three-year-olds recognize letterforms. Yet there are on the order of 50,000 typefaces in existence, each different. Subtle and not-so-subtle variations in the

10 point type, 11 point linespace

The alphabet is firmly fixed in the shapes of its letters. Three-year-olds recognize letterforms. Yet there are on the order of 50,000 typefaces in existence, each different. Subtle and not-so-subtle variations in the thickness of the lines, the curves and angles, the shapes of the serifs, the relative sizes of the parts of the letters, and other design features, all add up to individualities. The alphabet is firmly fixed in the shapes of its letters. Three-year-olds recognize letterforms. Yet there are on the order of 50,000 typefaces in existence, each different. Subtle and not-so-subtle variations in the thickness of the lines, the curves and angles, the shapes of the serifs, the relative sizes of the parts of the letters, and other design features, all add up to individualities. The alphabet is firmly fixed in the shapes of its letters. Three-year-olds recognize letterforms. Yet there are on the order of

12 point type, 13 point linespace

The alphabet is firmly fixed in the shapes of its letters. Three-year-olds recognize letterforms. Yet there are on the order of 50,000 typefaces in existence, each different. Subtle and not-so-subtle variations in the thick-ness of the lines, the curves and angles, the shapes of the serifs, the relative sizes of the parts of the let-ters, and other design features, all add up to individualities. The alphabet is firmly fixed in the shapes of its let-ters. Three-year-olds recognize letterforms. Yet there are on the order of 50,000 typefaces in exist-ence, each differ-ent. Subtle and not-so-subtle variations in the thickness of the lines, the curves and angles, the

A strange face with a lot of contrast in stroke thickness, should be used only in combo with other Garamonds. Hard to work with in large sizes, it’s fine for subheads or dramatic emphasis within text.

ABCDEFGHIJKLMNOPQRSTUVWXYZ
abcdefghijklmnopqrstuvwxyz
0123456789&?!$%“”.,/;()

8 point type, 9 point linespace

The alphabet is firmly fixed in the shapes of its letters. Three-year-olds recognize letterforms. Yet there are on the order of 50,000 typefaces in existence, each different. Subtle and not-so-subtle variations in the thickness of the lines, the curves and angles, the shapes of the serifs, the relative sizes of the parts of the letters, and other design features, all add up to individualities. The alphabet is firmly fixed in the shapes of its letters. Three-year-olds recognize letterforms. Yet there are on the order of 50,000 typefaces in existence, each different. Subtle and not-so-subtle variations in the thickness of the lines, the curves and angles, the shapes of the serifs, the relative sizes of the parts of the letters, and other design features, all add up to individualities. The alphabet is firmly fixed in the shapes of its letters. Three-year-olds recognize letterforms. Yet there are on the order of 50,000 typefaces in existence, each different. Subtle and not-so-subtle variations in the thickness of the lines, the curves and angles, the shapes of the serifs, the relative sizes of the parts of the letters, and other design features, all add up to individualities. The alphabet is firmly fixed in the shapes of its letters. Three-year-olds recognize letterforms. Yet there are on the order of 50,000 typefaces in existence, each different. Subtle and not-

10 point type, 11 point linespace

The alphabet is firmly fixed in the shapes of its letters. Three-year-olds recognize letterforms. Yet there are on the order of 50,000 typefaces in existence, each different. Subtle and not-so-subtle variations in the thickness of the lines, the curves and angles, the shapes of the serifs, the relative sizes of the parts of the letters, and other design features, all add up to individualities. The alphabet is firmly fixed in the shapes of its letters. Three-year-olds recognize letterforms. Yet there are on the order of 50,000 typefaces in existence, each different. Subtle and not-so-subtle variations in the thickness of the lines, the curves and angles, the shapes of the serifs, the relative sizes of the parts of the letters, and other design features, all add up to individualities. The alphabet is firmly fixed in the shapes of its letters. Three-year-olds recognize letterforms. Yet there are on the order of

12 point type, 13 point linespace

The alphabet is firmly fixed in the shapes of its letters. Three-year-olds recognize letterforms. Yet there are on the order of 50,000 typefaces in existence, each different. Subtle and not-so-subtle variations in the thickness of the lines, the curves and angles, the shapes of the serifs, the relative sizes of the parts of the letters, and other design features, all add up to individualities. The alphabet is firmly fixed in the shapes of its letters. Three-year-olds recognize letterforms. Yet there are on the order of 50,000 typefaces in existence, each differ-ent. Subtle and not-so-subtle variations in the thickness of the lines, the curves and angles,

Actually easier to work with than the roman, and probably the most readable Garamond, this face can be used more freely than most italics, even holding up well as a text face for small blocks of text. A dramatic face.

ABCDEFGHIJKLMNOPQRSTUVWXYZ
abcdefghijklmnopqrstuvwxyz
0123456789&?!$%“”.,/;()

8 point type, 9 point linespace

The alphabet is firmly fixed in the shapes of its letters. Three-year-olds recognize letterforms. Yet there are on the order of 50,000 typefaces in existence, each different. Subtle and not-so-subtle variations in the thickness of the lines, the curves and angles, the shapes of the serifs, the relative sizes of the parts of the letters, and other design features, all add up to individualities. The alphabet is firmly fixed in the shapes of its letters. Three-year-olds recognize letterforms. Yet there are on the order of 50,000 typefaces in existence, each different. Subtle and not-so-subtle variations in the thickness of the lines, the curves and angles, the shapes of the serifs, the relative sizes of the parts of the letters, and other design features, all add up to individualities. The alphabet is firmly fixed in the shapes of its letters. Three-year-olds recognize letterforms. Yet there are on the order of 50,000 typefaces in existence, each different. Subtle and not-so-subtle variations in the thickness of the lines, the curves and angles, the shapes of the serifs, the relative sizes of the parts of the letters, and other design features, all add up to individualities. The alphabet is firmly fixed in the shapes of its letters. Three-year-olds recognize letterforms. Yet there are on the order of 50,000 typefaces in

10 point type, 11 point linespace

The alphabet is firmly fixed in the shapes of its letters. Three-year-olds recognize letterforms. Yet there are on the order of 50,000 typefaces in existence, each different. Subtle and not-so-subtle variations in the thickness of the lines, the curves and angles, the shapes of the serifs, the relative sizes of the parts of the letters, and other design features, all add up to individualities. The alphabet is firmly fixed in the shapes of its letters. Three-year-olds recognize letterforms. Yet there are on the order of 50,000 typefaces in existence, each different. Subtle and not-so-subtle variations in the thickness of the lines, the curves and angles, the shapes of the serifs, the relative sizes of the parts of the letters, and other design features, all add up to individualities. The alphabet is firmly fixed in the shapes of its letters. Three-year-olds recognize letterforms. Yet

12 point type, 13 point linespace

The alphabet is firmly fixed in the shapes of its letters. Three-year-olds recognize letterforms. Yet there are on the order of 50,000 typefaces in existence, each different. Subtle and not-so-subtle variations in the thickness of the lines, the curves and angles, the shapes of the serifs, the relative sizes of the parts of the letters, and other design features, all add up to individualities. The alphabet is firmly fixed in the shapes of its letters. Three-year-olds recognize letterforms. Yet there are on the order of 50,000 typefaces in existence, each different. Subtle and not-so-subtle variations in the thick-

Very unwieldy, almost bloated. Hard to kern. Seldom defensible for normal use, but if you want to take the time to play with letter-spacing, can hit a reader hard as a megaton headline.

ABCDEFGHIJKLMNOPQRSTUVWXYZ
abcdefghijklmnopqrstuvwxyz
0123456789&?!$%“”.,/;()

8 point type, 9 point linespace

The alphabet is firmly fixed in the shapes of its letters. Three-year-olds recognize letterforms. Yet there are on the order of 50,000 typefaces in existence, each different. Subtle and not-so-subtle variations in the thickness of the lines, the curves and angles, the shapes of the serifs, the relative sizes of the parts of the letters, and other design features, all add up to individualities. The alphabet is firmly fixed in the shapes of its letters. Three-year-olds recognize letterforms. Yet there are on the order of 50,000 typefaces in existence, each different. Subtle and not-so-subtle variations in the thickness of the lines, the curves and angles, the shapes of the serifs, the relative sizes of the parts of the letters, and other design features, all add up to individualities. The alphabet is firmly fixed in the shapes of its letters. Three-year-olds recognize letterforms. Yet there are on the order of 50,000 typefaces in existence, each different. Subtle and not-so-subtle variations in the thickness of the lines, the curves and angles, the shapes of the serifs, the relative sizes of the parts of the letters, and other design features, all add up to individualities. The alphabet is firmly fixed in the shapes of its letters. Three-year-olds recognize letterforms. Yet there are on the order of 50,000

10 point type, 11 point linespace

The alphabet is firmly fixed in the shapes of its letters. Three-year-olds recognize letterforms. Yet there are on the order of 50,000 typefaces in existence, each different. Subtle and not-so-subtle variations in the thickness of the lines, the curves and angles, the shapes of the serifs, the relative sizes of the parts of the letters, and other design features, all add up to individualities. The alphabet is firmly fixed in the shapes of its letters. Three-year-olds recognize letterforms. Yet there are on the order of 50,000 typefaces in existence, each different. Subtle and not-so-subtle variations in the thickness of the lines, the curves and angles, the shapes of the serifs, the relative sizes of the parts of the letters, and other design features, all add up to individualities. The alphabet is firmly fixed in the shapes of its letters. Three-year-olds

12 point type, 13 point linespace

The alphabet is firmly fixed in the shapes of its letters. Three-year-olds recognize letterforms. Yet there are on the order of 50,000 typefaces in existence, each different. Subtle and not-so-subtle variations in the thickness of the lines, the curves and angles, the shapes of the serifs, the relative sizes of the parts of the letters, and other design features, all add up to individualities. The alphabet is firmly fixed in the shapes of its letters. Three-year-olds recognize letterforms. Yet there are on the order of 50,000 typefaces in existence, each different. Subtle and not-so-subtle variations in the

An almost useless face except when absolutely needed to stress a word against the roman. The numerals are strong by themselves and well designed, so have applications as graphic devices in a very dynamic piece.

ABCDEFGHIJKLMNOPQRSTUVWXYZ
abcdefghijklmnopqrstuvwxyz
0123456789&?!$%“”.,/;()

8 point type, 9 point linespace

The alphabet is firmly fixed in the shapes of its letters. Three-year-olds recognize letterforms. Yet there are on the order of 50,000 typefaces in existence, each different. Subtle and not-so-subtle variations in the thickness of the lines, the curves and angles, the shapes of the serifs, the relative sizes of the parts of the letters, and other design features, all add up to individualities. The alphabet is firmly fixed in the shapes of its letters. Three-year-olds recognize letterforms. Yet there are on the order of 50,000 typefaces in existence, each different. Subtle and not-so-subtle variations in the thickness of the lines, the curves and angles, the shapes of the serifs, the relative sizes of the parts of the letters, and other design features, all add up to individualities. The alphabet is firmly fixed in the shapes of its letters. Three-year-olds recognize letterforms. Yet there are on the order of 50,000 typefaces in existence, each different. Subtle and not-so-subtle variations in the thickness of the lines, the curves and angles, the shapes of the serifs, the relative sizes of the parts of the letters, and other design features, all add up to individualities. The alphabet is firmly fixed in the shapes of its letters. Three-year-olds recognize letterforms. Yet there are on the order of 50,000 typefaces in existence, each different. Subtle and not-so-subtle variations in the thickness of the lines, the curves and angles, the shapes of the serifs, the relative sizes of the parts of the letters, and other design features, all add up to individualities. The alphabet is firmly fixed in the shapes of its letters. Three-year-olds recognize letterforms. Yet there are on the order of 50,000 typefaces in existence, each different. Subtle and not-so-subtle variations in the thickness of the lines, the curves and angles, the shapes of the serifs, the relative sizes of the parts of the letters, and other design features, all add up to individualities. The alphabet is firmly fixed in the shapes of its letters. Three-year-olds

10 point type, 11 point linespace

The alphabet is firmly fixed in the shapes of its letters. Three-year-olds recognize letterforms. Yet there are on the order of 50,000 typefaces in existence, each different. Subtle and not-so-subtle variations in the thickness of the lines, the curves and angles, the shapes of the serifs, the relative sizes of the parts of the letters, and other design features, all add up to individualities. The alphabet is firmly fixed in the shapes of its letters. Three-year-olds recognize letterforms. Yet there are on the order of 50,000 typefaces in existence, each different. Subtle and not-so-subtle variations in the thickness of the lines, the curves and angles, the shapes of the serifs, the relative sizes of the parts of the letters, and other design features, all add up to individualities. The alphabet is firmly fixed in the shapes of its letters. Three-year-olds recognize letterforms. Yet there are on the order of 50,000 typefaces in existence, each different. Subtle and not-so-subtle variations in the thickness of the lines, the curves and angles, the shapes of the serifs, the relative sizes of the parts of the letters, and other design features, all add up to individualities. The alphabet is firmly fixed in the shapes of its letters. Three-year-olds recognize letterforms. Yet there are on the order of 50,000 typefaces in existence, each different. Subtle and not-

12 point type, 13 point linespace

The alphabet is firmly fixed in the shapes of its letters. Three-year-olds recognize letterforms. Yet there are on the order of 50,000 typefaces in existence, each different. Subtle and not-so-subtle variations in the thickness of the lines, the curves and angles, the shapes of the serifs, the relative sizes of the parts of the letters, and other design features, all add up to individualities. The alphabet is firmly fixed in the shapes of its letters. Three-year-olds recognize letterforms. Yet there are on the order of 50,000 typefaces in existence, each different. Subtle and not-so-subtle variations in the thickness of the lines, the curves and angles, the shapes of the serifs, the relative sizes of the parts of the letters, and other design features, all add up to individualities. The alphabet is firmly fixed in the shapes of its letters. Three-year-olds recognize letterforms. Yet there are on the order of 50,000 typefaces in existence, each different. Subtle

A surprisingly good text face for space-tight situations, from 10-point up to 18-point or so, it can be used if a condensed serif face is needed. It is not a first-choice typeface in most situations.

ABCDEFGHIJKLMNOPQRSTUVWXYZ
abcdefghijklmnopqrstuvwxyz
0123456789&?!$%“”.,/;()

8 point type, 9 point linespace

The alphabet is firmly fixed in the shapes of its letters. Three-year-olds recognize letterforms. Yet there are on the order of 50,000 typefaces in existence, each different. Subtle and not-so-subtle variations in the thickness of the lines, the curves and angles, the shapes of the serifs, the relative sizes of the parts of the letters, and other design features, all add up to individualities. The alphabet is firmly fixed in the shapes of its letters. Three-year-olds recognize letterforms. Yet there are on the order of 50,000 typefaces in existence, each different. Subtle and not-so-subtle variations in the thickness of the lines, the curves and angles, the shapes of the serifs, the relative sizes of the parts of the letters, and other design features, all add up to individualities. The alphabet is firmly fixed in the shapes of its letters. Three-year-olds recognize letterforms. Yet there are on the order of 50,000 typefaces in existence, each different. Subtle and not-so-subtle variations in the thickness of the lines, the curves and angles, the shapes of the serifs, the relative sizes of the parts of the letters, and other design features, all add up to individualities. The alphabet is firmly fixed in the shapes of its letters. Three-year-olds recognize letterforms. Yet there are on the order of 50,000 typefaces in existence, each different. Subtle and not-so-subtle variations in the shapes of the serifs, the relative sizes of the parts of the letters, and other design features, all add up to individualities. The alphabet is firmly fixed in the shapes of its letters. Three-year-olds recognize letterforms. Yet there are on the order of 50,000 typefaces in existence, each different. Subtle and not-so-subtle variations in the thickness of the lines, the curves and angles, the shapes of the serifs, the relative sizes of the parts of the letters, and other design features, all add up to individualities. The alphabet is firmly fixed in the shapes of its letters.

10 point type, 11 point linespace

The alphabet is firmly fixed in the shapes of its letters. Three-year-olds recognize letterforms. Yet there are on the order of 50,000 typefaces in existence, each different. Subtle and not-so-subtle variations in the thickness of the lines, the curves and angles, the shapes of the serifs, the relative sizes of the parts of the letters, and other design features, all add up to individualities. The alphabet is firmly fixed in the shapes of its letters. Three-year-olds recognize letterforms. Yet there are on the order of 50,000 typefaces in existence, each different. Subtle and not-so-subtle variations in the thickness of the lines, the curves and angles, the shapes of the serifs, the relative sizes of the parts of the letters, and other design features, all add up to individualities. The alphabet is firmly fixed in the shapes of its letters. Three-year-olds recognize letterforms. Yet there are on the order of 50,000 typefaces in existence, each different. Subtle and not-so-subtle variations in the thickness of the lines, the curves and angles, the shapes of the serifs, the relative sizes of the parts of the letters, and other design features, all add up to individualities. The alphabet is firmly fixed in the shapes of its letters. Three-year-olds recognize letterforms. Yet there are on the order of

12 point type, 13 point linespace

The alphabet is firmly fixed in the shapes of its letters. Three-year-olds recognize letterforms. Yet there are on the order of 50,000 typefaces in existence, each different. Subtle and not-so-subtle variations in the thickness of the lines, the curves and angles, the shapes of the serifs, the relative sizes of the parts of the letters, and other design features, all add up to individualities. The alphabet is firmly fixed in the shapes of its letters. Three-year-olds recognize letterforms. Yet there are on the order of 50,000 typefaces in existence, each different. Subtle and not-so-subtle variations in the thickness of the lines, the curves and angles, the shapes of the serifs, the relative sizes of the parts of the letters, and other design features, all add up to individualities. The alphabet is firmly fixed in the shapes of its letters. Three-year-olds recognize letterforms. Yet there are on the order of 50,000 typefaces in existence, each

Difficult to read and not as graceful or aesthetic as the roman, definitely not to be used as a text block. Prefers larger sizes, and the characters tend to blur together below 12-point.

ABCDEFGHIJKLMNOPQRSTUVWXYZ
abcdefghijklmnopqrstuvwxyz
0123456789&?!$%“”.,/;()

8 point type, 9 point linespace

The alphabet is firmly fixed in the shapes of its letters. Three-year-olds recognize letterforms. Yet there are on the order of 50,000 typefaces in existence, each different. Subtle and not-so-subtle variations in the thickness of the lines, the curves and angles, the shapes of the serifs, the relative sizes of the parts of the letters, and other design features, all add up to individualities. The alphabet is firmly fixed in the shapes of its letters. Three-year-olds recognize letterforms. Yet there are on the order of 50,000 typefaces in existence, each different. Subtle and not-so-subtle variations in the thickness of the lines, the curves and angles, the shapes of the serifs, the relative sizes of the parts of the letters, and other design features, all add up to individualities. The alphabet is firmly fixed in the shapes of its letters. Three-year-olds recognize letterforms. Yet there are on the order of 50,000 typefaces in existence, each different. Subtle and not-so-subtle variations in the thickness of the lines, the curves and angles, the shapes of the serifs, the relative sizes of the parts of the letters, and other design features, all add up to individualities. The alphabet is firmly fixed in the shapes of its letters. Three-year-olds recognize letterforms. Yet there are on the order of 50,000 typefaces in existence, each different. Subtle and not-so-subtle variations in the thickness of the lines, the curves and angles, the shapes of the serifs, the relative sizes of the parts of the letters, and other design features, all add up to individualities. The alphabet is firmly fixed in the shapes of its letters. Three-year-olds recognize letterforms. Yet there are on the order of 50,000 typefaces in existence, each different. Subtle and not-so-subtle variations in the thickness of the lines, the curves and angles, the shapes of the serifs, the relative sizes of the parts of the letters, and other design features, all add up to individualities. The alphabet is firmly fixed in the shapes of its letters.

10 point type, 11 point linespace

The alphabet is firmly fixed in the shapes of its letters. Three-year-olds recognize letterforms. Yet there are on the order of 50,000 typefaces in existence, each different. Subtle and not-so-subtle variations in the thickness of the lines, the curves and angles, the shapes of the serifs, the relative sizes of the parts of the letters, and other design features, all add up to individualities. The alphabet is firmly fixed in the shapes of its letters. Three-year-olds recognize letterforms. Yet there are on the order of 50,000 typefaces in existence, each different. Subtle and not-so-subtle variations in the thickness of the lines, the curves and angles, the shapes of the serifs, the relative sizes of the parts of the letters, and other design features, all add up to individualities. The alphabet is firmly fixed in the shapes of its letters. Three-year-olds recognize letterforms. Yet there are on the order of 50,000 typefaces in existence, each different. Subtle and not-so-subtle variations in the thickness of the lines, the curves and angles, the shapes of the serifs, the relative sizes of the parts of the letters, and other design features, all add up to individualities. The alphabet is firmly fixed in the shapes of its letters. Three-year-olds recognize letterforms. Yet there are on the order of 50,000 typefaces in existence, each different. Subtle

12 point type, 13 point linespace

The alphabet is firmly fixed in the shapes of its letters. Three-year-olds recognize letterforms. Yet there are on the order of 50,000 typefaces in existence, each different. Subtle and not-so-subtle variations in the thickness of the lines, the curves and angles, the shapes of the serifs, the relative sizes of the parts of the letters, and other design features, all add up to individualities. The alphabet is firmly fixed in the shapes of its letters. Three-year-olds recognize letterforms. Yet there are on the order of 50,000 typefaces in existence, each different. Subtle and not-so-subtle variations in the thickness of the lines, the curves and angles, the shapes of the serifs, the relative sizes of the parts of the letters, and other design features, all add up to individualities. The alphabet is firmly fixed in the shapes of its letters. Three-year-olds recognize letterforms. Yet there are on the order of 50,000 typefaces in existence, each different. Subtle

The most readable condensed serif face, this is the typeface of choice when space is at a premium and legibility is critical. Recommend it or use it with confidence and authority.

ABCDEFGHIJKLMNOPQRSTUVWXYZ
abcdefghijklmnopqrstuvwxyz
0123456789&?!$%“”.,/;()

8 point type, 9 point linespace

The alphabet is firmly fixed in the shapes of its letters. Three-year-olds recognize letterforms. Yet there are on the order of 50,000 typefaces in existence, each different. Subtle and not-so-subtle variations in the thickness of the lines, the curves and angles, the shapes of the serifs, the relative sizes of the parts of the letters, and other design features, all add up to individualities. The alphabet is firmly fixed in the shapes of its letters. Three-year-olds recognize letterforms. Yet there are on the order of 50,000 typefaces in existence, each different. Subtle and not-so-subtle variations in the thickness of the lines, the curves and angles, the shapes of the serifs, the relative sizes of the parts of the letters, and other design features, all add up to individualities. The alphabet is firmly fixed in the shapes of its letters. Three-year-olds recognize letterforms. Yet there are on the order of 50,000 typefaces in existence, each different. Subtle and not-so-subtle variations in the thickness of the lines, the curves and angles, the shapes of the serifs, the relative sizes of the parts of the letters, and other design features, all add up to individualities. The alphabet is firmly fixed in the shapes of its letters. Three-year-olds recognize letterforms. Yet there are on the order of 50,000 typefaces in existence, each different. Subtle and not-so-subtle variations in the thickness of the lines, the curves and angles, the shapes of the serifs, the relative sizes of the parts of the letters, and other design features, all add up to individualities. The alphabet is firmly fixed in the shapes of its letters. Three-year-olds recognize letterforms. Yet there are on the order of 50,000 typefaces in existence, each different. Subtle and not-so-subtle variations in the thickness of the lines, the curves and angles, the shapes of the serifs, the relative sizes of the parts of the letters, and other design

10 point type, 11 point linespace

The alphabet is firmly fixed in the shapes of its letters. Three-year-olds recognize letterforms. Yet there are on the order of 50,000 typefaces in existence, each different. Subtle and not-so-subtle variations in the thickness of the lines, the curves and angles, the shapes of the serifs, the relative sizes of the parts of the letters, and other design features, all add up to individualities. The alphabet is firmly fixed in the shapes of its letters. Three-year-olds recognize letterforms. Yet there are on the order of 50,000 typefaces in existence, each different. Subtle and not-so-subtle variations in the thickness of the lines, the curves and angles, the shapes of the serifs, the relative sizes of the parts of the letters, and other design features, all add up to individualities. The alphabet is firmly fixed in the shapes of its letters. Three-year-olds recognize letterforms. Yet there are on the order of 50,000 typefaces in existence, each different. Subtle and not-so-subtle variations in the thickness of the lines, the curves and angles, the shapes of the serifs, the relative sizes of the parts of the letters, and other design features, all add up to individualities. The alphabet is firmly fixed in the shapes of its letters. Three-year-olds recognize letterforms.

12 point type, 13 point linespace

The alphabet is firmly fixed in the shapes of its letters. Three-year-olds recognize letterforms. Yet there are on the order of 50,000 typefaces in existence, each different. Subtle and not-so-subtle variations in the thickness of the lines, the curves and angles, the shapes of the serifs, the relative sizes of the parts of the letters, and other design features, all add up to individualities. The alphabet is firmly fixed in the shapes of its letters. Three-year-olds recognize letterforms. Yet there are on the order of 50,000 typefaces in existence, each different. Subtle and not-so-subtle variations in the thickness of the lines, the curves and angles, the shapes of the serifs, the relative sizes of the parts of the letters, and other design features, all add up to individualities. The alphabet is firmly fixed in the shapes of its letters. Three-year-olds recognize letterforms. Yet there are on the order of 50,000

Not bad. It works with the roman without disturbing the overall feel of the type, and effectively emphasizes what needs to be emphasized. It is hard to read, though, so should be used sparingly.

ABCDEFGHIJKLMNOPQRSTUVWXYZ
abcdefghijklmnopqrstuvwxyz
0123456789&?!$%“”.,/;()

8 point type, 9 point linespace

The alphabet is firmly fixed in the shapes of its letters. Three-year-olds recognize letterforms. Yet there are on the order of 50,000 typefaces in existence, each different. Subtle and not-so-subtle variations in the thickness of the lines, the curves and angles, the shapes of the serifs, the relative sizes of the parts of the letters, and other design features, all add up to individualities. The alphabet is firmly fixed in the shapes of its letters. Three-year-olds recognize letterforms. Yet there are on the order of 50,000 typefaces in existence, each different. Subtle and not-so-subtle variations in the thickness of the lines, the curves and angles, the shapes of the serifs, the relative sizes of the parts of the letters, and other design features, all add up to individualities. The alphabet is firmly fixed in the shapes of its letters. Three-year-olds recognize letterforms. Yet there are on the order of 50,000 typefaces in existence, each different. Subtle and not-so-subtle variations in the thickness of the lines, the curves and angles, the shapes of the serifs, the relative sizes of the parts of the letters, and other design features, all add up to individualities. The alphabet is firmly fixed in the shapes of its letters. Three-year-olds recognize letterforms. Yet there are on the order of 50,000 typefaces in existence, each different. Subtle and not-so-subtle variations in the thickness of the lines, the curves and angles, the shapes of the serifs, the relative sizes of the parts of the letters, and other design features, all add up to individualities. The alphabet is firmly fixed in the shapes of its letters. Three-year-olds recognize letterforms. Yet there are on the order of 50,000 typefaces in existence, each different. Subtle and not-so-subtle

10 point type, 11 point linespace

The alphabet is firmly fixed in the shapes of its letters. Three-year-olds recognize letterforms. Yet there are on the order of 50,000 typefaces in existence, each different. Subtle and not-so-subtle variations in the thickness of the lines, the curves and angles, the shapes of the serifs, the relative sizes of the parts of the letters, and other design features, all add up to individualities. The alphabet is firmly fixed in the shapes of its letters. Three-year-olds recognize letterforms. Yet there are on the order of 50,000 typefaces in existence, each different. Subtle and not-so-subtle variations in the thickness of the lines, the curves and angles, the shapes of the serifs, the relative sizes of the parts of the letters, and other design features, all add up to individualities. The alphabet is firmly fixed in the shapes of its letters. Three-year-olds recognize letterforms. Yet there are on the order of 50,000 typefaces in existence, each different. Subtle and not-so-subtle variations in the thickness of the lines, the curves and angles, the shapes of the serifs, the relative sizes of the parts of the letters, and other design features, all add up to individualities.

12 point type, 13 point linespace

The alphabet is firmly fixed in the shapes of its letters. Three-year-olds recognize letterforms. Yet there are on the order of 50,000 typefaces in existence, each different. Subtle and not-so-subtle variations in the thickness of the lines, the curves and angles, the shapes of the serifs, the relative sizes of the parts of the letters, and other design features, all add up to individualities. The alphabet is firmly fixed in the shapes of its letters. Three-year-olds recognize letterforms. Yet there are on the order of 50,000 typefaces in existence, each different. Subtle and not-so-subtle variations in the thickness of the lines, the curves and angles, the shapes of the serifs, the relative sizes of the parts of the letters, and other design features, all add up to individualities. The alphabet is firmly fixed in the shapes of its letters. Three-

As nicely designed as the rest of the Garamond family, the Bold can be set tight or loose without detriment. It’s a safe emphatic face, and blends well with other weights. It doesn’t work well in contrast with sans serifs.

ABCDEFGHIJKLMNOPQRSTUVWXYZ
abcdefghijklmnopqrstuvwxyz
0123456789&?!$%“”.,/;()

8 point type, 9 point linespace

The alphabet is firmly fixed in the shapes of its letters. Three-year-olds recognize letterforms. Yet there are on the order of 50,000 typefaces in existence, each different. Subtle and not-so-subtle variations in the thickness of the lines, the curves and angles, the shapes of the serifs, the relative sizes of the parts of the letters, and other design features, all add up to individualities. The alphabet is firmly fixed in the shapes of its letters. Three-year-olds recognize letterforms. Yet there are on the order of 50,000 typefaces in existence, each different. Subtle and not-so-subtle variations in the thickness of the lines, the curves and angles, the shapes of the serifs, the relative sizes of the parts of the letters, and other design features, all add up to individualities. The alphabet is firmly fixed in the shapes of its letters. Three-year-olds recognize letterforms. Yet there are on the order of 50,000 typefaces in existence, each different. Subtle and not-so-subtle variations in the thickness of the lines, the curves and angles, the shapes of the serifs, the relative sizes of the parts of the letters, and other design features, all add up to individualities. The alphabet is firmly fixed in the shapes of its letters. Three-year-olds recognize letterforms. Yet there are on the order of 50,000 typefaces in existence, each different. Subtle and not-so-subtle variations in the shapes of the serifs, the the relative sizes of the parts of the letters, and other design features, all add up to individualities. The alphabet is firmly fixed in the shapes of its letters. Three-year-olds recognize

10 point type, 11 point linespace

The alphabet is firmly fixed in the shapes of its letters. Three-year-olds recognize letterforms. Yet there are on the order of 50,000 typefaces in existence, each different. Subtle and not-so-subtle variations in the thickness of the lines, the curves and angles, the shapes of the serifs, the relative sizes of the parts of the letters, and other design features, all add up to individualities. The alphabet is firmly fixed in the shapes of its letters. Three-year-olds recognize letterforms. Yet there are on the order of 50,000 typefaces in existence, each different. Subtle and not-so-subtle variations in the thickness of the lines, the curves and angles, the shapes of the serifs, the relative sizes of the parts of the letters, and other design features, all add up to individualities. The alphabet is firmly fixed in the shapes of its letters. Three-year-olds recognize letterforms. Yet there are on the order of 50,000 typefaces in existence, each different. Subtle and not-so-subtle variations in the thickness of the lines, the curves and angles, the shapes of the serifs, the relative sizes of the parts of

12 point type, 13 point linespace

The alphabet is firmly fixed in the shapes of its letters. Three-year-olds recognize letterforms. Yet there are on the order of 50,000 typefaces in existence, each different. Subtle and not-so-subtle variations in the thickness of the lines, the curves and angles, the shapes of the serifs, the relative sizes of the parts of the letters, and other design features, all add up to individualities. The alphabet is firmly fixed in the shapes of its letters. Three-year-olds recognize letterforms. Yet there are on the order of 50,000 typefaces in existence, each different. Subtle and not-so-subtle variations in the thickness of the lines, the curves and angles, the shapes of the serifs, the relative sizes of the parts of the letters, and other design features, all add up to individualities. The

This italic is not so distorted as the other Garamond italics, so is easier to read and can be used more frequently. Despite its weight, it is an elegant face. Use it freely, without misgivings.

ABCDEFGHIJKLMNOPQRSTUVWXYZ
abcdefghijklmnopqrstuvwxyz
0123456789&?!$%“”.,/;()

8 point type, 9 point linespace

The alphabet is firmly fixed in the shapes of its letters. Three-year-olds recognize letterforms. Yet there are on the order of 50,000 typefaces in existence, each different. Subtle and not-so-subtle variations in the thickness of the lines, the curves and angles, the shapes of the serifs, the relative sizes of the parts of the letters, and other design features, all add up to individualities. The alphabet is firmly fixed in the shapes of its letters. Three-year-olds recognize letterforms. Yet there are on the order of 50,000 typefaces in existence, each different. Subtle and not-so-subtle variations in the thickness of the lines, the curves and angles, the shapes of the serifs, the relative sizes of the parts of the letters, and other design features, all add up to individualities. The alphabet is firmly fixed in the shapes of its letters. Three-year-olds recognize letterforms. Yet there are on the order of 50,000 typefaces in existence, each different. Subtle and not-so-subtle variations in the thickness of the lines, the curves and angles, the shapes of the serifs, the relative sizes of the parts of the letters, and other design features, all add up to individualities. The alphabet is firmly fixed in the shapes of its letters. Three-year-olds recognize letterforms. Yet there are on the order of 50,000 typefaces in existence, each different. Subtle and not-so-subtle variations in the thickness of the lines, the curves and angles, the shapes of the serifs, the relative sizes of the parts of the of the letters, and other design features, all add up to individualities. The alphabet is firmly fixed in the shapes of its letters. Three-year-olds recognize letterforms. Yet

10 point type, 11 point linespace

The alphabet is firmly fixed in the shapes of its letters. Three-year-olds recognize letterforms. Yet there are on the order of 50,000 typefaces in existence, each different. Subtle and not-so-subtle variations in the thickness of the lines, the curves and angles, the shapes of the serifs, the relative sizes of the parts of the letters, and other design features, all add up to individualities. The alphabet is firmly fixed in the shapes of its letters. Three-year-olds recognize letterforms. Yet there are on the order of 50,000 typefaces in existence, each different. Subtle and not-so-subtle variations in the thickness of the lines, the curves and angles, the shapes of the serifs, the relative sizes of the parts of the letters, and other design features, all add up to individualities. The alphabet is firmly fixed in the shapes of its letters. Three-year-olds recognize letterforms. Yet there are on the order of 50,000 typefaces in existence, each different. Subtle and not-so-subtle variations in the thickness of the lines, the curves and angles, the shapes of the serifs, the relative sizes

12 point type, 13 point linespace

The alphabet is firmly fixed in the shapes of its letters. Three-year-olds recognize letterforms. Yet there are on the order of 50,000 typefaces in existence, each different. Subtle and not-so-subtle variations in the thickness of the lines, the curves and angles, the shapes of the serifs, the relative sizes of the parts of the letters, and other design features, all add up to individualities. The alphabet is firmly fixed in the shapes of its letters. Three-year-olds recognize letterforms. Yet there are on the order of 50,000 typefaces in existence, each different. Subtle and not-so-subtle variations in the thickness of the lines, the curves and angles, the shapes of the serifs, the relative sizes of the parts of the letters, and other design features, all add up to individualities. The

An overpowering face, a little of this goes a long way. Avoid using in screened or low-contrast situations, as the letters fill in easily. Definitely don’t use below 12-point if you can help it.

ABCDEFGHIJKLMNOPQRSTUVWXYZ
abcdefghijklmnopqrstuvwxyz
0123456789&?!$%“”.,/;()

8 point type, 9 point linespace

The alphabet is firmly fixed in the shapes of its letters. Three-year-olds recognize letterforms. Yet there are on the order of 50,000 typefaces in existence, each different. Subtle and not-so-subtle variations in the thickness of the lines, the curves and angles, the shapes of the serifs, the relative sizes of the parts of the letters, and other design features, all add up to individualities. The alphabet is firmly fixed in the shapes of its letters. Three-year-olds recognize letterforms. Yet there are on the order of 50,000 typefaces in existence, each different. Subtle and not-so-subtle variations in the thickness of the lines, the curves and angles, the shapes of the serifs, the relative sizes of the parts of the letters, and other design features, all add up to individualities. The alphabet is firmly fixed in the shapes of its letters. Three-year-olds recognize letterforms. Yet there are on the order of 50,000 typefaces in existence, each different. Subtle and not-so-subtle variations in the thickness of the lines, the curves and angles, the shapes of the serifs, the relative sizes of the parts of the letters, and other design features, all add up to individualities. The alphabet is firmly fixed in the shapes of its letters. Three-year-olds recognize letterforms. Yet there are on the order of 50,000 typefaces in existence, each different. Subtle and not-so-subtle variations in the thickness of the lines, the curves and angles, the shapes of the serifs, the relative sizes of the parts of the letters, and other design features, all add up to individualities. The alphabet is firmly fixed in the

10 point type, 11 point linespace

The alphabet is firmly fixed in the shapes of its letters. Three-year-olds recognize letterforms. Yet there are on the order of 50,000 typefaces in existence, each different. Subtle and not-so-subtle variations in the thickness of the lines, the curves and angles, the shapes of the serifs, the relative sizes of the parts of the letters, and other design features, all add up to individualities. The alphabet is firmly fixed in the shapes of its letters. Three-year-olds recognize letterforms. Yet there are on the order of 50,000 typefaces in existence, each different. Subtle and not-so-subtle variations in the thickness of the lines, the curves and angles, the shapes of the serifs, the relative sizes of the parts of the letters, and other design features, all add up to individualities. The alphabet is firmly fixed in the shapes of its letters. Three-year-olds recognize letterforms. Yet there are on the order of 50,000 typefaces in existence, each different. Subtle and not-so-subtle variations in the thickness of the lines, the curves and angles,

12 point type, 13 point linespace

The alphabet is firmly fixed in the shapes of its letters. Three-year-olds recognize letterforms. Yet there are on the order of 50,000 typefaces in existence, each different. Subtle and not-so-subtle variations in the thickness of the lines, the curves and angles, the shapes of the serifs, the relative sizes of the parts of the letters, and other design features, all add up to individualities. The alphabet is firmly fixed in the shapes of its letters. Three-year-olds recognize letterforms. Yet there are on the order of 50,000 typefaces in existence, each different. Subtle and not-so-subtle variations in the thickness of the lines, the curves and angles, the shapes of the serifs, the relative sizes of the parts of the letters, and other design features, all

This is a surprisingly soft italic, mixing much more smoothly with its roman counterpart than most. While neither is used a lot, normally, they can be used together to create very vibrant, powerful effects.

ABCDEFGHIJKLMNOPQRSTUVWXYZ
abcdefghijklmnopqrstuvwxyz
0123456789&?!$%“”.,/;()

8 point type, 9 point linespace

The alphabet is firmly fixed in the shapes of its letters. Three-year-olds recognize letterforms. Yet there are on the order of 50,000 typefaces in existence, each different. Subtle and not-so-subtle variations in the thickness of the lines, the curves and angles, the shapes of the serifs, the relative sizes of the parts of the letters, and other design features, all add up to individualities. The alphabet is firmly fixed in the shapes of its letters. Three-year-olds recognize letterforms. Yet there are on the order of 50,000 typefaces in existence, each different. Subtle and not-so-subtle variations in the thickness of the lines, the curves and angles, the shapes of the serifs, the relative sizes of the parts of the letters, and other design features, all add up to individualities. The alphabet is firmly fixed in the shapes of its letters. Three-year-olds recognize letterforms. Yet there are on the order of 50,000 typefaces in existence, each different. Subtle and not-so-subtle variations in the thickness of the lines, the curves and angles, the shapes of the serifs, the relative sizes of the parts of the letters, and other design features, all add up to individualities. The alphabet is firmly fixed in the shapes of its letters. Three-year-olds recognize letterforms. Yet there are on the order of 50,000 typefaces in existence, each different. Subtle and not-so-subtle variations in the thickness of the lines, the curves and angles, the shapes of the serifs, the relative sizes of the parts of the letters, and other design features, all add up to individualities. The alphabet is firmly fixed in the shapes of its letters. Three-year-olds recognize letterforms. Yet there are on the order of

10 point type, 11 point linespace

The alphabet is firmly fixed in the shapes of its letters. Three-year-olds recognize letterforms. Yet there are on the order of 50,000 typefaces in existence, each different. Subtle and not-so-subtle variations in the thickness of the lines, the curves and angles, the shapes of the serifs, the relative sizes of the parts of the letters, and other design features, all add up to individualities. The alphabet is firmly fixed in the shapes of its letters. Three-year-olds recognize letterforms. Yet there are on the order of 50,000 typefaces in existence, each different. Subtle and not-so-subtle variations in the thickness of the lines, the curves and angles, the shapes of the serifs, the relative sizes of the parts of the letters, and other design features, all add up to individualities. The alphabet is firmly fixed in the shapes of its letters. Three-year-olds recognize letterforms. Yet there are on the order of 50,000 typefaces in existence, each different. Subtle and not-so-subtle variations in the thickness of the lines, the curves and angles, the shapes of the serifs, the relative sizes of the parts of the letters, and other

12 point type, 13 point linespace

The alphabet is firmly fixed in the shapes of its letters. Three-year-olds recognize letterforms. Yet there are on the order of 50,000 typefaces in existence, each different. Subtle and not-so-subtle variations in the thickness of the lines, the curves and angles, the shapes of the serifs, the relative sizes of the parts of the letters, and other design features, all add up to individualities. The alphabet is firmly fixed in the shapes of its letters. Three-year-olds recognize letterforms. Yet there are on the order of 50,000 typefaces in existence, each different. Subtle and not-so-subtle variations in the thickness of the lines, the curves and angles, the shapes of the serifs, the relative sizes of the parts of the letters, and other design features, all add up to individualities. The alphabet is firmly fixed in

Goudy has to be one of the most beautiful typefaces ever designed, truly achieving the quality of elegance. Flaring graceful serifs invite the eye to follow along forever. Works best at 12-14 point.

ABCDEFGHIJKLMNOPQRSTUVWXYZ
abcdefghijklmnopqrstuvwxyz
0123456789&?!$%“”.,/;()

8 point type, 9 point linespace

The alphabet is firmly fixed in the shapes of its letters. Three-year-olds recognize letterforms. Yet there are on the order of 50,000 typefaces in existence, each different. Subtle and not-so-subtle variations in the thickness of the lines, the curves and angles, the shapes of the serifs, the relative sizes of the parts of the letters, and other design features, all add up to individualities. The alphabet is firmly fixed in the shapes of its letters. Three-year-olds recognize letterforms. Yet there are on the order of 50,000 typefaces in existence, each different. Subtle and not-so-subtle variations in the thickness of the lines, the curves and angles, the shapes of the serifs, the relative sizes of the parts of the letters, and other design features, all add up to individualities. The alphabet is firmly fixed in the shapes of its letters. Three-year-olds recognize letterforms. Yet there are on the order of 50,000 typefaces in existence, each different. Subtle and not-so-subtle variations in the thickness of the lines, the curves and angles, the shapes of the serifs, the relative sizes of the parts of the letters, and other design features, all add up to individualities. The alphabet is firmly fixed in the shapes of its letters. Three-year-olds recognize letterforms. Yet there are on the order of 50,000 typefaces in existence, each different. Subtle and not-so-subtle variations in the shapes of the serifs, the relative sizes of the parts of the letters, and other design features, all add up to individualities. The alphabet is firmly fixed in the shapes of its letters. Three-year-olds recognize letterforms. Yet there are on the order of 50,000 typefaces in existence, each different. Subtle and not-so-subtle variations in the shapes of the serifs, the relative sizes of the parts of the letters, and other designfeatures, all add up to individualities. The alphabet is firmly

10 point type, 11 point linespace

The alphabet is firmly fixed in the shapes of its letters. Three-year-olds recognize letterforms. Yet there are on the order of 50,000 typefaces in existence, each different. Subtle and not-so-subtle variations in the thickness of the lines, the curves and angles, the shapes of the serifs, the relative sizes of the parts of the letters, and other design features, all add up to individualities. The alphabet is firmly fixed in the shapes of its letters. Three-year-olds recognize letterforms. Yet there are on the order of 50,000 typefaces in existence, each different. Subtle and not-so-subtle variations in the thickness of the lines, the curves and angles, the shapes of the serifs, the relative sizes of the parts of the letters, and other design features, all add up to individualities. The alphabet is firmly fixed in the shapes of its letters. Three-year-olds recognize letterforms. Yet there are on the order of 50,000 typefaces in existence, each different. Subtle and not-so-subtle variations in the thickness of the lines, the curves and angles, the shapes of the serifs, the relative sizes of the parts of the letters, and other design features, all add up to individualities. The alphabet is firmly fixed in the shapes of its letters. Three-

12 point type, 13 point linespace

The alphabet is firmly fixed in the shapes of its letters. Three-year-olds recognize letterforms. Yet there are on the order of 50,000 typefaces in existence, each different. Subtle and not-so-subtle variations in the thickness of the lines, the curves and angles, the shapes of the serifs, the relative sizes of the parts of the letters, and other design features, all add up to individualities. The alphabet is firmly fixed in the shapes of its letters. Three-year-olds recognize letterforms. Yet there are on the order of 50,000 typefaces in existence, each different. Subtle and not-so-subtle variations in the thickness of the lines, the curves and angles, the shapes of the serifs, the relative sizes of the parts of the letters, and other design features, all add up to individualities. The alphabet is firmly fixed in the shapes of its letters. Three-year-olds recognize letterforms. Yet there are on the order of

Equally well designed as the roman, with pretty swoops and swirls, and very legible, this italic almost has to be included somewhere in any Goudy job, to bring out the full flavor of the family.

ABCDEFGHIJKLMNOPQRSTUVWXYZ
abcdefghijklmnopqrstuvwxyz
0123456789&?!$%“”.,/;()

8 point type, 9 point linespace

The alphabet is firmly fixed in the shapes of its letters. Three-year-olds recognize letterforms. Yet there are on the order of 50,000 typefaces in existence, each different. Subtle and not-so-subtle variations in the thickness of the lines, the curves and angles, the shapes of the serifs, the relative sizes of the parts of the letters, and other design features, all add up to individualities. The alphabet is firmly fixed in the shapes of its letters. Three-year-olds recognize letterforms. Yet there are on the order of 50,000 typefaces in existence, each different. Subtle and not-so-subtle variations in the thickness of the lines, the curves and angles, the shapes of the serifs, the relative sizes of the parts of the letters, and other design features, all add up to individualities. The alphabet is firmly fixed in the shapes of its letters. Three-year-olds recognize letterforms. Yet there are on the order of 50,000 typefaces in existence, each different. Subtle and not-so-subtle variations in the thickness of the lines, the curves and angles, the shapes of the serifs, the relative sizes of the parts of the letters, and other design features, all add up to individualities. The alphabet is firmly fixed in the shapes of its letters. Three-year-olds recognize letterforms. Yet there are on the order of 50,000 typefaces in existence, each different. Subtle and not-so-subtle variations in the thickness of the lines, the curves and angles, the shapes of the serifs, the relative sizes of the parts of the letters, and other design features, all add up to individualities. The alphabet is firmly fixed in the shapes of its letters. Three-

10 point type, 11 point linespace

The alphabet is firmly fixed in the shapes of its letters. Three-year-olds recognize letterforms. Yet there are on the order of 50,000 typefaces in existence, each different. Subtle and not-so-subtle variations in the thickness of the lines, the curves and angles, the shapes of the serifs, the relative sizes of the parts of the letters, and other design features, all add up to individualities. The alphabet is firmly fixed in the shapes of its letters. Three-year-olds recognize letterforms. Yet there are on the order of 50,000 typefaces in existence, each different. Subtle and not-so-subtle variations in the thickness of the lines, the curves and angles, the shapes of the serifs, the relative sizes of the parts of the letters, and other design features, all add up to individualities. The alphabet is firmly fixed in the shapes of its letters. Three-year-olds recognize letterforms. Yet there are on the order of 50,000 typefaces in existence, each different. Subtle and not-so-subtle variations in the thickness of the lines, the curves and angles, the shapes of the serifs, the relative sizes

12 point type, 13 point linespace

The alphabet is firmly fixed in the shapes of its letters. Three-year-olds recognize letterforms. Yet there are on the order of 50,000 typefaces in existence, each different. Subtle and not-so-subtle variations in the thickness of the lines, the curves and angles, the shapes of the serifs, the relative sizes of the parts of the letters, and other design features, all add up to individualities. The alphabet is firmly fixed in the shapes of its letters. Three-year-olds recognize letterforms. Yet there are on the order of 50,000 typefaces in existence, each different. Subtle and not-so-subtle variations in the thickness of the lines, the curves and angles, the shapes of the serifs, the relative sizes of the parts of the letters, and other design features, all add up to individualities.

Adding weight to a serif face often costs the diminution of its design concept, but not in this case. Mix Bold into the regular weight without the worry of changing mood or tempo. Frederic Goudy threw his heart into this one.

ABCDEFGHIJKLMNOPQRSTUVWXYZ
abcdefghijklmnopqrstuvwxyz
0123456789&?!$%“”.,/;()

8 point type, 9 point linespace

The alphabet is firmly fixed in the shapes of its letters. Three-year-olds recognize letterforms. Yet there are on the order of 50,000 typefaces in existence, each different. Subtle and not-so-subtle variations in the thickness of the lines, the curves and angles, the shapes of the serifs, the relative sizes of the parts of the letters, and other design features, all add up to individualities. The alphabet is firmly fixed in the shapes of its letters. Three-year-olds recognize letterforms. Yet there are on the order of 50,000 typefaces in existence, each different. Subtle and not-so-subtle variations in the thickness of the lines, the curves and angles, the shapes of the serifs, the relative sizes of the parts of the letters, and other design features, all add up to individualities. The alphabet is firmly fixed in the shapes of its letters. Three-year-olds recognize letterforms. Yet there are on the order of 50,000 typefaces in existence, each different. Subtle and not-so-subtle variations in the thickness of the lines, the curves and angles, the shapes of the serifs, the relative sizes of the parts of the letters, and other design features, all add up to individualities. The alphabet is firmly fixed in the shapes of its letters. Three-year-olds recognize letterforms. Yet there are on the order of 50,000 typefaces in existence, each different. Subtle and not-so-subtle variations in the thickness of the lines, the curves and angles, the shapes of the serifs, the relative sizes of the parts of the letters, and other design features, all add up to individualities. The alphabet is firmly fixed in the shapes of its letters. Three-year-olds recognize letterforms. Yet there are

10 point type, 11 point linespace

The alphabet is firmly fixed in the shapes of its letters. Three-year-olds recognize letterforms. Yet there are on the order of 50,000 typefaces in existence, each different. Subtle and not-so-subtle variations in the thickness of the lines, the curves and angles, the shapes of the serifs, the relative sizes of the parts of the letters, and other design features, all add up to individualities. The alphabet is firmly fixed in the shapes of its letters. Three-year-olds recognize letterforms. Yet there are on the order of 50,000 typefaces in existence, each different. Subtle and not-so-subtle variations in the thickness of the lines, the curves and angles, the shapes of the serifs, the relative sizes of the parts of the letters, and other design features, all add up to individualities. The alphabet is firmly fixed in the shapes of its letters. Three-year-olds recognize letterforms. Yet there are on the order of 50,000 typefaces in existence, each different. Subtle and not-so-subtle variations in the thickness of the lines, the curves and angles, the shapes of the serifs, the

12 point type, 13 point linespace

The alphabet is firmly fixed in the shapes of its letters. Three-year-olds recognize letterforms. Yet there are on the order of 50,000 typefaces in existence, each different. Subtle and not-so-subtle variations in the thickness of the lines, the curves and angles, the shapes of the serifs, the relative sizes of the parts of the letters, and other design features, all add up to individualities. The alphabet is firmly fixed in the shapes of its letters. Three-year-olds recognize letterforms. Yet there are on the order of 50,000 typefaces in existence, each different. Subtle and not-so-subtle variations in the thickness of the lines, the curves and angles, the shapes of the serifs, the relative sizes of the parts of the letters, and other design features, all add up to individualities.

As graceful as the rest of the family, the bold italic adds spice and liveliness to an already lively face. Variety for its own sake can be detrimental, except in this case. Use the bold italic for the pleasure of using it.

ABCDEFGHIJKLMNOPQRSTUVWXYZ
abcdefghijklmnopqrstuvwxyz
0123456789&?!$%“”.,/;()

8 point type, 9 point linespace

The alphabet is firmly fixed in the shapes of its letters. Three-year-olds recognize letterforms. Yet there are on the order of 50,000 typefaces in existence, each different. Subtle and not-so-subtle variations in the thickness of the lines, the curves and angles, the shapes of the serifs, the relative sizes of the parts of the letters, and other design features, all add up to individualities. The alphabet is firmly fixed in the shapes of its letters. Three-year-olds recognize letterforms. Yet there are on the order of 50,000 typefaces in existence, each different. Subtle and not-so-subtle variations in the thickness of the lines, the curves and angles, the shapes of the serifs, the relative sizes of the parts of the letters, and other design features, all add up to individualities. The alphabet is firmly fixed in the shapes of its letters. Three-year-olds recognize letterforms. Yet there are on the order of 50,000 typefaces in existence, each different. Subtle and not-so-subtle variations in the thickness of the lines, the curves and angles, the shapes of the serifs, the relative sizes of the parts of the letters, and other design features, all add up to individualities. The alphabet is firmly fixed in the shapes of its letters. Three-year-olds recognize letterforms. Yet there are on the order of 50,000 typefaces in existence, each different. Subtle and not-so-subtle variations in the thickness of the lines, the curves and angles, the shapes of the serifs, the relative sizes of the parts of the letters, and other design features,

10 point type, 11 point linespace

The alphabet is firmly fixed in the shapes of its letters. Three-year-olds recognize letterforms. Yet there are on the order of 50,000 typefaces in existence, each different. Subtle and not-so-subtle variations in the thickness of the lines, the curves and angles, the shapes of the serifs, the relative sizes of the parts of the letters, and other design features, all add up to individualities. The alphabet is firmly fixed in the shapes of its letters. Three-year-olds recognize letterforms. Yet there are on the order of 50,000 typefaces in existence, each different. Subtle and not-so-subtle variations in the thickness of the lines, the curves and angles, the shapes of the serifs, the relative sizes of the parts of the letters, and other design features, all add up to individualities. The alphabet is firmly fixed in the shapes of its letters. Three-year-olds recognize letterforms. Yet there are on the order of 50,000 typefaces in existence, each different. Subtle and not-so-subtle variations in the thickness of the lines,

12 point type, 13 point linespace

The alphabet is firmly fixed in the shapes of its letters. Three-year-olds recognize letterforms. Yet there are on the order of 50,000 typefaces in existence, each different. Subtle and not-so-subtle variations in the thickness of the lines, the curves and angles, the shapes of the serifs, the relative sizes of the parts of the letters, and other design features, all add up to individualities. The alphabet is firmly fixed in the shapes of its letters. Three-year-olds recognize letterforms. Yet there are on the order of 50,000 typefaces in existence, each different. Subtle and not-so-subtle variations in the thickness of the lines, the curves and angles, the shapes of the serifs, the relative sizes of the parts of the

A necessary complement for when weight is needed to make a design work, and fortunately true to the Goudy feel, this is a face to use as needed, and no more than that. Overuse wears thin quickly.

ABCDEFGHIJKLMNOPQRSTUVWXYZ
abcdefghijklmnopqrstuvwxyz
0123456789&?!$%“”.,/;()

8 point type, 9 point linespace

The alphabet is firmly fixed in the shapes of its letters. Three-year-olds recognize letterforms. Yet there are on the order of 50,000 typefaces in existence, each different. Subtle and not-so-subtle variations in the thickness of the lines, the curves and angles, the shapes of the serifs, the relative sizes of the parts of the letters, and other design features, all add up to individualities. The alphabet is firmly fixed in the shapes of its letters. Three-year-olds recognize letterforms. Yet there are on the order of 50,000 typefaces in existence, each different. Subtle and not-so-subtle variations in the thickness of the lines, the curves and angles, the shapes of the serifs, the relative sizes of the parts of the letters, and other design features, all add up to individualities. The alphabet is firmly fixed in the shapes of its letters. Three-year-olds recognize letterforms. Yet there are on the order of 50,000 typefaces in existence, each different. Subtle and not-so-subtle variations in the thickness of the lines, the curves and angles, the shapes of the serifs, the relative sizes of the parts of the letters, and other design features, all add up to individualities. The alphabet is firmly fixed in the shapes of its letters. Three-year-olds recognize letterforms. Yet there are on the order of 50,000 typefaces in existence, each different. Subtle and not-so-subtle variations in the shapes of the serifs, the the relative sizes of the parts of the letters, and other design features, all add up to individualities. The alphabet is firmly fixed in the shapes of its letters. Three-year-olds recognize

10 point type, 11 point linespace

The alphabet is firmly fixed in the shapes of its letters. Three-year-olds recognize letterforms. Yet there are on the order of 50,000 typefaces in existence, each different. Subtle and not-so-subtle variations in the thickness of the lines, the curves and angles, the shapes of the serifs, the relative sizes of the parts of the letters, and other design features, all add up to individualities. The alphabet is firmly fixed in the shapes of its letters. Three-year-olds recognize letterforms. Yet there are on the order of 50,000 typefaces in existence, each different. Subtle and not-so-subtle variations in the thickness of the lines, the curves and angles, the shapes of the serifs, the relative sizes of the parts of the letters, and other design features, all add up to individualities. The alphabet is firmly fixed in the shapes of its letters. Three-year-olds recognize letterforms. Yet there are on the order of 50,000 typefaces in existence, each different. Subtle and not-so-subtle variations in the thickness of the lines, the curves and angles, the shapes of the

12 point type, 13 point linespace

The alphabet is firmly fixed in the shapes of its letters. Three-year-olds recognize letterforms. Yet there are on the order of 50,000 typefaces in existence, each different. Subtle and not-so-subtle variations in the thickness of the lines, the curves and angles, the shapes of the serifs, the relative sizes of the parts of the letters, and other design features, all add up to individualities. The alphabet is firmly fixed in the shapes of its letters. Three-year-olds recognize letterforms. Yet there are on the order of 50,000 typefaces in existence, each different. Subtle and not-so-subtle variations in the thickness of the lines, the curves and angles, the shapes of the serifs, the relative sizes of the parts of the letters, and other design features, all

A lovely face to use when the design of a piece is such as to not require a dark type element. Suggests understated strength, self-confidence, and respect for others’ opinions. Do not set overtightly.

ABCDEFGHIJKLMNOPQRSTUVWXYZ
abcdefghijklmnopqrstuvwxyz
0123456789&?!$%“”.,/;()

8 point type, 9 point linespace

The alphabet is firmly fixed in the shapes of its letters. Three-year-olds recognize letterforms. Yet there are on the order of 50,000 typefaces in existence, each different. Subtle and not-so-subtle variations in the thickness of the lines, the curves and angles, the shapes of the serifs, the relative sizes of the parts of the letters, and other design features, all add up to individualities. The alphabet is firmly fixed in the shapes of its letters. Three-year-olds recognize letterforms. Yet there are on the order of 50,000 typefaces in existence, each different. Subtle and not-so-subtle variations in the thickness of the lines, the curves and angles, the shapes of the serifs, the relative sizes of the parts of the letters, and other design features, all add up to individualities. The alphabet is firmly fixed in the shapes of its letters. Three-year-olds recognize letterforms. Yet there are on the order of 50,000 typefaces in existence, each different. Subtle and not-so-subtle variations in the thickness of the lines, the curves and angles, the shapes of the serifs, the relative sizes of the parts of the letters, and other design features, all add up to individualities. The alphabet is firmly fixed in the shapes of its letters. Three-year-olds recognize letterforms. Yet there are on the order of 50,000 typefaces in existence, each different. Subtle and not-so-subtle variations in the thickness of the lines, the curves and angles, the shapes of the serifs, the relative sizes of the parts of the of the letters, and other design features, all add up to individualities. The alphabet is firmly fixed in the

10 point type, 11 point linespace

The alphabet is firmly fixed in the shapes of its letters. Three-year-olds recognize letterforms. Yet there are on the order of 50,000 typefaces in existence, each different. Subtle and not-so-subtle variations in the thickness of the lines, the curves and angles, the shapes of the serifs, the relative sizes of the parts of the letters, and other design features, all add up to individualities. The alphabet is firmly fixed in the shapes of its letters. Three-year-olds recognize letterforms. Yet there are on the order of 50,000 typefaces in existence, each different. Subtle and not-so-subtle variations in the thickness of the lines, the curves and angles, the shapes of the serifs, the relative sizes of the parts of the letters, and other design features, all add up to individualities. The alphabet is firmly fixed in the shapes of its letters. Three-year-olds recognize letterforms. Yet there are on the order of 50,000 typefaces in existence, each different. Subtle and not-so-subtle variations in the thickness of the lines, the curves and angles, the shapes of the

12 point type, 13 point linespace

The alphabet is firmly fixed in the shapes of its letters. Three-year-olds recognize letterforms. Yet there are on the order of 50,000 typefaces in existence, each different. Subtle and not-so-subtle variations in the thickness of the lines, the curves and angles, the shapes of the serifs, the relative sizes of the parts of the letters, and other design features, all add up to individualities. The alphabet is firmly fixed in the shapes of its letters. Three-year-olds recognize letterforms. Yet there are on the order of 50,000 typefaces in existence, each different. Subtle and not-so-subtle variations in the thickness of the lines, the curves and angles, the shapes of the serifs, the relative sizes of the parts of the letters, and other design features, all

Complements the roman beautifully, and can even stand on its own, as a more-legible-than-most italic. Wide effective size range, from 8-point on up. Use with impunity.

ABCDEFGHIJKLMNOPQRSTUVWXYZ
abcdefghijklmnopqrstuvwxyz
0123456789&?!$%“”.,/;()

8 point type, 9 point linespace

The alphabet is firmly fixed in the shapes of its letters. Three-year-olds recognize letterforms. Yet there are on the order of 50,000 typefaces in existence, each different. Subtle and not-so-subtle variations in the thickness of the lines, the curves and angles, the shapes of the serifs, the relative sizes of the parts of the letters, and other design features, all add up to individualities. The alphabet is firmly fixed in the shapes of its letters. Three-year-olds recognize letterforms. Yet there are on the order of 50,000 typefaces in existence, each different. Subtle and not-so-subtle variations in the thickness of the lines, the curves and angles, the shapes of the serifs, the relative sizes of the parts of the letters, and other design features, all add up to individualities. The alphabet is firmly fixed in the shapes of its letters. Three-year-olds recognize letterforms. Yet there are on the order of 50,000 typefaces in existence, each different. Subtle and not-so-subtle variations in the thickness of the lines, the curves and angles, the shapes of the serifs, the relative sizes of the parts of the letters, and other design features, all add up to individualities. The alphabet is firmly fixed in the shapes of its letters. Three-year-olds recognize letterforms. Yet there are on the order of 50,000 typefaces in existence, each different. Subtle and not-so-subtle variations in the thickness of the lines, the curves and angles, the shapes of the serifs, the relative sizes of the parts of the letters, and other design features,

10 point type, 11 point linespace

The alphabet is firmly fixed in the shapes of its letters. Three-year-olds recognize letterforms. Yet there are on the order of 50,000 typefaces in existence, each different. Subtle and not-so-subtle variations in the thickness of the lines, the curves and angles, the shapes of the serifs, the relative sizes of the parts of the letters, and other design features, all add up to individualities. The alphabet is firmly fixed in the shapes of its letters. Three-year-olds recognize letterforms. Yet there are on the order of 50,000 typefaces in existence, each different. Subtle and not-so-subtle variations in the thickness of the lines, the curves and angles, the shapes of the serifs, the relative sizes of the parts of the letters, and other design features, all add up to individualities. The alphabet is firmly fixed in the shapes of its letters. Three-year-olds recognize letterforms. Yet there are on the order of 50,000 typefaces in existence, each different. Subtle and not-so-subtle variations in the thickness of

12 point type, 13 point linespace

The alphabet is firmly fixed in the shapes of its letters. Three-year-olds recognize letterforms. Yet there are on the order of 50,000 typefaces in existence, each different. Subtle and not-so-subtle variations in the thickness of the lines, the curves and angles, the shapes of the serifs, the relative sizes of the parts of the letters, and other design features, all add up to individualities. The alphabet is firmly fixed in the shapes of its letters. Three-year-olds recognize letterforms. Yet there are on the order of 50,000 typefaces in existence, each different. Subtle and not-so-subtle variations in the thickness of the lines, the curves and angles, the shapes of the serifs, the relative sizes of the parts of

Easy to read, familiar to everyone from age five up, and useful in any sans serif situation, there’s nothing wrong with Helvetica. Don’t use sans serif faces for large blocks of text. Other than that, use Helvetica any time, unless you have a good reason to use another sans serif.

ABCDEFGHIJKLMNOPQRSTUVWXYZ
abcdefghijklmnopqrstuvwxyz
0123456789&?!$%“”.,/;()

8 point type, 9 point linespace

The alphabet is firmly fixed in the shapes of its letters. Three-year-olds recognize letterforms. Yet there are on the order of 50,000 typefaces in existence, each different. Subtle and not-so-subtle variations in the thickness of the lines, the curves and angles, the shapes of the serifs, the relative sizes of the parts of the letters, and other design features, all add up to individualities. The alphabet is firmly fixed in the shapes of its letters. Three-year-olds recognize letterforms. Yet there are on the order of 50,000 typefaces in existence, each different. Subtle and not-so-subtle variations in the thickness of the lines, the curves and angles, the shapes of the serifs, the relative sizes of the parts of the letters, and other design features, all add up to individualities. The alphabet is firmly fixed in the shapes of its letters. Three-year-olds recognize letterforms. Yet there are on the order of 50,000 typefaces in existence, each different. Subtle and not-so-subtle variations in the thickness of the lines, the curves and angles, the shapes of the serifs, the relative sizes of the parts of the letters, and other design features, all add up to individualities. The alphabet is firmly fixed in the shapes of its letters. Three-year-olds recognize letterforms. Yet there are on the order of 50,000 typefaces in existence, each different. Subtle and not-so-subtle variations in the thickness of the lines, the curves and angles, the shapes of the serifs, the relative sizes of the parts of the letters, and other design features,

10 point type, 11 point linespace

The alphabet is firmly fixed in the shapes of its letters. Three-year-olds recognize letterforms. Yet there are on the order of 50,000 typefaces in existence, each different. Subtle and not-so-subtle variations in the thickness of the lines, the curves and angles, the shapes of the serifs, the relative sizes of the parts of the letters, and other design features, all add up to individualities. The alphabet is firmly fixed in the shapes of its letters. Three-year-olds recognize letterforms. Yet there are on the order of 50,000 typefaces in existence, each different. Subtle and not-so-subtle variations in the thickness of the lines, the curves and angles, the shapes of the serifs, the relative sizes of the parts of the letters, and other design features, all add up to individualities. The alphabet is firmly fixed in the shapes of its letters. Three-year-olds recognize letterforms. Yet there are on the order of 50,000 typefaces in existence, each different. Subtle and not-so-subtle variations in the thickness of

12 point type, 13 point linespace

The alphabet is firmly fixed in the shapes of its letters. Three-year-olds recognize letterforms. Yet there are on the order of 50,000 typefaces in existence, each different. Subtle and not-so-subtle variations in the thickness of the lines, the curves and angles, the shapes of the serifs, the relative sizes of the parts of the letters, and other design features, all add up to individualities. The alphabet is firmly fixed in the shapes of its letters. Three-year-olds recognize letterforms. Yet there are on the order of 50,000 typefaces in existence, each different. Subtle and not-so-subtle variations in the thickness of the lines, the curves and angles, the shapes of the serifs, the relative sizes of the parts of

Not particularly emphatic, and certainly not readable in large quantities, Helvetica Italic works to point out the occasional word and has some dynamism as a headline face. Don’t count on it to carry an important message. It’s not very strong.

ABCDEFGHIJKLMNOPQRSTUVWXYZ
abcdefghijklmnopqrstuvwxyz
0123456789&?!$%“”.,/;()

8 point type, 9 point linespace

The alphabet is firmly fixed in the shapes of its letters. Three-year-olds recognize letterforms. Yet there are on the order of 50,000 typefaces in existence, each different. Subtle and not-so-subtle variations in the thickness of the lines, the curves and angles, the shapes of the serifs, the relative sizes of the parts of the letters, and other design features, all add up to individualities. The alphabet is firmly fixed in the shapes of its letters. Three-year-olds recognize letterforms. Yet there are on the order of 50,000 typefaces in existence, each different. Subtle and not-so-subtle variations in the thickness of the lines, the curves and angles, the shapes of the serifs, the relative sizes of the parts of the letters, and other design features, all add up to individualities. The alphabet is firmly fixed in the shapes of its letters. Three-year-olds recognize letterforms. Yet there are on the order of 50,000 typefaces in existence, each different. Subtle and not-so-subtle variations in the thickness of the lines, the curves and angles, the shapes of the serifs, the relative sizes of the parts of the letters, and other design features, all add up to individualities. The alphabet is firmly fixed in the shapes of its letters. Three-year-olds recognize letterforms. Yet there are on the order of 50,000 typefaces in existence, each different. Subtle and not-so-subtle variations in the thickness of the lines, the curves and angles, the shapes of the serifs, the relative sizes of the

10 point type, 11 point linespace

The alphabet is firmly fixed in the shapes of its letters. Three-year-olds recognize letterforms. Yet there are on the order of 50,000 typefaces in existence, each different. Subtle and not-so-subtle variations in the thickness of the lines, the curves and angles, the shapes of the serifs, the relative sizes of the parts of the letters, and other design features, all add up to individualities. The alphabet is firmly fixed in the shapes of its letters. Three-year-olds recognize letterforms. Yet there are on the order of 50,000 typefaces in existence, each different. Subtle and not-so-subtle variations in the thickness of the lines, the curves and angles, the shapes of the serifs, the relative sizes of the parts of the letters, and other design features, all add up to individualities. The alphabet is firmly fixed in the shapes of its letters. Three-year-olds recognize letterforms. Yet there are on the order of 50,000 typefaces in existence, each different. Subtle and not-so-subtle variations in

12 point type, 13 point linespace

The alphabet is firmly fixed in the shapes of its letters. Three-year-olds recognize letterforms. Yet there are on the order of 50,000 typefaces in existence, each different. Subtle and not-so-subtle variations in the thickness of the lines, the curves and angles, the shapes of the serifs, the relative sizes of the parts of the letters, and other design features, all add up to individualities. The alphabet is firmly fixed in the shapes of its letters. Three-year-olds recognize letterforms. Yet there are on the order of 50,000 typefaces in existence, each different. Subtle and not-so-subtle variations in the thickness of the lines, the curves and angles, the shapes of the serifs, the relative sizes of

Set with tight letterspace to achieve full impact. Use for headlines, subheads, column heads, and extracted quotes in larger sizes. While a bit too heavy for a text face, it is very legible and complements Helvetica perfectly.

ABCDEFGHIJKLMNOPQRSTUVWXYZ
abcdefghijklmnopqrstuvwxyz
0123456789&?!$%“”.,/;()

8 point type, 9 point linespace

The alphabet is firmly fixed in the shapes of its letters. Three-year-olds recognize letterforms. Yet there are on the order of 50,000 typefaces in existence, each different. Subtle and not-so-subtle variations in the thickness of the lines, the curves and angles, the shapes of the serifs, the relative sizes of the parts of the letters, and other design features, all add up to individualities. The alphabet is firmly fixed in the shapes of its letters. Three-year-olds recognize letterforms. Yet there are on the order of 50,000 typefaces in existence, each different. Subtle and not-so-subtle variations in the thickness of the lines, the curves and angles, the shapes of the serifs, the relative sizes of the parts of the letters, and other design features, all add up to individualities. The alphabet is firmly fixed in the shapes of its letters. Three-year-olds recognize letterforms. Yet there are on the order of 50,000 type-faces in existence, each different. Subtle and not-so-subtle variations in the thickness of the lines, the curves and angles, the shapes of the serifs, the relative sizes of the parts of the letters, and other design features, all add up to individualities. The alphabet is firmly fixed in the shapes of its letters. Three-year-olds recognize letterforms. Yet there are on the order of 50,000 type-faces in existence, each different. Subtle and not-so-subtle variations in the thickness of the lines, the curves and angles, the shapes of the serifs, the relative sizes of

10 point type, 11 point linespace

The alphabet is firmly fixed in the shapes of its letters. Three-year-olds recognize letterforms. Yet there are on the order of 50,000 typefaces in existence, each different. Subtle and not-so-subtle variations in the thickness of the lines, the curves and angles, the shapes of the serifs, the relative sizes of the parts of the letters, and other design features, all add up to individuali-ties. The alphabet is firmly fixed in the shapes of its letters. Three-year-olds recognize letterforms. Yet there are on the order of 50,000 typefaces in existence, each different. Subtle and not-so-subtle variations in the thickness of the lines, the curves and angles, the shapes of the serifs, the relative sizes of the parts of the letters, and other design features, all add up to individualities. The alphabet is firmly fixed in the shapes of its letters. Three-year-olds recognize letterforms. Yet there are on the order of 50,000 typefaces in existence, each different. Subtle and not-so-subtle

12 point type, 13 point linespace

The alphabet is firmly fixed in the shapes of its letters. Three-year-olds recognize letterforms. Yet there are on the order of 50,000 typefaces in exist-ence, each different. Subtle and not-so-subtle variations in the thickness of the lines, the curves and angles, the shapes of the serifs, the relative sizes of the parts of the letters, and other design features, all add up to individualities. The alphabet is firmly fixed in the shapes of its letters. Three-year-olds recognize letterforms. Yet there are on the order of 50,000 typefaces in exist-ence, each different. Subtle and not-so-subtle variations in the thickness of the lines, the curves and angles, the shapes of the serifs, the relative sizes of the

Weaker than Helvetica 65 Medium, the Italic form must be set tightly to achieve any impact. Otherwise, it will detract from the Medium type it usually accompanies, and weaken a message rather than strengthen it.

ABCDEFGHIJKLMNOPQRSTUVWXYZ
abcdefghijklmnopqrstuvwxyz
0123456789&?!$%“”.,/;()

8 point type, 9 point linespace

The alphabet is firmly fixed in the shapes of its letters. Three-year-olds recognize letterforms. Yet there are on the order of 50,000 typefaces in existence, each different. Subtle and not-so-subtle variations in the thickness of the lines, the curves and angles, the shapes of the serifs, the relative sizes of the parts of the letters, and other design features, all add up to individualities. The alphabet is firmly fixed in the shapes of its letters. Three-year-olds recognize letterforms. Yet there are on the order of 50,000 typefaces in existence, each different. Subtle and not-so-subtle variations in the thickness of the lines, the curves and angles, the shapes of the serifs, the relative sizes of the parts of the letters, and other design features, all add up to individualities. The alphabet is firmly fixed in the shapes of its letters. Three-year-olds recognize letterforms. Yet there are on the order of 50,000 typefaces in existence, each different. Subtle and not-so-subtle variations in the thickness of the lines, the curves and angles, the shapes of the serifs, the relative sizes of the parts of the letters, and other design features, all add up to individualities. The alphabet is firmly fixed in the shapes of its letters. Three-year-olds recognize letterforms. Yet there are on the order of 50,000 typefaces in existence, each different. Subtle and not-so-subtle variations in the

10 point type, 11 point linespace

The alphabet is firmly fixed in the shapes of its letters. Three-year-olds recognize letterforms. Yet there are on the order of 50,000 typefaces in existence, each different. Subtle and not-so-subtle variations in the thickness of the lines, the curves and angles, the shapes of the serifs, the relative sizes of the parts of the letters, and other design features, all add up to individualities. The alphabet is firmly fixed in the shapes of its letters. Three-year-olds recognize letterforms. Yet there are on the order of 50,000 typefaces in existence, each different. Subtle and not-so-subtle variations in the thickness of the lines, the curves and angles, the shapes of the serifs, the relative sizes of the parts of the letters, and other design features, all add up to individualities. The alphabet is firmly fixed in the shapes of its letters. Three-year-olds recognize letterforms. Yet there are on the order of

12 point type, 13 point linespace

The alphabet is firmly fixed in the shapes of its letters. Three-year-olds recognize letterforms. Yet there are on the order of 50,000 typefaces in existence, each different. Subtle and not-so-subtle variations in the thick-ness of the lines, the curves and angles, the shapes of the serifs, the relative sizes of the parts of the let-ters, and other design features, all add up to individualities. The alpha-bet is firmly fixed in the shapes of its letters. Three-year-olds recognize letterforms. Yet there are on the order of 50,000 typefaces in existence, each different. Subtle and not-so-subtle variations in the thickness of the lines, the curves and angles, the

The workhorse of headlines, column heads, subheads, any heads at all, giving the perfect balance of mass and significance. It should be set very tightly to fully bring out its flavor, and it holds up well in reverse.

ABCDEFGHIJKLMNOPQRSTUVWXYZ
abcdefghijklmnopqrstuvwxyz
0123456789&?!$%“”.,/;()

8 point type, 9 point linespace

The alphabet is firmly fixed in the shapes of its letters. Three-year-olds recognize letterforms. Yet there are on the order of 50,000 typefaces in existence, each different. Subtle and not-so-subtle variations in the thickness of the lines, the curves and angles, the shapes of the serifs, the relative sizes of the parts of the letters, and other design features, all add up to individualities. The alphabet is firmly fixed in the shapes of its letters. Three-year-olds recognize letterforms. Yet there are on the order of 50,000 typefaces in existence, each different. Subtle and not-so-subtle variations in the thickness of the lines, the curves and angles, the shapes of the serifs, the relative sizes of the parts of the letters, and other design features, all add up to individualities. The alphabet is firmly fixed in the shapes of its letters. Three-year-olds recognize letterforms. Yet there are on the order of 50,000 typefaces in existence, each different. Subtle and not-so-subtle variations in the thickness of the lines, the curves and angles, the shapes of the serifs, the relative sizes of the parts of the letters, and other design features, all add up to individualities. The alphabet is firmly fixed in the shapes of its letters. Three-year-olds recognize letterforms. Yet there are on the order of 50,000 typefaces in existence, each different. Subtle and not-so-subtle variations in the

10 point type, 11 point linespace

The alphabet is firmly fixed in the shapes of its letters. Three-year-olds recognize letterforms. Yet there are on the order of 50,000 typefaces in existence, each different. Subtle and not-so-subtle variations in the thickness of the lines, the curves and angles, the shapes of the serifs, the relative sizes of the parts of the letters, and other design features, all add up to individualities. The alphabet is firmly fixed in the shapes of its letters. Three-year-olds recognize letterforms. Yet there are on the order of 50,000 typefaces in existence, each different. Subtle and not-so-subtle variations in the thickness of the lines, the curves and angles, the shapes of the serifs, the relative sizes of the parts of the letters, and other design features, all add up to individualities. The alphabet is firmly fixed in the shapes of its letters. Three-year-olds recognize letterforms. Yet there are on the order of

12 point type, 13 point linespace

The alphabet is firmly fixed in the shapes of its letters. Three-year-olds recognize letterforms. Yet there are on the order of 50,000 typefaces in existence, each different. Subtle and not-so-subtle variations in the thick-ness of the lines, the curves and angles, the shapes of the serifs, the relative sizes of the parts of the let-ters, and other design features, all add up to individualities. The alpha-bet is firmly fixed in the shapes of its letters. Three-year-olds recognize letterforms. Yet there are on the order of 50,000 typefaces in existence, each different. Subtle and not-so-subtle variations in the thickness of the lines, the curves and angles, the

This loses a little bit of punch compared to the roman, so does not pro-vide the emphasis you might expect. Better to use it against Helvetica 65 Medium to really make a point.

ABCDEFGHIJKLMNOPQRSTUVWXYZ
abcdefghijklmnopqrstuvwxyz
0123456789&?!$%“”.,/;()

8 point type, 9 point linespace

The alphabet is firmly fixed in the shapes of its letters. Three-year-olds recognize letterforms. Yet there are on the order of 50,000 typefaces in existence, each different. Subtle and not-so-subtle variations in the thickness of the lines, the curves and angles, the shapes of the serifs, the relative sizes of the parts of the letters, and other design features, all add up to individualities. The alphabet is firmly fixed in the shapes of its letters. Three-year-olds recognize letterforms. Yet there are on the order of 50,000 typefaces in existence, each different. Subtle and not-so-subtle variations in the thickness of the lines, the curves and angles, the shapes of the serifs, the relative sizes of the parts of the letters, and other design features, all add up to individualities. The alphabet is firmly fixed in the shapes of its letters. Three-year-olds recognize letterforms. Yet there are on the order of 50,000 typefaces in existence, each different. Subtle and not-so-subtle variations in the thickness of the lines, the curves and angles, the shapes of the serifs, the relative sizes of the parts of the letters, and other design features, all add up to individualities. The alphabet is firmly fixed in the shapes of its letters. Three-year-olds recognize letterforms. Yet there are on the order of 50,000 typefaces in existence, each

10 point type, 11 point linespace

The alphabet is firmly fixed in the shapes of its letters. Three-year-olds recognize letterforms. Yet there are on the order of 50,000 typefaces in existence, each different. Subtle and not-so-subtle variations in the thickness of the lines, the curves and angles, the shapes of the serifs, the relative sizes of the parts of the letters, and other design features, all add up to individualities. The alphabet is firmly fixed in the shapes of its letters. Three-year-olds recognize letterforms. Yet there are on the order of 50,000 typefaces in existence, each different. Subtle and not-so-subtle variations in the thickness of the lines, the curves and angles, the shapes of the serifs, the relative sizes of the parts of the letters, and other design features, all add up to individualities. The alphabet is firmly fixed in the shapes of its letters. Three-year-olds recognize letterforms. Yet

12 point type, 13 point linespace

The alphabet is firmly fixed in the shapes of its letters. Three-year-olds recognize letterforms. Yet there are on the order of 50,000 typefaces in existence, each different. Subtle and not-so-subtle variations in the thickness of the lines, the curves and angles, the shapes of the serifs, the relative sizes of the parts of the letters, and other design features, all add up to individualities. The alphabet is firmly fixed in the shapes of its letters. Three-year-olds recognize letterforms. Yet there are on the order of 50,000 typefaces in existence, each different. Subtle and not-so-subtle variations in the thick-

Solely for use in large sizes, but not *very* large. Use in 18-36 point situations. For the biggest blackest heads, it still contains too much white space in its design.

ABCDEFGHIJKLMNOPQRSTUVWXYZ
abcdefghijklmnopqrstuvwxyz
0123456789&?!$%“”.,/;()

8 point type, 9 point linespace

The alphabet is firmly fixed in the shapes of its letters. Three-year-olds recognize letterforms. Yet there are on the order of 50,000 typefaces in existence, each different. Subtle and not-so-subtle variations in the thickness of the lines, the curves and angles, the shapes of the serifs, the relative sizes of the parts of the letters, and other design features, all add up to individualities. The alphabet is firmly fixed in the shapes of its letters. Three-year-olds recognize letterforms. Yet there are on the order of 50,000 typefaces in existence, each different. Subtle and not-so-subtle variations in the thickness of the lines, the curves and angles, the shapes of the serifs, the relative sizes of the parts of the letters, and other design features, all add up to individualities. The alphabet is firmly fixed in the shapes of its letters. Three-year-olds recognize letterforms. Yet there are on the order of 50,000 typefaces in existence, each different. Subtle and not-so-subtle variations in the thickness of the lines, the curves and angles, the shapes of the serifs, the relative sizes of the parts of the letters, and other design features, all add up to individualities. The alphabet is firmly fixed in the shapes of its letters. Three-year-olds recognize letterforms. Yet there are on the order of 50,000 typefaces in existence, each

10 point type, 11 point linespace

The alphabet is firmly fixed in the shapes of its letters. Three-year-olds recognize letterforms. Yet there are on the order of 50,000 typefaces in existence, each different. Subtle and not-so-subtle variations in the thickness of the lines, the curves and angles, the shapes of the serifs, the relative sizes of the parts of the letters, and other design features, all add up to individualities. The alphabet is firmly fixed in the shapes of its letters. Three-year-olds recognize letterforms. Yet there are on the order of 50,000 typefaces in existence, each different. Subtle and not-so-subtle variations in the thickness of the lines, the curves and angles, the shapes of the serifs, the relative sizes of the parts of the letters, and other design features, all add up to individualities. The alphabet is firmly fixed in the shapes of its letters. Three-year-olds recognize letterforms. Yet

12 point type, 13 point linespace

The alphabet is firmly fixed in the shapes of its letters. Three-year-olds recognize letterforms. Yet there are on the order of 50,000 typefaces in existence, each different. Subtle and not-so-subtle variations in the thickness of the lines, the curves and angles, the shapes of the serifs, the relative sizes of the parts of the letters, and other design features, all add up to individualities. The alphabet is firmly fixed in the shapes of its letters. Three-year-olds recognize letterforms. Yet there are on the order of 50,000 typefaces in existence, each different. Subtle and not-so-subtle variations in the thick-

One of the few italics that carries as much weight as the roman version, but still needs tight setting. Best used in small complete blocks of type, not mixed with roman, as its contrast to roman is fairly low.

ABCDEFGHIJKLMNOPQRSTUVWXYZ
abcdefghijklmnopqrstuvwxyz
0123456789&?!$%“”.,/;()

8 point type, 9 point linespace

The alphabet is firmly fixed in the shapes of its letters. Three-year-olds recognize letterforms. Yet there are on the order of 50,000 typefaces in existence, each different. Subtle and not-so-subtle variations in the thickness of the lines, the curves and angles, the shapes of the serifs, the relative sizes of the parts of the letters, and other design features, all add up to individualities. The alphabet is firmly fixed in the shapes of its letters. Three-year-olds recognize letterforms. Yet there are on the order of 50,000 typefaces in existence, each different. Subtle and not-so-subtle variations in the thickness of the lines, the curves and angles, the shapes of the serifs, the relative sizes of the parts of the letters, and other design features, all add up to individualities. The alphabet is firmly fixed in the shapes of its letters. Three-year-olds recognize letterforms. Yet there are on the order of 50,000 typefaces in existence, each different. Subtle and not-so-subtle variations in the thickness of the lines, the curves and angles, the shapes of the serifs, the relative sizes of the parts of the letters, and other design features, all add up to individualities. The alphabet is firmly fixed in the shapes of its letters. Three-year-olds recognize letterforms. Yet there are on the order of

10 point type, 11 point linespace

The alphabet is firmly fixed in the shapes of its letters. Three-year-olds recognize letterforms. Yet there are on the order of 50,000 typefaces in existence, each different. Subtle and not-so-subtle variations in the thickness of the lines, the curves and angles, the shapes of the serifs, the relative sizes of the parts of the letters, and other design features, all add up to individualities. The alphabet is firmly fixed in the shapes of its letters. Three-year-olds recognize letterforms. Yet there are on the order of 50,000 typefaces in existence, each different. Subtle and not-so-subtle variations in the thickness of the lines, the curves and angles, the shapes of the serifs, the relative sizes of the parts of the letters, and other design features, all add up to individualities. The alphabet is firmly fixed in the shapes of its letters. Three-

12 point type, 13 point linespace

The alphabet is firmly fixed in the shapes of its letters. Three-year-olds recognize letterforms. Yet there are on the order of 50,000 typefaces in existence, each different. Subtle and not-so-subtle variations in the thickness of the lines, the curves and angles, the shapes of the serifs, the relative sizes of the parts of the letters, and other design features, all add up to individualities. The alphabet is firmly fixed in the shapes of its letters. Three-year-olds recognize letterforms. Yet there are on the order of 50,000 typefaces in existence, each different. Subtle and not-so-subtle variations in the

For the largest headlines, or as an occasional type element (numbers on a list; initial letters to introduce a block of text; a word here or there). Easy to read, meant to be noticed, denotes more than ordinary significance.

ABCDEFGHIJKLMNOPQRSTUVWXYZ
abcdefghijklmnopqrstuvwxyz
0123456789&?!$%“”.,/;()

8 point type, 9 point linespace

The alphabet is firmly fixed in the shapes of its letters. Three-year-olds recognize letterforms. Yet there are on the order of 50,000 typefaces in existence, each different. Subtle and not-so-subtle variations in the thickness of the lines, the curves and angles, the shapes of the serifs, the relative sizes of the parts of the letters, and other design features, all add up to individualities. The alphabet is firmly fixed in the shapes of its letters. Three-year-olds recognize letterforms. Yet there are on the order of 50,000 typefaces in existence, each different. Subtle and not-so-subtle variations in the thickness of the lines, the curves and angles, the shapes of the serifs, the relative sizes of the parts of the letters, and other design features, all add up to individualities. The alphabet is firmly fixed in the shapes of its letters. Three-year-olds recognize letterforms. Yet there are on the order of 50,000 typefaces in existence, each different. Subtle and not-so-subtle variations in the thickness of the lines, the curves and angles, the shapes of the serifs, the relative sizes of the parts of the letters, and other design features, all add up to individualities. The alphabet is firmly fixed in the shapes of its letters. Three-year-olds recognize letterforms. Yet there are on the order of

10 point type, 11 point linespace

The alphabet is firmly fixed in the shapes of its letters. Three-year-olds recognize letterforms. Yet there are on the order of 50,000 typefaces in existence, each different. Subtle and not-so-subtle variations in the thickness of the lines, the curves and angles, the shapes of the serifs, the relative sizes of the parts of the letters, and other design features, all add up to individualities. The alphabet is firmly fixed in the shapes of its letters. Three-year-olds recognize letterforms. Yet there are on the order of 50,000 typefaces in existence, each different. Subtle and not-so-subtle variations in the thickness of the lines, the curves and angles, the shapes of the serifs, the relative sizes of the parts of the letters, and other design features, all add up to individualities. The alphabet is firmly fixed in the shapes of its letters. Three-

12 point type, 13 point linespace

The alphabet is firmly fixed in the shapes of its letters. Three-year-olds recognize letterforms. Yet there are on the order of 50,000 typefaces in existence, each different. Subtle and not-so-subtle variations in the thickness of the lines, the curves and angles, the shapes of the serifs, the relative sizes of the parts of the letters, and other design features, all add up to individualities. The alphabet is firmly fixed in the shapes of its letters. Three-year-olds recognize letterforms. Yet there are on the order of 50,000 typefaces in existence, each different. Subtle and not-so-subtle variations in the

Use similarly to the roman, but when more urgency is required. This face strains the limits of a reader’s patience, almost forcing an immediate response, when used judiciously.

ABCDEFGHIJKLMNOPQRSTUVWXYZ
abcdefghijklmnopqrstuvwxyz
0123456789&?!$%“”.,/;()

8 point type, 9 point linespace

The alphabet is firmly fixed in the shapes of its letters. Three-year-olds recognize letterforms. Yet there are on the order of 50,000 typefaces in existence, each different. Subtle and not-so-subtle variations in the thickness of the lines, the curves and angles, the shapes of the serifs, the relative sizes of the parts of the letters, and other design features, all add up to individualities. The alphabet is firmly fixed in the shapes of its letters. Three-year-olds recognize letterforms. Yet there are on the order of 50,000 typefaces in existence, each different. Subtle and not-so-subtle variations in the thickness of the lines, the curves and angles, the shapes of the serifs, the relative sizes of the parts of the letters, and other design features, all add up to individualities. The alphabet is firmly fixed in the shapes of its letters. Three-year-olds recognize letterforms. Yet there are on the order of 50,000 typefaces in existence, each different. Subtle and not-so-subtle variations in the thickness of the lines, the curves and angles, the shapes of the serifs, the relative sizes of the parts of the letters, and other design features, all add up to individualities. The alphabet is firmly fixed in the shapes of its letters. Three-year-olds recognize letterforms. Yet there are on the order of 50,000 typefaces in existence, each different. Subtle and not-so-subtle variations in the thickness of the lines, the curves and angles, the shapes of the serifs, the relative sizes of the parts of the letters, and other design features, all add up to individualities. The alphabet is firmly fixed in the shapes of its letters. Three-year-olds recognize letterforms. Yet there are on the order of 50,000

10 point type, 11 point linespace

The alphabet is firmly fixed in the shapes of its letters. Three-year-olds recognize letterforms. Yet there are on the order of 50,000 typefaces in existence, each different. Subtle and not-so-subtle variations in the thickness of the lines, the curves and angles, the shapes of the serifs, the relative sizes of the parts of the letters, and other design features, all add up to individualities. The alphabet is firmly fixed in the shapes of its letters. Three-year-olds recognize letterforms. Yet there are on the order of 50,000 typefaces in existence, each different. Subtle and not-so-subtle variations in the thickness of the lines, the curves and angles, the shapes of the serifs, the relative sizes of the parts of the letters, and other design features, all add up to individualities. The alphabet is firmly fixed in the shapes of its letters. Three-year-olds recognize letterforms. Yet there are on the order of 50,000 typefaces in existence, each different. Subtle and not-so-subtle variations in the thickness of the lines, the curves and angles, the shapes of the serifs, the relative sizes of the parts of the letters, and other

12 point type, 13 point linespace

The alphabet is firmly fixed in the shapes of its letters. Three-year-olds recognize letterforms. Yet there are on the order of 50,000 typefaces in existence, each different. Subtle and not-so-subtle variations in the thickness of the lines, the curves and angles, the shapes of the serifs, the relative sizes of the parts of the letters, and other design features, all add up to individualities. The alphabet is firmly fixed in the shapes of its letters. Three-year-olds recognize letterforms. Yet there are on the order of 50,000 typefaces in existence, each different. Subtle and not-so-subtle variations in the thickness of the lines, the curves and angles, the shapes of the serifs, the relative sizes of the parts of the letters, and other design features, all add up to individualities. The alphabet is firmly fixed

For use in narrow places, or when a certain amount of type *must* fit onto one line. Excellent in charts, financial statements or for marginal notes in a book or brochure.

ABCDEFGHIJKLMNOPQRSTUVWXYZ
abcdefghijklmnopqrstuvwxyz
0123456789&?!$%“”.,/;()

8 point type, 9 point linespace

The alphabet is firmly fixed in the shapes of its letters. Three-year-olds recognize letterforms. Yet there are on the order of 50,000 typefaces in existence, each different. Subtle and not-so-subtle variations in the thickness of the lines, the curves and angles, the shapes of the serifs, the relative sizes of the parts of the letters, and other design features, all add up to individualities. The alphabet is firmly fixed in the shapes of its letters. Three-year-olds recognize letterforms. Yet there are on the order of 50,000 typefaces in existence, each different. Subtle and not-so-subtle variations in the thickness of the lines, the curves and angles, the shapes of the serifs, the relative sizes of the parts of the letters, and other design features, all add up to individualities. The alphabet is firmly fixed in the shapes of its letters. Three-year-olds recognize letterforms. Yet there are on the order of 50,000 typefaces in existence, each different. Subtle and not-so-subtle variations in the thickness of the lines, the curves and angles, the shapes of the serifs, the relative sizes of the parts of the letters, and other design features, all add up to individualities. The alphabet is firmly fixed in the shapes of its letters. Three-year-olds recognize letterforms. Yet there are on the order of 50,000 typefaces in existence, each different. Subtle and not-so-subtle variations in the thickness of the lines, the curves and angles, the shapes of the serifs, the relative sizes of the parts of the letters, and other design features, all add up to individualities. The alphabet is firmly fixed in the shapes of its letters. Three-year-olds recognize letterforms. Yet there are on the order of 50,000

10 point type, 11 point linespace

The alphabet is firmly fixed in the shapes of its letters. Three-year-olds recognize letterforms. Yet there are on the order of 50,000 typefaces in existence, each different. Subtle and not-so-subtle variations in the thickness of the lines, the curves and angles, the shapes of the serifs, the relative sizes of the parts of the letters, and other design features, all add up to individualities. The alphabet is firmly fixed in the shapes of its letters. Three-year-olds recognize letterforms. Yet there are on the order of 50,000 typefaces in existence, each different. Subtle and not-so-subtle variations in the thickness of the lines, the curves and angles, the shapes of the serifs, the relative sizes of the parts of the letters, and other design features, all add up to individualities. The alphabet is firmly fixed in the shapes of its letters. Three-year-olds recognize letterforms. Yet there are on the order of 50,000 typefaces in existence, each different. Subtle and not-so-subtle variations in the thickness of the lines, the curves and angles, the shapes of the serifs, the relative sizes of the parts of the letters, and other

12 point type, 13 point linespace

The alphabet is firmly fixed in the shapes of its letters. Three-year-olds recognize letterforms. Yet there are on the order of 50,000 typefaces in existence, each different. Subtle and not-so-subtle variations in the thickness of the lines, the curves and angles, the shapes of the serifs, the relative sizes of the parts of the letters, and other design features, all add up to individualities. The alphabet is firmly fixed in the shapes of its letters. Three-year-olds recognize letterforms. Yet there are on the order of 50,000 typefaces in existence, each different. Subtle and not-so-subtle variations in the thickness of the lines, the curves and angles, the shapes of the serifs, the relative sizes of the parts of the letters, and other design features, all add up to individualities. The alphabet is firmly fixed

With good contrast to the roman, this can be used freely for emphasis in combination with roman. Not particularly readable on its own.

ABCDEFGHIJKLMNOPQRSTUVWXYZ
abcdefghijklmnopqrstuvwxyz
0123456789&?!$%“”.,/;()

8 point type, 9 point linespace

The alphabet is firmly fixed in the shapes of its letters. Three-year-olds recognize letterforms. Yet there are on the order of 50,000 typefaces in existence, each different. Subtle and not-so-subtle variations in the thickness of the lines, the curves and angles, the shapes of the serifs, the relative sizes of the parts of the letters, and other design features, all add up to individualities. The alphabet is firmly fixed in the shapes of its letters. Three-year-olds recognize letterforms. Yet there are on the order of 50,000 typefaces in existence, each different. Subtle and not-so-subtle variations in the thickness of the lines, the curves and angles, the shapes of the serifs, the relative sizes of the parts of the letters, and other design features, all add up to individualities. The alphabet is firmly fixed in the shapes of its letters. Three-year-olds recognize letterforms. Yet there are on the order of 50,000 typefaces in existence, each different. Subtle and not-so-subtle variations in the thickness of the lines, the curves and angles, the shapes of the serifs, the relative sizes of the parts of the letters, and other design features, all add up to individualities. The alphabet is firmly fixed in the shapes of its letters. Three-year-olds recognize letterforms. Yet there are on the order of 50,000 typefaces in existence, each different. Subtle and not-so-subtle variations in the thickness of the lines, the curves and angles, the shapes of the serifs, the relative sizes of the parts of the letters, and other design features, all add up to individualities. The alphabet is firmly fixed in the shapes of its letters. Three-year-olds recognize

10 point type, 11 point linespace

The alphabet is firmly fixed in the shapes of its letters. Three-year-olds recognize letterforms. Yet there are on the order of 50,000 typefaces in existence, each different. Subtle and not-so-subtle variations in the thickness of the lines, the curves and angles, the shapes of the serifs, the relative sizes of the parts of the letters, and other design features, all add up to individualities. The alphabet is firmly fixed in the shapes of its letters. Three-year-olds recognize letterforms. Yet there are on the order of 50,000 typefaces in existence, each different. Subtle and not-so-subtle variations in the thickness of the lines, the curves and angles, the shapes of the serifs, the relative sizes of the parts of the letters, and other design features, all add up to individualities. The alphabet is firmly fixed in the shapes of its letters. Three-year-olds recognize letterforms. Yet there are on the order of 50,000 typefaces in existence, each different. Subtle and not-so-subtle variations in the thickness of the lines, the curves and angles, the shapes of the serifs, the

12 point type, 13 point linespace

The alphabet is firmly fixed in the shapes of its letters. Three-year-olds recognize letterforms. Yet there are on the order of 50,000 typefaces in existence, each different. Subtle and not-so-subtle variations in the thickness of the lines, the curves and angles, the shapes of the serifs, the relative sizes of the parts of the letters, and other design features, all add up to individualities. The alphabet is firmly fixed in the shapes of its letters. Three-year-olds recognize letterforms. Yet there are on the order of 50,000 typefaces in existence, each different. Subtle and not-so-subtle variations in the thickness of the lines, the curves and angles, the shapes of its letters. Three-year-olds recognize letterforms. Yet there are on the order of 50,000 typefaces in

A very clean well-balanced typeface with a wide range of effective sizes, from 6-point to 60. Cleanly cut, easy to read, fairly easy to set (set tight). Play with this face in many situations where “nothing seems to work.”

ABCDEFGHIJKLMNOPQRSTUVWXYZ
abcdefghijklmnopqrstuvwxyz
0123456789&?!$%“”.,/;()

8 point type, 9 point linespace

The alphabet is firmly fixed in the shapes of its letters. Three-year-olds recognize letterforms. Yet there are on the order of 50,000 typefaces in existence, each different. Subtle and not-so-subtle variations in the thickness of the lines, the curves and angles, the shapes of the serifs, the relative sizes of the parts of the letters, and other design features, all add up to individualities. The alphabet is firmly fixed in the shapes of its letters. Three-year-olds recognize letterforms. Yet there are on the order of 50,000 typefaces in existence, each different. Subtle and not-so-subtle variations in the thickness of the lines, the curves and angles, the shapes of the serifs, the relative sizes of the parts of the letters, and other design features, all add up to individualities. The alphabet is firmly fixed in the shapes of its letters. Three-year-olds recognize letterforms. Yet there are on the order of 50,000 typefaces in existence, each different. Subtle and not-so-subtle variations in the thickness of the lines, the curves and angles, the shapes of the serifs, the relative sizes of the parts of the letters, and other design features, all add up to individualities. The alphabet is firmly fixed in the shapes of its letters. Three-year-olds recognize letterforms. Yet there are on the order of 50,000 typefaces in existence, each different. Subtle and not-so-subtle variations in the thickness of the lines, the curves and angles, the shapes of the serifs, the relative sizes of the parts of the letters, and other design features, all add up to individualities. The alphabet is firmly fixed in the shapes of its letters. Three-year-olds recognize

10 point type, 11 point linespace

The alphabet is firmly fixed in the shapes of its letters. Three-year-olds recognize letterforms. Yet there are on the order of 50,000 typefaces in existence, each different. Subtle and not-so-subtle variations in the thickness of the lines, the curves and angles, the shapes of the serifs, the relative sizes of the parts of the letters, and other design features, all add up to individualities. The alphabet is firmly fixed in the shapes of its letters. Three-year-olds recognize letterforms. Yet there are on the order of 50,000 typefaces in existence, each different. Subtle and not-so-subtle variations in the thickness of the lines, the curves and angles, the shapes of the serifs, the relative sizes of the parts of the letters, and other design features, all add up to individualities. The alphabet is firmly fixed in the shapes of its letters. Three-year-olds recognize letterforms. Yet there are on the order of 50,000 typefaces in existence, each different. Subtle and not-so-subtle variations in the thickness of the lines, the curves and angles, the shapes of the serifs, the

12 point type, 13 point linespace

The alphabet is firmly fixed in the shapes of its letters. Three-year-olds recognize letterforms. Yet there are on the order of 50,000 typefaces in existence, each different. Subtle and not-so-subtle variations in the thickness of the lines, the curves and angles, the shapes of the serifs, the relative sizes of the parts of the letters, and other design features, all add up to individualities. The alphabet is firmly fixed in the shapes of its letters. Three-year-olds recognize letterforms. Yet there are on the order of 50,000 typefaces in existence, each different. Subtle and not-so-subtle variations in the thickness of the lines, the curves and angles, the shapes of its letters. Three-year-olds recognize letterforms. Yet there are on the order of 50,000 typefaces in

The marriage of roman and italic here is strong and enduring. Combine the two with confidence—neither overshadows the other, and both gain by the alliance.

ABCDEFGHIJKLMNOPQRSTUVWXYZ
abcdefghijklmnopqrstuvwxyz
0123456789&?!$%“”.,/;()

8 point type, 9 point linespace

The alphabet is firmly fixed in the shapes of its letters. Three-year-olds recognize letterforms. Yet there are on the order of 50,000 typefaces in existence, each different. Subtle and not-so-subtle variations in the thickness of the lines, the curves and angles, the shapes of the serifs, the relative sizes of the parts of the letters, and other design features, all add up to individualities. The alphabet is firmly fixed in the shapes of its letters. Three-year-olds recognize letterforms. Yet there are on the order of 50,000 typefaces in existence, each different. Subtle and not-so-subtle variations in the thickness of the lines, the curves and angles, the shapes of the serifs, the relative sizes of the parts of the letters, and other design features, all add up to individualities. The alphabet is firmly fixed in the shapes of its letters. Three-year-olds recognize letterforms. Yet there are on the order of 50,000 typefaces in existence, each different. Subtle and not-so-subtle variations in the thickness of the lines, the curves and angles, the shapes of the serifs, the relative sizes of the parts of the letters, and other design features, all add up to individualities. The alphabet is firmly fixed in the shapes of its letters. Three-year-olds recognize letterforms. Yet there are on the order of 50,000 typefaces in existence, each different. Subtle and not-so-subtle variations in the thickness of the lines, the curves and angles, the shapes of the serifs, the relative sizes of the parts of the letters, and other design features, all add up to individualities. The alphabet is firmly fixed in the shapes of its

10 point type, 11 point linespace

The alphabet is firmly fixed in the shapes of its letters. Three-year-olds recognize letterforms. Yet there are on the order of 50,000 typefaces in existence, each different. Subtle and not-so-subtle variations in the thickness of the lines, the curves and angles, the shapes of the serifs, the relative sizes of the parts of the letters, and other design features, all add up to individualities. The alphabet is firmly fixed in the shapes of its letters. Three-year-olds recognize letterforms. Yet there are on the order of 50,000 typefaces in existence, each different. Subtle and not-so-subtle variations in the thickness of the lines, the curves and angles, the shapes of the serifs, the relative sizes of the parts of the letters, and other design features, all add up to individualities. The alphabet is firmly fixed in the shapes of its letters. Three-year-olds recognize letterforms. Yet there are on the the order of 50,000 typefaces in existence, each different. Subtle and not-so-subtle variations in the thickness of the lines, the curves and angles, the shapes of the

12 point type, 13 point linespace

The alphabet is firmly fixed in the shapes of its letters. Three-year-olds recognize letterforms. Yet there are on the order of 50,000 typefaces in existence, each different. Subtle and not-so-subtle variations in the thickness of the lines, the curves and angles, the shapes of the serifs, the relative sizes of the parts of the letters, and other design features, all add up to individualities. The alphabet is firmly fixed in the shapes of its letters. Three-year-olds recognize letterforms. Yet there are on the order of 50,000 typefaces in existence, each different. Subtle and not-so-subtle variations in the thickness of the lines, the curves and angles, the shapes of its letters. Three-year-olds recognize letterforms. Yet there are on the order of 50,000 typefaces

A bit overbearing, even somewhat awkward, use only in large sizes, preferably in headlines of more than one line, usually short lines. Good in tall narrow spaces for strong immediate impact.

ABCDEFGHIJKLMNOPQRSTUVWXYZ
abcdefghijklmnopqrstuvwxyz
0123456789&?!$%“”.,/;()

8 point type, 9 point linespace

The alphabet is firmly fixed in the shapes of its letters. Three-year-olds recognize letterforms. Yet there are on the order of 50,000 typefaces in existence, each different. Subtle and not-so-subtle variations in the thickness of the lines, the curves and angles, the shapes of the serifs, the relative sizes of the parts of the letters, and other design features, all add up to individualities. The alphabet is firmly fixed in the shapes of its letters. Three-year-olds recognize letterforms. Yet there are on the order of 50,000 typefaces in existence, each different. Subtle and not-so-subtle variations in the thickness of the lines, the curves and angles, the shapes of the serifs, the relative sizes of the parts of the letters, and other design features, all add up to individualities. The alphabet is firmly fixed in the shapes of its letters. Three-year-olds recognize letterforms. Yet there are on the order of 50,000 typefaces in existence, each different. Subtle and not-so-subtle variations in the thickness of the lines, the curves and angles, the shapes of the serifs, the relative sizes of the parts of the letters, and other design features, all add up to individualities. The alphabet is firmly fixed in the shapes of its letters. Three-year-olds recognize letterforms. Yet there are on the order of 50,000 typefaces in existence, each different. Subtle and not-so-subtle variations in the thickness of the lines, the curves and angles, the shapes of the serifs, the relative sizes of the parts of the letters, and other design features, all add up to individualities. The alphabet is firmly fixed in the shapes of its

10 point type, 11 point linespace

The alphabet is firmly fixed in the shapes of its letters. Three-year-olds recognize letterforms. Yet there are on the order of 50,000 typefaces in existence, each different. Subtle and not-so-subtle variations in the thickness of the lines, the curves and angles, the shapes of the serifs, the relative sizes of the parts of the letters, and other design features, all add up to individualities. The alphabet is firmly fixed in the shapes of its letters. Three-year-olds recognize letterforms. Yet there are on the order of 50,000 typefaces in existence, each different. Subtle and not-so-subtle variations in the thickness of the lines, the curves and angles, the shapes of the serifs, the relative sizes of the parts of the letters, and other design features, all add up to individualities. The alphabet is firmly fixed in the shapes of its letters. Three-year-olds recognize letterforms. Yet there are on the the order of 50,000 typefaces in existence, each different. Subtle and not-so-subtle variations in the thickness of the lines, the curves and angles, the shapes of the

12 point type, 13 point linespace

The alphabet is firmly fixed in the shapes of its letters. Three-year-olds recognize letterforms. Yet there are on the order of 50,000 typefaces in existence, each different. Subtle and not-so-subtle variations in the thickness of the lines, the curves and angles, the shapes of the serifs, the relative sizes of the parts of the letters, and other design features, all add up to individualities. The alphabet is firmly fixed in the shapes of its letters. Three-year-olds recognize letterforms. Yet there are on the order of 50,000 typefaces in existence, each different. Subtle and not-so-subtle variations in the thickness of the lines, the curves and angles, the shapes of its letters. Three-year-olds recognize letterforms. Yet there are on the order of 50,000 typefaces

Almost a “specialty” face, it may be useful if a whole concept is based on italics, but otherwise there’s not a lot of reason to use this face. It doesn’t contrast that well with roman.

ABCDEFGHIJKLMNOPQRSTUVWXYZ
abcdefghijklmnopqrstuvwxyz
0123456789&?!$%"".,/;()

8 point type, 9 point linespace

The alphabet is firmly fixed in the shapes of its letters. Three-year-olds recognize letterforms. Yet there are on the order of 50,000 typefaces in existence, each different. Subtle and not-so-subtle variations in the thickness of the lines, the curves and angles, the shapes of the serifs, the relative sizes of the parts of the letters, and other design features, all add up to individualities. The alphabet is firmly fixed in the shapes of its letters. Three-year-olds recognize letterforms. Yet there are on the order of 50,000 typefaces in existence, each different. Subtle and not-so-subtle variations in the thickness of the lines, the curves and angles, the shapes of the serifs, the relative sizes of the parts of the letters, and other design features, all add up to individualities. The alphabet is firmly fixed in the shapes of its letters. Three-year-olds recognize letterforms. Yet there are on the order of 50,000 typefaces in existence, each different. Subtle and not-so-subtle variations in the thickness of the lines, the curves and angles, the shapes of the serifs, the relative sizes of the parts of the letters, and other design features, all add up to individualities. The alphabet is firmly fixed in the shapes of its letters. Three-year-olds recognize letterforms. Yet there are on the order of 50,000 typefaces in existence, each different. Subtle and not-so-subtle variations in the thickness of the lines, the curves and angles, the shapes of the serifs, the relative sizes of the parts of the letters, and other design

10 point type, 11 point linespace

The alphabet is firmly fixed in the shapes of its letters. Three-year-olds recognize letterforms. Yet there are on the order of 50,000 typefaces in existence, each different. Subtle and not-so-subtle variations in the thickness of the lines, the curves and angles, the shapes of the serifs, the relative sizes of the parts of the letters, and other design features, all add up to individualities. The alphabet is firmly fixed in the shapes of its letters. Three-year-olds recognize letterforms. Yet there are on the order of 50,000 typefaces in existence, each different. Subtle and not-so-subtle variations in the thickness of the lines, the curves and angles, the shapes of the serifs, the relative sizes of the parts of the letters, and other design features, all add up to individualities. The alphabet is firmly fixed in the shapes of its letters. Three-year-olds recognize letterforms. Yet there are on the the order of 50,000 typefaces in existence, each different. Subtle and not-so-subtle variations in the

12 point type, 13 point linespace

The alphabet is firmly fixed in the shapes of its letters. Three-year-olds recognize letterforms. Yet there are on the order of 50,000 typefaces in existence, each different. Subtle and not-so-subtle variations in the thickness of the lines, the curves and angles, the shapes of the serifs, the relative sizes of the parts of the letters, and other design features, all add up to individualities. The alphabet is firmly fixed in the shapes of its letters. Three-year-olds recognize letterforms. Yet there are on the order of 50,000 typefaces in existence, each different. Subtle and not-so-subtle variations in the thickness of the lines, the curves and angles, the shapes of its letters. Three-year-olds recognize

An odd combination of delicacy, because of its light strokes, and sturdiness, with its square serifs. This weight should be used as an accent to the other weights of Memphis.

ABCDEFGHIJKLMNOPQRSTUVWXYZ
abcdefghijklmnopqrstuvwxyz
0123456789&?!$%"".,/;()

8 point type, 9 point linespace

The alphabet is firmly fixed in the shapes of its letters. Three-year-olds recognize letterforms. Yet there are on the order of 50,000 typefaces in existence, each different. Subtle and not-so-subtle variations in the thickness of the lines, the curves and angles, the shapes of the serifs, the relative sizes of the parts of the letters, and other design features, all add up to individualities. The alphabet is firmly fixed in the shapes of its letters. Three-year-olds recognize letterforms. Yet there are on the order of 50,000 typefaces in existence, each different. Subtle and not-so-subtle variations in the thickness of the lines, the curves and angles, the shapes of the serifs, the relative sizes of the parts of the letters, and other design features, all add up to individualities. The alphabet is firmly fixed in the shapes of its letters. Three-year-olds recognize letterforms. Yet there are on the order of 50,000 typefaces in existence, each different. Subtle and not-so-subtle variations in the thickness of the lines, the curves and angles, the shapes of the serifs, the relative sizes of the parts of the letters, and other design features, all add up to individualities. The alphabet is firmly fixed in the shapes of its letters. Three-year-olds recognize letterforms. Yet there are on the order of 50,000 typefaces in existence, each different. Subtle and not-so-subtle variations in the thickness of the lines, the curves and angles, the shapes of the serifs, the relative sizes of the parts of the letters, and other design

10 point type, 11 point linespace

The alphabet is firmly fixed in the shapes of its letters. Three-year-olds recognize letterforms. Yet there are on the order of 50,000 typefaces in existence, each different. Subtle and not-so-subtle variations in the thickness of the lines, the curves and angles, the shapes of the serifs, the relative sizes of the parts of the letters, and other design features, all add up to individualities. The alphabet is firmly fixed in the shapes of its letters. Three-year-olds recognize letterforms. Yet there are on the order of 50,000 typefaces in existence, each different. Subtle and not-so-subtle variations in the thickness of the lines, the curves and angles, the shapes of the serifs, the relative sizes of the parts of the letters, and other design features, all add up to individualities. The alphabet is firmly fixed in the shapes of its letters. Three-year-olds recognize letterforms. Yet there are on the the order of 50,000 typefaces in existence, each different. Subtle and not-so-subtle variations in

12 point type, 13 point linespace

The alphabet is firmly fixed in the shapes of its letters. Three-year-olds recognize letterforms. Yet there are on the order of 50,000 typefaces in existence, each different. Subtle and not-so-subtle variations in the thickness of the lines, the curves and angles, the shapes of the serifs, the relative sizes of the parts of the letters, and other design features, all add up to individualities. The alphabet is firmly fixed in the shapes of its letters. Three-year-olds recognize letterforms. Yet there are on the order of 50,000 typefaces in existence, each different. Subtle and not-so-subtle variations in the thickness of the lines, the curves and angles, the shapes of its letters. Three-year-olds recognize

The various Memphis italics are little more than normal Memphis with a slant applied. As such, and this face is a good example, the slant compromises the essential stability of the face and weakens it. Use in small doses.

ABCDEFGHIJKLMNOPQRSTUVWXYZ
abcdefghijklmnopqrstuvwxyz
0123456789&?!$%“”.,/;()

8 point type, 9 point linespace

The alphabet is firmly fixed in the shapes of its letters. Three-year-olds recognize letterforms. Yet there are on the order of 50,000 typefaces in existence, each different. Subtle and not-so-subtle variations in the thickness of the lines, the curves and angles, the shapes of the serifs, the relative sizes of the parts of the letters, and other design features, all add up to individualities. The alphabet is firmly fixed in the shapes of its letters. Three-year-olds recognize letterforms. Yet there are on the order of 50,000 typefaces in existence, each different. Subtle and not-so-subtle variations in the thickness of the lines, the curves and angles, the shapes of the serifs, the relative sizes of the parts of the letters, and other design features, all add up to individualities. The alphabet is firmly fixed in the shapes of its letters. Three-year-olds recognize letterforms. Yet there are on the order of 50,000 typefaces in existence, each different. Subtle and not-so-subtle variations in the thickness of the lines, the curves and angles, the shapes of the serifs, the relative sizes of the parts of the letters, and other design features, all add up to individualities. The alphabet is firmly fixed in the shapes of its letters. Three-year-olds recognize letterforms. Yet there are on the order of 50,000 typefaces in existence, each different. Subtle and not-so-subtle variations in the thickness of the lines, the curves and angles, the shapes of the serifs,

10 point type, 11 point linespace

The alphabet is firmly fixed in the shapes of its letters. Three-year-olds recognize letterforms. Yet there are on the order of 50,000 typefaces in existence, each different. Subtle and not-so-subtle variations in the thickness of the lines, the curves and angles, the shapes of the serifs, the relative sizes of the parts of the letters, and other design features, all add up to individualities. The alphabet is firmly fixed in the shapes of its letters. Three-year-olds recognize letterforms. Yet there are on the order of 50,000 typefaces in existence, each different. Subtle and not-so-subtle variations in the thickness of the lines, the curves and angles, the shapes of the serifs, the relative sizes of the parts of the letters, and other design features, all add up to individualities. The alphabet is firmly fixed in the shapes of its letters. Three-year-olds recognize letterforms. Yet there are on the order of 50,000 typefaces in existence, each

12 point type, 13 point linespace

The alphabet is firmly fixed in the shapes of its letters. Three-year-olds recognize letterforms. Yet there are on the order of 50,000 typefaces in exist-ence, each different. Subtle and not-so-subtle variations in the thickness of the lines, the curves and angles, the shapes of the serifs, the relative sizes of the parts of the letters, and other design features, all add up to indi-vidualities. The alphabet is firmly fixed in the shapes of its letters. Three-year-olds recognize letterforms. Yet there are on the order of 50,000 type-faces in existence, each different. Subtle and not-so-subtle variations in the thickness of the lines, the curves and angles, the shapes of the serifs,

Much easier to read than Memphis Light, an excellent face for no-nonsense text: instruction manuals, data sheets, economics essays, etc. This face is not used as much as it could and should be.

ABCDEFGHIJKLMNOPQRSTUVWXYZ
abcdefghijklmnopqrstuvwxyz
0123456789&?!$%"".,/;()

8 point type, 9 point linespace

The alphabet is firmly fixed in the shapes of its letters. Three-year-olds recognize letterforms. Yet there are on the order of 50,000 typefaces in existence, each different. Subtle and not-so-subtle variations in the thickness of the lines, the curves and angles, the shapes of the serifs, the relative sizes of the parts of the letters, and other design features, all add up to individualities. The alphabet is firmly fixed in the shapes of its letters. Three-year-olds recognize letterforms. Yet there are on the order of 50,000 typefaces in existence, each different. Subtle and not-so-subtle variations in the thickness of the lines, the curves and angles, the shapes of the serifs, the relative sizes of the parts of the letters, and other design features, all add up to individualities. The alphabet is firmly fixed in the shapes of its letters. Three-year-olds recognize letterforms. Yet there are on the order of 50,000 typefaces in existence, each different. Subtle and not-so-subtle variations in the thickness of the lines, the curves and angles, the shapes of the serifs, the relative sizes of the parts of the letters, and other design features, all add up to individualities. The alphabet is firmly fixed in the shapes of its letters. Three-year-olds recognize letterforms. Yet there are on the order of 50,000 typefaces in existence, each different. Subtle and not-so-subtle variations in the thickness of the lines, the curves and angles, the shapes of the serifs,

10 point type, 11 point linespace

The alphabet is firmly fixed in the shapes of its letters. Three-year-olds recognize letterforms. Yet there are on the order of 50,000 typefaces in existence, each different. Subtle and not-so-subtle variations in the thickness of the lines, the curves and angles, the shapes of the serifs, the relative sizes of the parts of the letters, and other design features, all add up to individualities. The alphabet is firmly fixed in the shapes of its letters. Three-year-olds recognize letterforms. Yet there are on the order of 50,000 typefaces in existence, each different. Subtle and not-so-subtle variations in the thickness of the lines, the curves and angles, the shapes of the serifs, the relative sizes of the parts of the letters, and other design features, all add up to individualities. The alphabet is firmly fixed in the shapes of its letters. Three-year-olds recognize letterforms. Yet there are on the order of 50,000 typefaces in existence, each different. Subtle

12 point type, 13 point linespace

The alphabet is firmly fixed in the shapes of its letters. Three-year-olds recognize letterforms. Yet there are on the order of 50,000 typefaces in exist-ence, each different. Subtle and not-so-subtle variations in the thickness of the lines, the curves and angles, the shapes of the serifs, the relative sizes of the parts of the letters, and other de-sign features, all add up to individuali-ties. The alphabet is firmly fixed in the shapes of its letters. Three-year-olds recognize letterforms. Yet there are on the order of 50,000 typefaces in exist-ence, each different. Subtle and not-so-subtle variations in the thickness of the lines, the curves and angles, the shapes of the serifs, the relative sizes of

As with all the Memphis italics, use sparingly. This face offers little contrast to its roman version, so doesn't work to highlight an important word, for instance. Underlining is much more appropriate to this type family.

ABCDEFGHIJKLMNOPQRSTUVWXYZ
abcdefghijklmnopqrstuvwxyz
0123456789&?!$%"".,/;()

8 point type, 9 point linespace

The alphabet is firmly fixed in the shapes of its letters. Three-year-olds recognize letterforms. Yet there are on the order of 50,000 typefaces in existence, each different. Subtle and not-so-subtle variations in the thickness of the lines, the curves and angles, the shapes of the serifs, the relative sizes of the parts of the letters, and other design features, all add up to individualities. The alphabet is firmly fixed in the shapes of its letters. Three-year-olds recognize letterforms. Yet there are on the order of 50,000 typefaces in existence, each different. Subtle and not-so-subtle variations in the thickness of the lines, the curves and angles, the shapes of the serifs, the relative sizes of the parts of the letters, and other design features, all add up to individualities. The alphabet is firmly fixed in the shapes of its letters. Three-year-olds recognize letterforms. Yet there are on the order of 50,000 typefaces in existence, each different. Subtle and not-so-subtle variations in the thickness of the lines, the curves and angles, the shapes of the serifs, the relative sizes of the parts of the letters, and other design features, all add up to individualities. The alphabet is firmly fixed in the shapes of its letters. Three-year-olds recognize letterforms. Yet there are on the order of 50,000 typefaces in existence, each different. Subtle and not-so-subtle variations in the thickness of the lines, the curves and angles, the shapes of the serifs,

10 point type, 11 point linespace

The alphabet is firmly fixed in the shapes of its letters. Three-year-olds recognize letterforms. Yet there are on the order of 50,000 typefaces in existence, each different. Subtle and not-so-subtle variations in the thickness of the lines, the curves and angles, the shapes of the serifs, the relative sizes of the parts of the letters, and other design features, all add up to individualities. The alphabet is firmly fixed in the shapes of its letters. Three-year-olds recognize letterforms. Yet there are on the order of 50,000 typefaces in existence, each different. Subtle and not-so-subtle variations in the thickness of the lines, the curves and angles, the shapes of the serifs, the relative sizes of the parts of the letters, and other design features, all add up to individualities. The alphabet is firmly fixed in the shapes of its letters. Three-year-olds recognize letterforms. Yet there are on the order of 50,000 typefaces in existence, each

12 point type, 13 point linespace

The alphabet is firmly fixed in the shapes of its letters. Three-year-olds recognize letterforms. Yet there are on the order of 50,000 typefaces in existence, each different. Subtle and not-so-subtle variations in the thickness of the lines, the curves and angles, the shapes of the serifs, the relative sizes of the parts of the letters, and other design features, all add up to individualities. The alphabet is firmly fixed in the shapes of its letters. Three-year-olds recognize letterforms. Yet there are on the order of 50,000 typefaces in existence, each different. Subtle and not-so-subtle variations in the thickness of the lines, the curves and angles, the shapes of the serifs,

The weight gradation in this family is excellent, so the various weights mix and match and work together well. Bold can be used to highlight words in a Medium text block, instead of using italic.

ABCDEFGHIJKLMNOPQRSTUVWXYZ
abcdefghijklmnopqrstuvwxyz
0123456789&?!$%"" .,/;:()

8 point type, 9 point linespace

The alphabet is firmly fixed in the shapes of its letters. Three-year-olds recognize letterforms. Yet there are on the order of 50,000 typefaces in existence, each different. Subtle and not-so-subtle variations in the thickness of the lines, the curves and angles, the shapes of the serifs, the relative sizes of the parts of the letters, and other design features, all add up to individualities. The alphabet is firmly fixed in the shapes of its letters. Three-year-olds recognize letterforms. Yet there are on the order of 50,000 typefaces in existence, each different. Subtle and not-so-subtle variations in the thickness of the lines, the curves and angles, the shapes of the serifs, the relative sizes of the parts of the letters, and other design features, all add up to individualities. The alphabet is firmly fixed in the shapes of its letters. Three-year-olds recognize letterforms. Yet there are on the order of 50,000 typefaces in existence, each different. Subtle and not-so-subtle variations in the thickness of the lines, the curves and angles, the shapes of the serifs, the relative sizes of the parts of the letters, and other design features, all add up to individualities. The alphabet is firmly fixed in the shapes of its letters. Three-year-olds recognize letterforms. Yet there are on the order of 50,000 typefaces in existence, each different. Subtle and not-so-subtle variations in the thickness of the lines, the curves and angles, the shapes of the serifs,

10 point type, 11 point linespace

The alphabet is firmly fixed in the shapes of its letters. Three-year-olds recognize letterforms. Yet there are on the order of 50,000 typefaces in existence, each different. Subtle and not-so-subtle variations in the thickness of the lines, the curves and angles, the shapes of the serifs, the relative sizes of the parts of the letters, and other design features, all add up to individualities. The alphabet is firmly fixed in the shapes of its letters. Three-year-olds recognize letterforms. Yet there are on the order of 50,000 typefaces in existence, each different. Subtle and not-so-subtle variations in the thickness of the lines, the curves and angles, the shapes of the serifs, the relative sizes of the parts of the letters, and other design features, all add up to individualities. The alphabet is firmly fixed in the shapes of its letters. Three-year-olds recognize letterforms. Yet there are on the order of 50,000 typefaces in existence, each different. Subtle

12 point type, 13 point linespace

The alphabet is firmly fixed in the shapes of its letters. Three-year-olds recognize letterforms. Yet there are on the order of 50,000 typefaces in exist-ence, each different. Subtle and not-so-subtle variations in the thickness of the lines, the curves and angles, the shapes of the serifs, the relative sizes of the parts of the letters, and other de-sign features, all add up to individuali-ties. The alphabet is firmly fixed in the shapes of its letters. Three-year-olds recognize letterforms. Yet there are on the order of 50,000 typefaces in exist-ence, each different. Subtle and not-so-subtle variations in the thickness of the lines, the curves and angles, the shapes of the serifs, the relative sizes of

Because of the greater weight, the italic does not hurt the essential stability of Memphis Bold as much as in lighter weights, but it is still a bit disconcerting. Not for general use.

ABCDEFGHIJKLMNOPQRSTUVWX YZabcdefghijklmnopqrstuvwxyz 0123456789&?!$%"" .,/;()

8 point type, 9 point linespace

The alphabet is firmly fixed in the shapes of its letters. Three-year-olds recognize letterforms. Yet there are on the order of 50,000 typefaces in existence, each different. Subtle and not-so-subtle variations in the thickness of the lines, the curves and angles, the shapes of the serifs, the relative sizes of the parts of the letters, and other design features, all add up to individualities. The alphabet is firmly fixed in the shapes of its letters. Three-year-olds recognize letterforms. Yet there are on the order of 50,000 typefaces in existence, each different. Subtle and not-so-subtle variations in the thickness of the lines, the curves and angles, the shapes of the serifs, the relative sizes of the parts of the letters, and other design features, all add up to individualities. The alphabet is firmly fixed in the shapes of its letters. Three-year-olds recognize letterforms. Yet there are on the order of 50,000 typefaces in existence, each different. Subtle and not-so-subtle variations in the thickness of the lines, the curves and angles, the shapes of the serifs, the relative sizes of the parts of the letters, and other design features, all add up to individualities. The alphabet is firmly fixed in

10 point type, 11 point linespace

The alphabet is firmly fixed in the shapes of its letters. Three-year-olds recognize letterforms. Yet there are on the order of 50,000 typefaces in existence, each different. Subtle and not-so-subtle variations in the thickness of the lines, the curves and angles, the shapes of the serifs, the relative sizes of the parts of the letters, and other design features, all add up to individualities. The alphabet is firmly fixed in the shapes of its letters. Three-year-olds recognize letterforms. Yet there are on the order of 50,000 typefaces in existence, each different. Subtle and not-so-subtle variations in the thickness of the lines, the curves and angles, the shapes of the serifs, the relative sizes of the parts of the letters, and other design features, all add up to individualities.

12 point type, 13 point linespace

The alphabet is firmly fixed in the shapes of its letters. Three-year-olds recognize letterforms. Yet there are on the order of 50,000 typefaces in existence, each different. Subtle and not-so-subtle variations in the thickness of the lines, the curves and angles, the shapes of the serifs, the relative sizes of the parts of the letters, and other design features, all add up to individualities. The alphabet is firmly fixed in the shapes of its letters. Three-year-olds recognize letterforms. Yet there are on the order of 50,000 typefaces in existence, each different. Subtle

Wide, heavy characters that fit together well. A good solid headline face, especially useful in a horizontal design format. Doesn't need excessive size to create an impact, so is economical in a smaller space.

ABCDEFGHIJKLMNOPQRSTUVWXYZ
abcdefghijklmnopqrstuvwxyz
0123456789&?!$%“”.,/;()

8 point type, 9 point linespace

The alphabet is firmly fixed in the shapes of its letters. Three-year-olds recognize letterforms. Yet there are on the order of 50,000 typefaces in existence, each different. Subtle and not-so-subtle variations in the thickness of the lines, the curves and angles, the shapes of the serifs, the relative sizes of the parts of the letters, and other design features, all add up to individualities. The alphabet is firmly fixed in the shapes of its letters. Three-year-olds recognize letterforms. Yet there are on the order of 50,000 typefaces in existence, each different. Subtle and not-so-subtle variations in the lines, the curves and angles, the shapes of the serifs, the relative sizes of the parts of the letters, and other design features, all add up to individualities. The alphabet is firmly fixed in the shapes of its letters. Three-year-olds recognize letterforms. Yet there are on the order of 50,000 typefaces in existence, each different. Subtle and not-so-subtle variations in the thickness of the lines, the curves and angles, the shapes of the serifs, the relative sizes of the parts of the letters, and other design features, all add up to individualities. The alphabet is firmly fixed in the shapes of its letters. Three-year-olds recognize letterforms. Yet there are on the order of 50,000 typefaces in existence, each different. Subtle and not-so-subtle variations in the thickness of the lines, the curves and angles, the shapes of the serifs, the relative sizes of the parts of the letters, and other design features, all add up to individualities. The alphabet is firmly fixed in the shapes of its letters. Three-year-olds recognize letterforms. Yet there are on the order of 50,000 typefaces in existence, each different. Subtle and not-so-subtle variations in the thickness of the lines, the curves and angles, the shapes of the serifs, the relative sizes of the parts of the letters, and

10 point type, 11 point linespace

The alphabet is firmly fixed in the shapes of its letters. Three-year-olds recognize letterforms. Yet there are on the order of 50,000 typefaces in existence, each different. Subtle and not-so-subtle variations in the thickness of the lines, the curves and angles, the shapes of the serifs, the relative sizes of the parts of the letters, and other design features, all add up to individualities. The alphabet is firmly fixed in the shapes of its letters. Three-year-olds recognize letterforms. Yet there are on the order of 50,000 typefaces in existence, each different. Subtle and not-so-subtle variations in the thickness of the lines, the curves and angles, the shapes of the serifs, the relative sizes of the parts of the letters, and other design features, all add up to individualities. The alphabet is firmly fixed in the shapes of its letters. Three-year-olds recognize letterforms. Yet there are on the order of 50,000 typefaces in existence, each different. Subtle and not-so-subtle variations in the thickness of the lines, the curves and angles, the shapes of the serifs, the relative sizes of the parts of the letters, and other design features, all add up to individualities. The alphabet is firmly fixed in the shapes of its letters. Three-

12 point type, 13 point linespace

The alphabet is firmly fixed in the shapes of its letters. Three-year-olds recognize letterforms. Yet there are on the order of 50,000 typefaces in existence, each different. Subtle and not-so-subtle variations in the thickness of the lines, the curves and angles, the shapes of the serifs, the relative sizes of the parts of the letters, and other design features, all add up to individualities. The alphabet is firmly fixed in the shapes of its letters. Three-year-olds recognize letterforms. Yet there are on the order of 50,000 typefaces in existence, each different. Subtle and not-so-subtle variations in the thickness of the lines, the curves and angles, the shapes of the serifs, the relative sizes of the parts of the letters, and other design features, all add up to individualities. The alphabet is firmly fixed in the shapes of its letters. Three-year-olds recognize letterforms. Yet there are on the order of 50,000

Every library should have one free-wheeling casual hand-scrawling face, and Mistral fills the bill. Definitely not pretentious, Mistral does not forsake typographic principles: it is legible while it wanders. This is a fun face.

ABCDEFGHIJKLMNOPQRSTUVWXYZ
abcdefghijklmnopqrstuvwxyz
0123456789&?!$%“”.,/;()

8 point type, 9 point linespace

The alphabet is firmly fixed in the shapes of its letters. Three-year-olds recognize letterforms. Yet there are on the order of 50,000 typefaces in existence, each different. Subtle and not-so-subtle variations in the thickness of the lines, the curves and angles, the shapes of the serifs, the relative sizes of the parts of the letters, and other design features, all add up to individualities. The alphabet is firmly fixed in the shapes of its letters. Three-year-olds recognize letterforms. Yet there are on the order of 50,000 typefaces in existence, each different. Subtle and not-so-subtle variations in the thickness of the lines, the curves and angles, the shapes of the serifs, the relative sizes of the parts of the letters, and other design features, all add up to individualities. The alphabet is firmly fixed in the shapes of its letters. Three-year-olds recognize letterforms. Yet there are on the order of 50,000 typefaces in existence, each different. Subtle and not-so-subtle variations in the thickness of the lines, the curves and angles, the shapes of the serifs, the relative sizes of the parts of the letters, and other design features, all add up to individualities. The alphabet is firmly fixed in the shapes of its letters. Three-year-olds recognize letterforms. Yet there are on the order of 50,000 typefaces in existence, each different. Subtle and not-so-subtle variations in the thickness of the lines, the curves and angles, the shapes of the serifs, the relative sizes of the parts of the letters, and other design features, all add up to individualities. The alphabet is firmly fixed in the shapes of its

10 point type, 11 point linespace

The alphabet is firmly fixed in the shapes of its letters. Three-year-olds recognize letterforms. Yet there are on the order of 50,000 typefaces in existence, each different. Subtle and not-so-subtle variations in the thickness of the lines, the curves and angles, the shapes of the serifs, the relative sizes of the parts of the letters, and other design features, all add up to individualities. The alphabet is firmly fixed in the shapes of its letters. Three-year-olds recognize letterforms. Yet there are on the order of 50,000 typefaces in existence, each different. Subtle and not-so-subtle variations in the thickness of the lines, the curves and angles, the shapes of the serifs, the relative sizes of the parts of the letters, and other design features, all add up to individualities. The alphabet is firmly fixed in the shapes of its letters. Three-year-olds recognize letterforms. Yet there are on the order of 50,000 typefaces in existence, each different. Subtle and not-so-subtle variations in the thickness of the lines, the curves and angles, the shapes of the

12 point type, 13 point linespace

The alphabet is firmly fixed in the shapes of its letters. Three-year-olds recognize letterforms. Yet there are on the order of 50,000 typefaces in existence, each different. Subtle and not-so-subtle variations in the thickness of the lines, the curves and angles, the shapes of the serifs, the relative sizes of the parts of the letters, and other design features, all add up to individualities. The alphabet is firmly fixed in the shapes of its letters. Three-year-olds recognize letterforms. Yet there are on the order of 50,000 typefaces in existence, each different. Subtle and not-so-subtle variations in the thickness of the lines, the curves and angles, the shapes of the serifs, the relative sizes of the parts of the letters, and other design features, all add up to

Clean, readable, sophisticated. This weight is a bit light for sizes below 9-point or for use with colored backgrounds, but serves well for clean, minimal-copy advertising and large sizes.

ABCDEFGHIJKLMNOPQRSTUVWXYZ
abcdefghijklmnopqrstuvwxyz
0123456789&?!$%“”.,/;()

8 point type, 9 point linespace

The alphabet is firmly fixed in the shapes of its letters. Three-year-olds recognize letterforms. Yet there are on the order of 50,000 typefaces in existence, each different. Subtle and not-so subtle variations in the thickness of the lines, the curves and angles, the shapes of the serifs, the relative sizes of the parts of the letters, and other design features, all add up to individualities. The alphabet is firmly fixed in the shapes of its letters. Three-year-olds recognize letterforms. Yet there are on the order of 50,000 typefaces in existence, each different. Subtle and not-so-subtle variations in the thickness of the lines, the curves and angles, the shapes of the serifs, the relative sizes of the parts of the letters, and other design features, all add up to individualities. The alphabet is firmly fixed in the shapes of its letters. Three-year-olds recognize letterforms. Yet there are on the order of 50,000 typefaces in existence, each different. Subtle and not-so-subtle variations in the thickness of the lines, the curves and angles, the shapes of the serifs, the relative sizes of the parts of the letters, and other design features, all add up to individualities. The alphabet is firmly fixed in the shapes of its letters. Three-year-olds recognize letterforms. Yet there are on the order of 50,000 typefaces in existence, each different. Subtle and not-so-subtle variations in the thickness of the lines, the curves and angles, the shapes of the serifs, the relative sizes of the parts of the letters, and other design features, all add up to

10 point type, 11 point linespace

The alphabet is firmly fixed in the shapes of its letters. Three-year-olds recognize letterforms. Yet there are on the order of 50,000 typefaces in existence, each different. Subtle and not-so-subtle variations in the thickness of the lines, the curves and angles, the shapes of the serifs, the relative sizes of the parts of the letters, and other design features, all add up to individualities. The alphabet is firmly fixed in the shapes of its letters. Three year-olds recognize letterforms. Yet there are on the order of 50,000 typefaces in existence, each different. Subtle and not-so-subtle variations in the thickness of the lines, the curves and angles, the shapes of the serifs, the relative sizes of the parts of the letters, and other design features, all add up to individualities. The alphabet is firmly fixed in the shapes of its letters. Three-year-olds recognize letterforms. Yet there are on the order of 50,000 typefaces in existence, each different. Subtle and not-so-subtle variations in the thickness of the lines, the curves and angles, the shapes of the

12 point type, 13 point linespace

The alphabet is firmly fixed in the shapes of its letters. Three-year-olds recognize letterforms. Yet there are on the order of 50,000 typefaces in existence, each different. Subtle and not-so-subtle variations in the thickness of the lines, the curves and angles, the shapes of the serifs, the relative sizes of the parts of the letters, and other design features, all add up to individualities. The alphabet is firmly fixed in the shapes of its letters. Three-year-olds recognize letterforms. Yet there are on the order of 50,000 typefaces in existence, each different. Subtle and not-so-subtle variations in the thickness of the lines, the curves and angles, the shapes of the serifs, the relative sizes of the parts of the letters, and other design features, all add up to

Not that different from the roman face, this italic does not carry the emphatic qualities of most italics. Use lightly underlined roman for emphasis, and use this face as a text face when more energy is needed.

ABCDEFGHIJKLMNOPQRSTUVWXYZ
abcdefghijklmnopqrstuvwxyz
0123456789&?!$%“”.,/;()

8 point type, 9 point linespace

The alphabet is firmly fixed in the shapes of its letters. Three-year-olds recognize letterforms. Yet there are on the order of 50,000 typefaces in existence, each different. Subtle and not-so-subtle variations in the thickness of the lines, the curves and angles, the shapes of the serifs, the relative sizes of the parts of the letters, and other design features, all add up to individualities. The alphabet is firmly fixed in the shapes of its letters. Three-year-olds recognize letterforms. Yet there are on the order of 50,000 typefaces in existence, each different. Subtle and not-so-subtle variations in the thickness of the lines, the curves and angles, the shapes of the serifs, the relative sizes of the parts of the letters, and other design features, all add up to individualities. The alphabet is firmly fixed in the shapes of its letters. Three-year-olds recognize letterforms. Yet there are on the order of 50,000 typefaces in existence, each different. Subtle and not-so-subtle variations in the thickness of the lines, the curves and angles, the shapes of the serifs, the relative sizes of the parts of the letters, and other design features, all add up to individualities. The alphabet is firmly fixed in the shapes of its letters. Three-year-olds recognize letterforms. Yet there are on the order of 50,000 typefaces in existence, each different. Subtle and not-so-subtle variations in the thickness of the lines, the curves and angles, the shapes of the serifs, the relative sizes of the parts of the letters, and other design features, all add up to individualities. The

10 point type, 11 point linespace

The alphabet is firmly fixed in the shapes of its letters. Three-year-olds recognize letterforms. Yet there are on the order of 50,000 typefaces in existence, each different. Subtle and not-so-subtle variations in the thickness of the lines, the curves and angles, the shapes of the serifs, the relative sizes of the parts of the letters, and other design features, all add up to individualities. The alphabet is firmly fixed in the shapes of its letters. Three-year-olds recognize letterforms. Yet there are on the order of 50,000 typefaces in existence, each different. Subtle and not-so-subtle variations in the thickness of the lines, the curves and angles, the shapes of the serifs, the relative sizes of the parts of the letters, and other design features, all add up to individualities. The alphabet is firmly fixed in the shapes of its letters. Three-year-olds recognize letterforms. Yet there are on the order of 50,000 typefaces in existence, each different. Subtle and not-so-subtle variations in the thickness of the lines, the curves and

12 point type, 13 point linespace

The alphabet is firmly fixed in the shapes of its letters. Three-year-olds recognize letterforms. Yet there are on the order of 50,000 typefaces in existence, each different. Subtle and not-so-subtle variations in the thickness of the lines, the curves and angles, the shapes of the serifs, the relative sizes of the parts of the letters, and other design features, all add up to individualities. The alphabet is firmly fixed in the shapes of its letters. Three-year-olds recognize letterforms. Yet there are on the order of 50,000 typefaces in existence, each different. Subtle and not-so-subtle variations in the thickness of the lines, the curves and angles, the shapes of the serifs, the relative sizes of the parts of the letters, and

This is more than just a darker Optima, though it clearly complements Optima for subheads, etc. Optima Bold can be set looser than most sans serif faces because its purpose is not to slam the reader, but to touch him firmly. A self-assured face.

ABCDEFGHIJKLMNOPQRSTUVWXYZ
abcdefghijklmnopqrstuvwxyz
0123456789&?!$%“”.,/;()

8 point type, 9 point linespace

The alphabet is firmly fixed in the shapes of its letters. Three-year-olds recognize letterforms. Yet there are on the order of 50,000 typefaces in existence, each different. Subtle and not-so-subtle variations in the thickness of the lines, the curves and angles, the shapes of the serifs, the relative sizes of the parts of the letters, and other design features, all add up to individualities. The alphabet is firmly fixed in the shapes of its letters. Three-year-olds recognize letterforms. Yet there are on the order of 50,000 typefaces in existence, each different. Subtle and not-so-subtle variations in the thickness of the lines, the curves and angles, the shapes of the serifs, the relative sizes of the parts of the letters, and other design features, all add up to individualities. The alphabet is firmly fixed in the shapes of its letters. Three-year-olds recognize letterforms. Yet there are on the order of 50,000 typefaces in existence, each different. Subtle and not-so-subtle variations in the thickness of the lines, the curves and angles, the shapes of the serifs, the relative sizes of the parts of the letters, and other design features, all add up to individualities. The alphabet is firmly fixed in the shapes of its letters. Three-year-olds recognize letterforms. Yet there are on the order of 50,000 typefaces in existence, each different. Subtle and not-so-subtle variations in the thickness of the lines, the curves and angles, the shapes of the serifs, the relative sizes of the parts of the letters, and other design features, all add up to individualities. The

10 point type, 11 point linespace

The alphabet is firmly fixed in the shapes of its letters. Three-year-olds recognize letterforms. Yet there are on the order of 50,000 typefaces in existence, each different. Subtle and not-so-subtle variations in the thickness of the lines, the curves and angles, the shapes of the serifs, the relative sizes of the parts of the letters, and other design features, all add up to individualities. The alphabet is firmly fixed in the shapes of its letters. Three-year-olds recognize letterforms. Yet there are on the order of 50,000 typefaces in existence, each different. Subtle and not-so-subtle variations in the thickness of the lines, the curves and angles, the shapes of the serifs, the relative sizes of the parts of the letters, and other design features, all add up to individualities. The alphabet is firmly fixed in the shapes of its letters. Three-year-olds recognize letterforms. Yet there are on the order of 50,000 typefaces in existence, each different. Subtle and not-so-subtle variations in the thickness of the lines, the curves and

12 point type, 13 point linespace

The alphabet is firmly fixed in the shapes of its letters. Three-year-olds recognize letterforms. Yet there are on the order of 50,000 typefaces in existence, each different. Subtle and not-so-subtle variations in the thickness of the lines, the curves and angles, the shapes of the serifs, the relative sizes of the parts of the letters, and other design features, all add up to individualities. The alphabet is firmly fixed in the shapes of its letters. Three-year-olds recognize letterforms. Yet there are on the order of 50,000 typefaces in existence, each different. Subtle and not-so-subtle variations in the thickness of the lines, the curves and angles, the shapes of the serifs, the relative sizes of the parts of the letters, and

There is little excuse for this face—it rounds out the set. Useful in specialty color situations, or for an artificial, overstated intensity. If it is electronically slanted further, and set tightly, it can suggest desperate motion, if you want that.

ABCDEFGHIJKLMNOPQRSTUVWXYZ
abcdefghijklmnopqrstuvwxyz
0123456789&?!$%“”.,/;()

8 point type, 9 point linespace

The alphabet is firmly fixed in the shapes of its letters. Three-year-olds recognize letterforms. Yet there are on the order of 50,000 typefaces in existence, each different. Subtle and not-so-subtle variations in the thickness of the lines, the curves and angles, the shapes of the serifs, the relative sizes of the parts of the letters, and other design features, all add up to individualities. The alphabet is firmly fixed in the shapes of its letters. Three-year-olds recognize letterforms. Yet there are on the order of 50,000 typefaces in existence, each different. Subtle and not-so-subtle variations in the thickness of the lines, the curves and angles, the shapes of the serifs, the relative sizes of the parts of the letters, and other design features, all add up to individualities. The alphabet is firmly fixed in the shapes of its letters. Three-year-olds recognize letterforms. Yet there are on the order of 50,000 typefaces in existence, each different. Subtle and not-so-subtle variations in the thickness of the lines, the curves and angles, the shapes of the serifs, the relative sizes of the parts of the letters, and other design features, all add up to individualities. The alphabet is firmly fixed in the shapes of its letters. Three-year-olds recognize letterforms. Yet there are on the order of 50,000 typefaces in existence, each different. Subtle and not-so-subtle variations in the thickness of the lines, the curves and angles, the shapes of the serifs, the relative sizes of the parts of the letters, and other design features, all add up to individualities. The

10 point type, 11 point linespace

The alphabet is firmly fixed in the shapes of its letters. Three-year-olds recognize letterforms. Yet there are on the order of 50,000 typefaces in existence, each different. Subtle and not-so-subtle variations in the thickness of the lines, the curves and angles, the shapes of the serifs, the relative sizes of the parts of the letters, and other design features, all add up to individualities. The alphabet is firmly fixed in the shapes of its letters. Three-year-olds recognize letterforms. Yet there are on the order of 50,000 typefaces in existence, each different. Subtle and not-so-subtle variations in the thickness of the lines, the curves and angles, the shapes of the serifs, the relative sizes of the parts of the letters, and other design features, all add up to individualities. The alphabet is firmly fixed in the shapes of its letters. Three-year-olds recognize letterforms. Yet there are on the order of 50,000 typefaces in existence, each different. Subtle and not-so-subtle variations in the thickness of the lines, the curves and

12 point type, 13 point linespace

The alphabet is firmly fixed in the shapes of its letters. Three-year-olds recognize letterforms. Yet there are on the order of 50,000 typefaces in existence, each different. Subtle and not-so-subtle variations in the thickness of the lines, the curves and angles, the shapes of the serifs, the relative sizes of the parts of the letters, and other design features, all add up to individualities. The alphabet is firmly fixed in the shapes of its letters. Three-year-olds recognize letterforms. Yet there are on the order of 50,000 typefaces in existence, each different. Subtle and not-so-subtle variations in the thickness of the lines, the curves and angles, the shapes of the serifs, the relative sizes of the parts of the letters, and other design features, all

Perhaps not the *most* readable face, Palatino more than makes up for it by being interesting. It's easy on the eye, and appeals to an aesthetic sense. It requires at least 10% more linespace than most faces (*never* set it solid). Use Palatino for the not-quite-conservative clients.

ABCDEFGHIJKLMNOPQRSTUVWXYZ
abcdefghijklmnopqrstuvwxyz
0123456789&?!$%“” .,/;()

8 point type, 9 point linespace

The alphabet is firmly fixed in the shapes of its letters. Three-year-olds recognize letterforms. Yet there are on the order of 50,000 typefaces in existence, each different. Subtle and not-so-subtle variations in the thickness of the lines, the curves and angles, the shapes of the serifs, the relative sizes of the parts of the letters, and other design features, all add up to individualities. The alphabet is firmly fixed in the shapes of its letters. Three-year-olds recognize letterforms. Yet there are on the order of 50,000 typefaces in existence, each different. Subtle and not-so-subtle variations in the thickness of the lines, the curves and angles, the shapes of the serifs, the relative sizes of the parts of the letters, and other design features, all add up to individualities. The alphabet is firmly fixed in the shapes of its letters. Three-year-olds recognize letterforms. Yet there are on the order of 50,000 typefaces in existence, each different. Subtle and not-so-subtle variations in the thickness of the lines, the curves and angles, the shapes of the serifs, the relative sizes of the parts of the letters, and other design features, all add up to individualities. The alphabet is firmly fixed in the shapes of its letters. Three-year-olds recognize letterforms. Yet there are on the order of 50,000 typefaces in existence, each different. Subtle and not-so-subtle variations in the thickness of the lines, the curves and angles, the shapes of the serifs, the relative sizes of the parts of the letters, and other design features, all add up to individualities. The alphabet is firmly fixed in the shapes of its letters. Three-year-olds recognize letterforms. Yet there are on the order of 50,000 typefaces in existence, each

10 point type, 11 point linespace

The alphabet is firmly fixed in the shapes of its letters. Three-year-olds recognize letterforms. Yet there are on the order of 50,000 typefaces in existence, each different. Subtle and not-so-subtle variations in the thickness of the lines, the curves and angles, the shapes of the serifs, the relative sizes of the parts of the letters, and other design features, all add up to individualities. The alphabet is firmly fixed in the shapes of its letters. Three-year-olds recognize letterforms. Yet there are on the order of 50,000 typefaces in existence, each different. Subtle and not-so-subtle variations in the thickness of the lines, the curves and angles, the shapes of the serifs, the relative sizes of the parts of the letters, and other design features, all add up to individualities. The alphabet is firmly fixed in the shapes of its letters. Three-year-olds recognize letterforms. Yet there are on the order of 50,000 typefaces in existence, each different. Subtle and not-so-subtle variations in the thickness of the lines, the curves and angles, the shapes of the serifs, the relative sizes of the parts of the letters, and other design features, all add up to individualities.

12 point type, 13 point linespace

The alphabet is firmly fixed in the shapes of its letters. Three-year-olds recognize letterforms. Yet there are on the order of 50,000 typefaces in existence, each different. Subtle and not-so-subtle variations in the thickness of the lines, the curves and angles, the shapes of the serifs, the relative sizes of the parts of the letters, and other design features, all add up to individualities. The alphabet is firmly fixed in the shapes of its letters. Three-year-olds recognize letterforms. Yet there are on the order of 50,000 typefaces in existence, each different. Subtle and not-so-subtle variations in the thickness of the lines, the curves and angles, the shapes of the serifs, the relative sizes of the parts of the letters, and other design features, all add up to individualities. The alphabet is firmly fixed in the shapes of its letters. Three-

A true italic, which does what italic should do: convey significance. Use this italic freely when stress on a word or phrase is important. It not only carries the idea of importance: it also creates a personalized effect.

ABCDEFGHIJKLMNOPQRSTUVWXYZ
abcdefghijklmnopqrstuvwxyz
0123456789&?!$%“”.,/;()

8 point type, 9 point linespace

The alphabet is firmly fixed in the shapes of its letters. Three-year-olds recognize letterforms. Yet there are on the order of 50,000 typefaces in existence, each different. Subtle and not-so-subtle variations in the thickness of the lines, the curves and angles, the shapes of the serifs, the relative sizes of the parts of the letters, and other design features, all add up to individualities. The alphabet is firmly fixed in the shapes of its letters. Three-year-olds recognize letterforms. Yet there are on the order of 50,000 typefaces in existence, each different. Subtle and not-so-subtle variations in the thickness of the lines, the curves and angles, the shapes of the serifs, the relative sizes of the parts of the letters, and other design features, all add up to individualities. The alphabet is firmly fixed in the shapes of its letters. Three-year-olds recognize letterforms. Yet there are on the order of 50,000 typefaces in existence, each different. Subtle and not-so-subtle variations in the thickness of the lines, the curves and angles, the shapes of the serifs, the relative sizes of the parts of the letters, and other design features, all add up to individualities. The alphabet is firmly fixed in the shapes of its letters. Three-year-olds recognize letterforms. Yet there are on the order of 50,000 typefaces in existence, each different. Subtle and not-so-subtle variations in the thickness of the lines, the curves and angles, the shapes of the serifs, the relative sizes of the parts of the letters, and other design features,

10 point type, 11 point linespace

The alphabet is firmly fixed in the shapes of its letters. Three-year-olds recognize letterforms. Yet there are on the order of 50,000 typefaces in existence, each different. Subtle and not-so-subtle variations in the thickness of the lines, the curves and angles, the shapes of the serifs, the relative sizes of the parts of the letters, and other design features, all add up to individualities. The alphabet is firmly fixed in the shapes of its letters. Three-year-olds recognize letterforms. Yet there are on the order of 50,000 typefaces in existence, each different. Subtle and not-so-subtle variations in the thickness of the lines, the curves and angles, the shapes of the serifs, the relative sizes of the parts of the letters, and other design features, all add up to individualities. The alphabet is firmly fixed in the shapes of its letters. Three-year-olds recognize letterforms. Yet there are on the order of 50,000 typefaces in existence, each different. Subtle and not-so-subtle variations in the

12 point type, 13 point linespace

The alphabet is firmly fixed in the shapes of its letters. Three-year-olds recognize letterforms. Yet there are on the order of 50,000 typefaces in existence, each different. Subtle and not-so-subtle variations in the thickness of the lines, the curves and angles, the shapes of the serifs, the relative sizes of the parts of the letters, and other design features, all add up to individualities. The alphabet is firmly fixed in the shapes of its letters. Three-year-olds recognize letterforms. Yet there are on the order of 50,000 typefaces in existence, each different. Subtle and not-so-subtle variations in the thickness of the lines, the curves and angles, the shapes of the serifs, the relative sizes of the

A slightly awkward face, this should be used sparingly and not as a headline. As a subhead it works, and it takes a little compression (up to 10%) very well. To look really good, though, it needs a lot of kerning, so it is not an easy face to work with.

ABCDEFGHIJKLMNOPQRSTUVWXYZ
abcdefghijklmnopqrstuvwxyz
0123456789&?!$% "" .,/;()

8 point type, 9 point linespace

The alphabet is firmly fixed in the shapes of its letters. Three-year-olds recognize letterforms. Yet there are on the order of 50,000 typefaces in existence, each different. Subtle and not-so-subtle variations in the thickness of the lines, the curves and angles, the shapes of the serifs, the relative sizes of the parts of the letters, and other design features, all add up to individualities. The alphabet is firmly fixed in the shapes of its letters. Three-year-olds recognize letterforms. Yet there are on the order of 50,000 typefaces in existence, each different. Subtle and not-so-subtle variations in the thickness of the lines, the curves and angles, the shapes of the serifs, the relative sizes of the parts of the letters, and other design features, all add up to individualities. The alphabet is firmly fixed in the shapes of its letters. Three-year-olds recognize letterforms. Yet there are on the order of 50,000 typefaces in existence, each different. Subtle and not-so-subtle variations in the thickness of the lines, the curves and angles, the shapes of the serifs, the relative sizes of the parts of the letters, and other design features, all add up to individualities. The alphabet is firmly fixed in the shapes of its letters. Three-year-olds recognize letterforms. Yet there are on the order of 50,000 typefaces in existence, each different. Subtle and not-so-subtle variations in the thickness of the lines, the curves and angles, the shapes of the serifs, the relative sizes of the parts of the letters, and other design features, all add up to individualities. The

10 point type, 11 point linespace

The alphabet is firmly fixed in the shapes of its letters. Three-year-olds recognize letterforms. Yet there are on the order of 50,000 typefaces in existence, each different. Subtle and not-so-subtle variations in the thickness of the lines, the curves and angles, the shapes of the serifs, the relative sizes of the parts of the letters, and other design features, all add up to individualities. The alphabet is firmly fixed in the shapes of its letters. Three-year-olds recognize letterforms. Yet there are on the order of 50,000 typefaces in existence, each different. Subtle and not-so-subtle variations in the thickness of the lines, the curves and angles, the shapes of the serifs, the relative sizes of the parts of the letters, and other design features, all add up to individualities. The alphabet is firmly fixed in the shapes of its letters. Three-year-olds recognize letterforms. Yet there are on the order of 50,000 typefaces in existence, each different. Subtle and not so subtle variations in the thickness of the lines, the curves

12 point type, 13 point linespace

The alphabet is firmly fixed in the shapes of its letters. Three-year-olds recognize letterforms. Yet there are on the order of 50,000 typefaces in existence, each different. Subtle and not-so-subtle variations in the thickness of the lines, the curves and angles, the shapes of the serifs, the relative sizes of the parts of the letters, and other design features, all add up to individualities. The alphabet is firmly fixed in the shapes of its letters. Three-year-olds recognize letterforms. Yet there are on the order of 50,000 typefaces in existence, each different. Subtle and not-so-subtle variations in the thickness of the lines, the curves and angles, the shapes of the serifs, the relative sizes of the parts of the letters, and other design

As opposed to Palatino Bold, this is a pleasantly active face, vibrating with energy. Use in small doses, as it's not terribly readable, but it impinges, and carries the message of "Notice This!" very well. The numerals carry the scent of exotica, as in numerology.

ABCDEFGHIJKLMNOPQRSTUVWXYZ

abcdefghijklmnopqrstuvwxyz

0123456789&?!$%“”.,/;()

8 point type, 9 point linespace

The alphabet is firmly fixed in the shapes of its letters. Three-year-olds recognize letterforms. Yet there are on the order of 50,000 typefaces in existence, each different. Subtle and not-so-subtle variations in the thickness of the lines, the curves and angles, the shapes of the serifs, the relative sizes of the parts of the letters, and other design features, all add up to individualities. The alphabet is firmly fixed in the shapes of its letters. Three-year-olds recognize letterforms. Yet there are on the order of 50,000 typefaces in existence, each different. Subtle and not-so-subtle variations in the thickness of the lines, the curves and angles, the shapes of the serifs, the relative sizes of the parts of the letters, and other design features, all add up to individualities. The alphabet is firmly fixed in the shapes of its letters. Three-year-olds recognize letterforms. Yet there are on the order of 50,000 typefaces in existence, each different. Subtle and not-so-subtle variations in the thickness of the lines, the curves and angles, the shapes of the serifs, the relative sizes of the parts of the letters, and other design features, all add up to individualities. The alphabet is firmly fixed in the shapes of its letters. Three-year-olds recognize letterforms. Yet there are on the order of 50,000 typefaces in existence, each different. Subtle and not-so-subtle variations in the thickness of the lines, the curves and angles, the shapes of the serifs, the relative sizes of the parts of the letters, and other design features, all add up to individualities. The alphabet is firmly fixed in the shapes of its letters. Three-year-olds recognize letterforms. Yet there are on the order of 50,000 typefaces in existence, each different.Subtle and not-so-subtle variations in the thickness of the lines, the curves and angles, the shapes of the serifs, the relative sizes of the parts of the letters, and other design features, all add up to individualities. The alphabet is firmly fixed in the shapes of its letters. Three-year-olds recognize letterforms. Yet there are on the order of 50,000 typefaces in existence, each different. Subtle and not-so-subtle variations in the thickness of the lines, the curves and angles, the shapes of the serifs, the relative sizes of the parts of the letters, and other design features, all add up to individualities. The alphabet is firmly fixed in the shapes of its letters. Three-year-olds recognize letterforms. Yet there are on the order of 50,000 typefaces in existence, each different. Subtle and not-so-

10 point type, 11 point linespace

The alphabet is firmly fixed in the shapes of its letters. Three-year-olds recognize letterforms. Yet there are on the order of 50,000 typefaces in existence, each different. Subtle and not-so-subtle variations in the thickness of the lines, the curves and angles, the shapes of the serifs, the relative sizes of the parts of the letters, and other design features, all add up to individualities. The alphabet is firmly fixed in the shapes of its letters. Three-year-olds recognize letterforms. Yet there are on the order of 50,000 typefaces in existence, each different. Subtle and not-so-subtle variations in the thickness of the lines, the curves and angles, the shapes of the serifs, the relative sizes of the parts of the letters, and other design features, all add up to individualities. The alphabet is firmly fixed in the shapes of its letters. Three-year-olds recognize letterforms. Yet there are on the order of 50,000 typefaces in existence, each different. Subtle and not-so-subtle variations in the thickness of the lines, the curves and angles, the shapes of the serifs, the relative sizes of the parts of the letters, and other design features, all add up to individualities. The alphabet is firmly fixed in the shapes of its letters. Three-year-olds recognize letterforms. Yet there are on the order of 50,000 typefaces in existence, each different. Subtle and not-so-subtle variations in the thickness of the lines, the curves and angles, the shapes of the serifs, the relative sizes of the parts of the letters, and other design features, all add up to individualities. The alphabet is firmly fixed in the shapes of its letters. Three-year-olds recognize letterforms. Yet there are on the order

12 point type, 13 point linespace

The alphabet is firmly fixed in the shapes of its letters. Three-year-olds recognize letterforms. Yet there are on the order of 50,000 typefaces in existence, each different. Subtle and not-so-subtle variations in the thickness of the lines, the curves and angles, the shapes of the serifs, the relative sizes of the parts of the letters, and other design features, all add up to individualities. The alphabet is firmly fixed in the shapes of its letters. Three-year-olds recognize letterforms. Yet there are on the order of 50,000 typefaces in existence, each different. Subtle and not-so-subtle variations in the thickness of the lines, the curves and angles, the shapes of the serifs, the relative sizes of the parts of the letters, and other design features, all add up to individualities. The alphabet is firmly fixed in the shapes of its letters. Three-year-olds recognize letterforms. Yet there are on the order of 50,000 typefaces in existence, each different. Subtle and not-so-subtle variations in the thickness of the lines, the curves and angles, the shapes of the serifs, the relative sizes of the parts of the letters, and other design features, all add up to individualities. The alphabet is firmly fixed in the shapes of its

Very formal, almost painfully so, but sometimes only Park Avenue will do. Social Register invitations, for instance. You gotta have it, whether or not you like it, and that's just how it is.

ABCDEFGHIJKLMNOPQRSTUVWXY
Zabcdefghijklmnopqrstuvwxyz
0123456789&?!$%“” .,/;()

8 point type, 9 point linespace

The alphabet is firmly fixed in the shapes of its letters. Three-year-olds recognize letterforms. Yet there are on the order of 50,000 typefaces in existence, each different. Subtle and not-so-subtle variations in the thickness of the lines, the curves and angles, the shapes of the serifs, the relative sizes of the parts of the letters, and other design features, all add up to individualities. The alphabet is firmly fixed in the shapes of its letters. Three-year-olds recognize letterforms. Yet there are on the order of 50,000 typefaces in existence, each different. Subtle and not-so-subtle variations in the thickness of the lines, the curves and angles, the shapes of the serifs, the relative sizes of the parts of the letters, and other design features, all add up to individualities. The alphabet is firmly fixed in the shapes of its letters. Three-year-olds recognize letterforms. Yet there are on the order of 50,000 typefaces in existence, each different. Subtle and not-so-subtle variations in the thickness of the lines, the curves and angles, the shapes of the serifs, the relative sizes of the parts of the letters, and other design features, all add up to individualities. The alphabet is firmly fixed in the shapes of its letters. Three-year-olds recognize letterforms. Yet there are on the order of 50,000 typefaces in existence, each different. Subtle and not-so-subtle variations in the thickness of the lines, the curves and angles, the shapes of the serifs, the relative sizes of the parts of the letters, and other design features, all add up to individualities. The alphabet is firmly fixed in the shapes of its letters. Three-year-olds recognize letterforms. Yet there are on the order of 50,000 typefaces in existence, each different. Subtle and not-so-subtle variations in the thickness of the lines, the curves and

10 point type, 11 point linespace

The alphabet is firmly fixed in the shapes of its letters. Three-year-olds recognize letterforms. Yet there are on the order of 50,000 typefaces in existence, each different. Subtle and not-so-subtle variations in the thickness of the lines, the curves and angles, the shapes of the serifs, the relative sizes of the parts of the letters, and other design features, all add up to individualities. The alphabet is firmly fixed in the shapes of its letters. Three-year-olds recognize letterforms. Yet there are on the order of 50,000 typefaces in existence, each different. Subtle and not-so-subtle variations in the thickness of the lines, the curves and angles, the shapes of the serifs, the relative sizes of the parts of the letters, and other design features, all add up to individualities. The alphabet is firmly fixed in the shapes of its letters. Three-year-olds recognize letterforms. Yet there are on the order of 50,000 typefaces in existence, each different. Subtle and not-so-subtle variations in the thickness of the lines, the curves and angles, the shapes of the serifs, the relative sizes of the parts of the letters, and other design features, all add up to individualities. The alphabet is firmly fixed in the

12 point type, 13 point linespace

The alphabet is firmly fixed in the shapes of its letters. Three-year-olds recognize letterforms. Yet there are on the order of 50,000 typefaces in existence, each different. Subtle and not-so-subtle variations in the thickness of the lines, the curves and angles, the shapes of the serifs, the relative sizes of the parts of the letters, and other design features, all add up to individualities. The alphabet is firmly fixed in the shapes of its letters. Three-year-olds recognize letterforms. Yet there are on the order of 50,000 typefaces in existence, each different. Subtle and not-so-subtle variations in the thickness of the lines, the curves and angles, the shapes of the serifs, the relative sizes of the parts of the letters, and other design features, all add up to individualities. The alphabet is firmly fixed in the shapes of its letters. Three-year-olds recognize letterforms.

Many script faces are overly ornate. Snell is relatively legible. It should be set much larger than you would expect, as it has very small lower case letters. A black-tie face.

ABCDEFGHIJKLMNOPQRSTUVWX

YZabcdefghijklmnopqrstuvwxyz

0123456789&?!$%“”.,/;()

8 point type, 9 point linespace

The alphabet is firmly fixed in the shapes of its letters. Three-year-olds recognize letterforms. Yet there are on the order of 50,000 typefaces in existence, each different. Subtle and not-so-subtle variations in the thickness of the lines, the curves and angles, the shapes of the serifs, the relative sizes of the parts of the letters, and other design features, all add up to individualities. The alphabet is firmly fixed in the shapes of its letters. Three-year-olds recognize letterforms. Yet there are on the order of 50,000 typefaces in existence, each different. Subtle and not-so-subtle variations in the thickness of the lines, the curves and angles, the shapes of the serifs, the relative sizes of the parts of the letters, and other design features, all add up to individualities. The alphabet is firmly fixed in the shapes of its letters. Three-year-olds recognize letterforms. Yet there are on the order of 50,000 typefaces in existence, each different. Subtle and not-so-subtle variations in the thickness of the lines, the curves and angles, the shapes of the serifs, the relative sizes of the parts of the letters, and other design features, all add up to individualities. The alphabet is firmly fixed in the shapes of its letters. Three-year-olds recognize letterforms. Yet there are on the order of 50,000 typefaces in existence, each different. Subtle and not-so-subtle variations in the thickness of the lines, the curves and angles, the shapes of the serifs, the relative sizes of the parts of the letters, and other design features, all add up to individualities. The alphabet is firmly fixed in the shapes of its letters. Three-year-olds recognize letterforms. Yet there are on the order of

10 point type, 11 point linespace

The alphabet is firmly fixed in the shapes of its letters. Three-year-olds recognize letterforms. Yet there are on the order of 50,000 typefaces in existence, each different. Subtle and not-so-subtle variations in the thickness of the lines, the curves and angles, the shapes of the serifs, the relative sizes of the parts of the letters, and other design features, all add up to individualities. The alphabet is firmly fixed in the shapes of its letters. Three-year-olds recognize letterforms. Yet there are on the order of 50,000 typefaces in existence, each different. Subtle and not-so-subtle variations in the thickness of the lines, the curves and angles, the shapes of the serifs, the relative sizes of the parts of the letters, and other design features, all add up to individualities. The alphabet is firmly fixed in the shapes of its letters. Three-year-olds recognize letterforms. Yet there are on the order of 50,000 typefaces in existence, each different. Subtle and not-so-subtle variations in the thickness of the lines, the curves and angles, the shapes of the serifs, the relative sizes of the parts of the letters, and other design features, all add up to individualities.

12 point type, 13 point linespace

The alphabet is firmly fixed in the shapes of its letters. Three-year-olds recognize letterforms. Yet there are on the order of 50,000 typefaces in existence, each different. Subtle and not-so-subtle variations in the thickness of the lines, the curves and angles, the shapes of the serifs, the relative sizes of the parts of the letters, and other design features, all add up to individualities. The alphabet is firmly fixed in the shapes of its letters. Three-year-olds recognize letterforms. Yet there are on the order of 50,000 typefaces in existence, each different. Subtle and not-so-subtle variations in the thickness of the lines, the curves and angles, the shapes of the serifs, the relative sizes of the parts of the letters, and other design features, all add up to individualities. The alphabet is firmly fixed in the

Actually preferable to plain Snell, this face holds up to printing much better, without looking ungainly. In smaller sizes, this face is the required choice. Compare the two.

ABCDEFGHIJKLMNOPQRSTUVWXYZ
abcdefghijklmnopqrstuvwxyz
0123456789&?!$%“”.,/;()

8 point type, 9 point linespace

The alphabet is firmly fixed in the shapes of its letters. Three-year-olds recognize letterforms. Yet there are on the order of 50,000 typefaces in existence, each different. Subtle and not-so-subtle variations in the thickness of the lines, the curves and angles, the shapes of the serifs, the relative sizes of the parts of the letters, and other design features, all add up to individualities. The alphabet is firmly fixed in the shapes of its letters. Three-year-olds recognize letterforms. Yet there are on the order of 50,000 typefaces in existence, each different. Subtle and not-so-subtle variations in the thickness of the lines, the curves and angles, the shapes of the serifs, the relative sizes of the parts of the letters, and other design features, all add up to individualities. The alphabet is firmly fixed in the shapes of its letters. Three-year-olds recognize letterforms. Yet there are on the order of 50,000 typefaces in existence, each different. Subtle and not-so-subtle variations in the thickness of the lines, the curves and angles, the shapes of the serifs, the relative sizes of the parts of the letters, and other design features, all add up to individualities. The alphabet is firmly fixed in the shapes of its letters. Three-year-olds recognize letterforms. Yet there are on the order of 50,000 typefaces in existence, each different. Subtle and not-so-subtle variations in the thickness of the lines, the curves and angles, the shapes of the serifs, the relative sizes of the parts of the of the letters, and other design features, all add up to individualities. The alphabet is firmly fixed in the

10 point type, 11 point linespace

The alphabet is firmly fixed in the shapes of its letters. Three-year-olds recognize letterforms. Yet there are on the order of 50,000 typefaces in existence, each different. Subtle and not-so-subtle variations in the thickness of the lines, the curves and angles, the shapes of the serifs, the relative sizes of the parts of the letters, and other design features, all add up to individualities. The alphabet is firmly fixed in the shapes of its letters. Three-year-olds recognize letterforms. Yet there are on the order of 50,000 typefaces in existence, each different. Subtle and not-so-subtle variations in the thickness of the lines, the curves and angles, the shapes of the serifs, the relative sizes of the parts of the letters, and other design features, all add up to individualities. The alphabet is firmly fixed in the shapes of its letters. Three-year-olds recognize letterforms. Yet there are on the order of 50,000 typefaces in existence, each different. Subtle and not-so-subtle variations in the thickness of the lines, the curves and angles, the shapes of the

12 point type, 13 point linespace

The alphabet is firmly fixed in the shapes of its letters. Three-year-olds recognize letterforms. Yet there are on the order of 50,000 typefaces in existence, each different. Subtle and not-so-subtle variations in the thickness of the lines, the curves and angles, the shapes of the serifs, the relative sizes of the parts of the letters, and other design features, all add up to individualities. The alphabet is firmly fixed in the shapes of its letters. Three-year-olds recognize letterforms. Yet there are on the order of 50,000 typefaces in existence, each different. Subtle and not-so-subtle variations in the thickness of the lines, the curves and angles, the shapes of the serifs, the relative sizes of the parts of the letters, and other design features, all add up to

The ultimate “soft serif,” the idea behind Souvenir is to be non-threatening. It’s a family face, rated G. Warm and friendly. Very popular in the late 70’s, it yet retains its winning features. Approved for general consumption.

ABCDEFGHIJKLMNOPQRSTUVWXYZ
abcdefghijklmnopqrstuvwxyz
0123456789&?!$%“”.,/;()

8 point type, 9 point linespace

The alphabet is firmly fixed in the shapes of its letters. Three-year-olds recognize letterforms. Yet there are on the order of 50,000 typefaces in existence, each different. Subtle and not-so-subtle variations in the thickness of the lines, the curves and angles, the shapes of the serifs, the relative sizes of the parts of the letters, and other design features, all add up to individualities. The alphabet is firmly fixed in the shapes of its letters. Three-year-olds recognize letterforms. Yet there are on the order of 50,000 typefaces in existence, each different. Subtle and not-so-subtle variations in the thickness of the lines, the curves and angles, the shapes of the serifs, the relative sizes of the parts of the letters, and other design features, all add up to individualities. The alphabet is firmly fixed in the shapes of its letters. Three-year-olds recognize letterforms. Yet there are on the order of 50,000 typefaces in existence, each different. Subtle and not-so-subtle variations in the thickness of the lines, the curves and angles, the shapes of the serifs, the relative sizes of the parts of the letters, and other design features, all add up to individualities. The alphabet is firmly fixed in the shapes of its letters. Three-year-olds recognize letterforms. Yet there are on the order of 50,000 typefaces in existence, each different. Subtle and not-so-subtle variations in the thickness of the lines, the curves and angles, the shapes of the serifs, the relative sizes of the

10 point type, 11 point linespace

The alphabet is firmly fixed in the shapes of its letters. Three-year-olds recognize letterforms. Yet there are on the order of 50,000 typefaces in existence, each different. Subtle and not-so-subtle variations in the thickness of the lines, the curves and angles, the shapes of the serifs, the relative sizes of the parts of the letters, and other design features, all add up to individualities. The alphabet is firmly fixed in the shapes of its letters. Three-year-olds recognize letterforms. Yet there are on the order of 50,000 typefaces in existence, each different. Subtle and not-so-subtle variations in the thickness of the lines, the curves and angles, the shapes of the serifs, the relative sizes of the parts of the letters, and other design features, all add up to individualities. The alphabet is firmly fixed in the shapes of its letters. Three-year-olds recognize letterforms. Yet there are on the order of 50,000 typefaces in existence, each different. Subtle and not-so-subtle variations in

12 point type, 13 point linespace

The alphabet is firmly fixed in the shapes of its letters. Three-year-olds recognize letterforms. Yet there are on the order of 50,000 typefaces in existence, each different. Subtle and not-so-subtle variations in the thickness of the lines, the curves and angles, the shapes of the serifs, the relative sizes of the parts of the letters, and other design features, all add up to individualities. The alphabet is firmly fixed in the shapes of its letters. Three-year-olds recognize letterforms. Yet there are on the order of 50,000 typefaces in existence, each different. Subtle and not-so-subtle variations in the thickness of the lines, the curves and angles, the shapes of the serifs, the relative sizes of the

Nicely done, even if technically a bit unimaginative. This does an italic's job, of adding significance without disturbing the reader's rhythm. The visual weight between roman and italic is almost identical, a definite plus in any roman/italic combo.

ABCDEFGHIJKLMNOPQRSTUVWXYZ
abcdefghijklmnopqrstuvwxyz
0123456789&?!$%“”.,/;()

8 point type, 9 point linespace

The alphabet is firmly fixed in the shapes of its letters. Three-year-olds recognize letterforms. Yet there are on the order of 50,000 typefaces in existence, each different. Subtle and not-so-subtle variations in the thickness of the lines, the curves and angles, the shapes of the serifs, the relative sizes of the parts of the letters, and other design features, all add up to individualities. The alphabet is firmly fixed in the shapes of its letters. Three-year-olds recognize letterforms. Yet there are on the order of 50,000 typefaces in existence, each different. Subtle and not-so-subtle variations in the thickness of the lines, the curves and angles, the shapes of the serifs, the relative sizes of the parts of the letters, and other design features, all add up to individualities. The alphabet is firmly fixed in the shapes of its letters. Three-year-olds recognize letterforms. Yet there are on the order of 50,000 typefaces in existence, each different. Subtle and not-so-subtle variations in the thickness of the lines, the curves and angles, the shapes of the serifs, the relative sizes of the parts of the letters, and other design features, all add up to individualities. The alphabet is firmly fixed in the shapes of its letters. Three-year-olds recognize letterforms. Yet there are on the order of 50,000 typefaces in existence, each different. Subtle and not-so-subtle variations in the thickness of the lines, the curves and angles, the shapes

10 point type, 11 point linespace

The alphabet is firmly fixed in the shapes of its letters. Three-year-olds recognize letterforms. Yet there are on the order of 50,000 typefaces in existence, each different. Subtle and not-so-subtle variations in the thickness of the lines, the curves and angles, the shapes of the serifs, the relative sizes of the parts of the letters, and other design features, all add up to individualities. The alphabet is firmly fixed in the shapes of its letters. Three-year-olds recognize letter-forms. Yet there are on the order of 50,000 typefaces in existence, each different. Subtle and not-so-subtle variations in the thickness of the lines, the curves and angles, the shapes of the serifs, the relative sizes of the parts of the letters, and other design features, all add up to individualities. The alphabet is firmly fixed in the shapes of its letters. Three-year-olds recognize letterforms. Yet there are on the order of 50,000 typefaces in existence, each different. Subtle and

12 point type, 13 point linespace

The alphabet is firmly fixed in the shapes of its letters. Three-year-olds recognize letterforms. Yet there are on the order of 50,000 typefaces in existence, each different. Subtle and not-so-subtle variations in the thickness of the lines, the curves and angles, the shapes of the serifs, the relative sizes of the parts of the letters, and other design features, all add up to individualities. The alphabet is firmly fixed in the shapes of its letters. Three-year-olds recognize letterforms. Yet there are on the order of 50,000 typefaces in existence, each different. Subtle and not-so-subtle variations in the thickness of the lines, the curves and angles, the shapes of the serifs, the relative sizes of the

Kind of “spiky” compared to the other Souvenirs. This weight is not so soft, though hardly hard. Good for small sizes or for somewhat less comfortable subject matter. Might work for a brochure on AIDS directed to parents, for instance.

ABCDEFGHIJKLMNOPQRSTUVWXYZ
abcdefghijklmnopqrstuvwxyz
0123456789&?!$%“”.,/;()

8 point type, 9 point linespace

The alphabet is firmly fixed in the shapes of its letters. Three-year-olds recognize letterforms. Yet there are on the order of 50,000 typefaces in existence, each different. Subtle and not-so-subtle variations in the thickness of the lines, the curves and angles, the shapes of the serifs, the relative sizes of the parts of the letters, and other design features, all add up to individualities. The alphabet is firmly fixed in the shapes of its letters. Three-year-olds recognize letterforms. Yet there are on the order of 50,000 typefaces in existence, each different. Subtle and not-so-subtle variations in the thickness of the lines, the curves and angles, the shapes of the serifs, the relative sizes of the parts of the letters, and other design features, all add up to individualities. The alphabet is firmly fixed in the shapes of its letters. Three-year-olds recognize letterforms. Yet there are on the order of 50,000 typefaces in existence, each different. Subtle and not-so-subtle variations in the thickness of the lines, the curves and angles, the shapes of the serifs, the relative sizes of the parts of the letters, and other design features, all add up to individualities. The alphabet is firmly fixed in the shapes of its letters. Three-year-olds recognize letterforms. Yet there are on the order of 50,000 typefaces in existence, each different. Subtle and not-

10 point type, 11 point linespace

The alphabet is firmly fixed in the shapes of its letters. Three-year-olds recognize letterforms. Yet there are on the order of 50,000 typefaces in existence, each differ-ent. Subtle and not-so-subtle variations in the thickness of the lines, the curves and angles, the shapes of the serifs, the relative sizes of the parts of the letters, and other design features, all add up to individuali-ties. The alphabet is firmly fixed in the shapes of its letters. Three-year-olds recog-nize letter-forms. Yet there are on the order of 50,000 typefaces in existence, each different. Subtle and not-so-subtle varia-tions in the thickness of the lines, the curves and angles, the shapes of the serifs, the relative sizes of the parts of the letters, and other design features, all add up to individualities. The alphabet is firmly fixed in the shapes of its letters. Three-year-olds recognize letterforms. Yet there are on the

12 point type, 13 point linespace

The alphabet is firmly fixed in the shapes of its letters. Three-year-olds recognize letterforms. Yet there are on the order of 50,000 typefaces in existence, each different. Subtle and not-so-subtle variations in the thick-ness of the lines, the curves and angles, the shapes of the serifs, the relative sizes of the parts of the letters, and other design features, all add up to individualities. The alpha-bet is firmly fixed in the shapes of its letters. Three-year-olds recognize letterforms. Yet there are on the order of 50,000 typefaces in exist-ence, each different. Subtle and not-so-subtle variations in the thickness of the lines, the curves and angles,

In contrast to the roman, this italic is as flowy and gentle as the other Souvenir italics. As such it can be contrapuntal to the roman, perhaps soften it if things get too serious.

ABCDEFGHIJKLMNOPQRSTUVWXYZ
abcdefghijklmnopqrstuvwxyz
0123456789&?!$%“”.,/;()

8 point type, 9 point linespace

The alphabet is firmly fixed in the shapes of its letters. Three-year-olds recognize letterforms. Yet there are on the order of 50,000 typefaces in existence, each different. Subtle and not-so-subtle variations in the thickness of the lines, the curves and angles, the shapes of the serifs, the relative sizes of the parts of the letters, and other design features, all add up to individualities. The alphabet is firmly fixed in the shapes of its letters. Three-year-olds recognize letterforms. Yet there are on the order of 50,000 typefaces in existence, each different. Subtle and not-so-subtle variations in the thickness of the lines, the curves and angles, the shapes of the serifs, the relative sizes of the parts of the letters, and other design features, all add up to individualities. The alphabet is firmly fixed in the shapes of its letters. Three-year-olds recognize letterforms. Yet there are on the order of 50,000 typefaces in existence, each different. Subtle and not-so-subtle variations in the thickness of the lines, the curves and angles, the shapes of the serifs, the relative sizes of the parts of the letters, and other design features, all add up to individualities. The alphabet is firmly fixed in the shapes of its letters. Three-year-olds recognize letterforms. Yet there are on the order of 50,000 typefaces in existence, each different. Subtle and

10 point type, 11 point linespace

The alphabet is firmly fixed in the shapes of its letters. Three-year-olds recognize letterforms. Yet there are on the order of 50,000 typefaces in existence, each different. Subtle and not-so-subtle variations in the thickness of the lines, the curves and angles, the shapes of the serifs, the relative sizes of the parts of the letters, and other design features, all add up to individualities. The alphabet is firmly fixed in the shapes of its letters. Three-year-olds recognize letterforms. Yet there are on the order of 50,000 typefaces in existence, each different. Subtle and not-so-subtle variations in the thickness of the lines, the curves and angles, the shapes of the serifs, the relative sizes of the parts of the letters, and other design features, all add up to individualities. The alphabet is firmly fixed in the shapes of its letters. Three-year-olds recognize letterforms. Yet there are on the

12 point type, 13 point linespace

The alphabet is firmly fixed in the shapes of its letters. Three-year-olds recognize letterforms. Yet there are on the order of 50,000 typefaces in existence, each different. Subtle and not-so-subtle variations in the thickness of the lines, the curves and angles, the shapes of the serifs, the relative sizes of the parts of the letters, and other design features, all add up to individualities. The alphabet is firmly fixed in the shapes of its letters. Three-year-olds recognize letterforms. Yet there are on the order of 50,000 typefaces in existence, each different. Subtle and not-so-subtle variations in the thickness of the lines, the curves and angles,

Now this face works; it earns its keep. A pleasant balance of stroke contrast makes it easy to view and inviting to read. It is still a soft face, but is so easily read that it is an excellent face to build on.

ABCDEFGHIJKLMNOPQRSTUVWXYZ
abcdefghijklmnopqrstuvwxyz
0123456789&?!$%“”.,/;()

8 point type, 9 point linespace

The alphabet is firmly fixed in the shapes of its letters. Three-year-olds recognize letterforms. Yet there are on the order of 50,000 typefaces in existence, each different. Subtle and not-so-subtle variations in the thickness of the lines, the curves and angles, the shapes of the serifs, the relative sizes of the parts of the letters, and other design features, all add up to individualities. The alphabet is firmly fixed in the shapes of its letters. Three-year-olds recognize letterforms. Yet there are on the order of 50,000 typefaces in existence, each different. Subtle and not-so-subtle variations in the thickness of the lines, the curves and angles, the shapes of the serifs, the relative sizes of the parts of the letters, and other design features, all add up to individualities. The alphabet is firmly fixed in the shapes of its letters. Three-year-olds recognize letterforms. Yet there are on the order of 50,000 typefaces in existence, each different. Subtle and not-so-subtle variations in the thickness of the lines, the curves and angles, the shapes of the serifs, the relative sizes of the parts of the letters, and other design features, all add up to individualities. The alphabet is firmly fixed in the shapes of its letters. Three-year-olds recognize letterforms. Yet there

10 point type, 11 point linespace

The alphabet is firmly fixed in the shapes of its letters. Three-year-olds recognize letterforms. Yet there are on the order of 50,000 typefaces in exist-ence, each different. Subtle and not-so-subtle variations in the thickness of the lines, the curves and angles, the shapes of the serifs, the relative sizes of the parts of the letters, and other design features, all add up to individualities. The alphabet is firmly fixed in the shapes of its letters. Three-year-olds recognize letterforms. Yet there are on the order of 50,000 typefaces in exist-ence, each different. Subtle and not-so-subtle variations in the thickness of the lines, the curves and angles, the shapes of the serifs, the relative sizes of the parts of the letters, and other design features, all add up to individualities. The alphabet is firmly fixed in the

12 point type, 13 point linespace

The alphabet is firmly fixed in the shapes of its letters. Three-year-olds recognize letterforms. Yet there are on the order of 50,000 typefaces in existence, each differ-ent. Subtle and not-so-subtle variations in the thickness of the lines, the curves and angles, the shapes of the serifs, the relative sizes of the parts of the letters, and other design features, all add up to individualities. The alphabet is firmly fixed in the shapes of its letters. Three-year-olds recognize letterforms. Yet there are on the order of 50,000 typefaces in exist-ence, each different. Subtle and not-so-subtle variations in the

Just barely more lightweight than the roman, this face cannot carry its own weight for long. Minimize its use against the roman. In itself, however, it’s quite legible and good for headlines in “artistic” or “homey” circumstances.

ABCDEFGHIJKLMNOPQRSTUVWXYZ
abcdefghijklmnopqrstuvwxyz
0123456789&?!$%“”.,/;()

8 point type, 9 point linespace

The alphabet is firmly fixed in the shapes of its letters. Three-year-olds recognize letterforms. Yet there are on the order of 50,000 typefaces in existence, each different. Subtle and not-so-subtle variations in the thickness of the lines, the curves and angles, the shapes of the serifs, the relative sizes of the parts of the letters, and other design features, all add up to individualities. The alphabet is firmly fixed in the shapes of its letters. Three-year-olds recognize letterforms. Yet there are on the order of 50,000 typefaces in existence, each different. Subtle and not-so-subtle variations in the thickness of the lines, the curves and angles, the shapes of the serifs, the relative sizes of the parts of the letters, and other design features, all add up to individualities. The alphabet is firmly fixed in the shapes of its letters. Three-year-olds recognize letterforms. Yet there are on the order of 50,000 typefaces in existence, each different. Subtle and not-so-subtle variations in the thickness of the lines, the curves and angles, the shapes of the serifs, the relative sizes of the parts of the letters, and other design features, all add up to individualities. The alphabet is firmly fixed in the shapes of its letters. Three-year-olds recognize letterforms. Yet

10 point type, 11 point linespace

The alphabet is firmly fixed in the shapes of its letters. Three-year-olds recognize letterforms. Yet there are on the order of 50,000 typefaces in exist-ence, each different. Subtle and not-so-subtle variations in the thickness of the lines, the curves and angles, the shapes of the serifs, the relative sizes of the parts of the letters, and other design features, all add up to individualities. The alphabet is firmly fixed in the shapes of its letters. Three-year-olds recognize letterforms. Yet there are on the order of 50,000 typefaces in exist-ence, each different. Subtle and not-so-subtle variations in the thickness of the lines, the curves and angles, the shapes of the serifs, the relative sizes of the parts of the letters, and other design features, all add up to individualities. The alphabet is firmly fixed in the

12 point type, 13 point linespace

The alphabet is firmly fixed in the shapes of its letters. Three-year-olds recognize letterforms. Yet there are on the order of 50,000 typefaces in existence, each differ-ent. Subtle and not-so-subtle variations in the thickness of the lines, the curves and angles, the shapes of the serifs, the relative sizes of the parts of the letters, and other design features, all add up to individualities. The alphabet is firmly fixed in the shapes of its letters. Three-year-olds recognize letterforms. Yet there are on the order of 50,000 typefaces in existence, each different. Subtle and not-so-subtle variations in the

One of the few heavy faces that works. Sure, it looks overweight, but so does Santa. This is a smiley face, very noticeable (impos-sible to ignore, in fact), but would only consider carrying good news.

ABCDEFGHIJKLMNOPQRSTUVWXYZ
abcdefghijklmnopqrstuvwxyz
0123456789&?!$%“”.,/;()

8 point type, 9 point linespace

The alphabet is firmly fixed in the shapes of its letters. Three-year-olds recognize letterforms. Yet there are on the order of 50,000 typefaces in existence, each different. Subtle and not-so-subtle variations in the thickness of the lines, the curves and angles, the shapes of the serifs, the relative sizes of the parts of the letters, and other design features, all add up to individualities. The alphabet is firmly fixed in the shapes of its letters. Three-year-olds recognize letterforms. Yet there are on the order of 50,000 typefaces in existence, each different. Subtle and not-so-subtle variations in the thickness of the lines, the curves and angles, the shapes of the serifs, the relative sizes of the parts of the letters, and other design features, all add up to individualities. The alphabet is firmly fixed in the shapes of its letters. Three-year-olds recognize letterforms. Yet there are on the order of 50,000 typefaces in existence, each different. Subtle and not-so-subtle variations in the thickness of the lines, the curves and angles, the shapes of the serifs, the relative sizes of the parts of the letters, and other design features, all add up to individualities. The alphabet is firmly fixed in

10 point type, 11 point linespace

The alphabet is firmly fixed in the shapes of its letters. Three-year-olds recognize letterforms. Yet there are on the order of 50,000 typefaces in existence, each different. Subtle and not-so-subtle variations in the thickness of the lines, the curves and angles, the shapes of the serifs, the relative sizes of the parts of the letters, and other design features, all add up to individualities. The alphabet is firmly fixed in the shapes of its letters. Three-year-olds recognize letterforms. Yet there are on the order of 50,000 typefaces in existence, each different. Subtle and not-so-subtle variations in the thickness of the lines, the curves and angles, the shapes of the serifs, the relative sizes of the parts of the letters, and other design features, all add up to indi-

12 point type, 13 point linespace

The alphabet is firmly fixed in the shapes of its letters. Three-year-olds recognize letterforms. Yet there are on the order of 50,000 typefaces in existence, each different. Subtle and not-so-subtle variations in the thickness of the lines, the curves and angles, the shapes of the serifs, the relative sizes of the parts of the letters, and other design features, all add up to individualities. The alphabet is firmly fixed in the shapes of its letters. Three-year-olds recognize letterforms. Yet there are on the order of 50,000 typefaces in existence, each different. Subtle

Complementary to the bold, not a standalone face at all. This is the uncle who tries too hard to make you feel good. He’s much better in the background, supporting his brother’s important points. But not a bad guy.

ABCDEFGHIJKLMNOPQRSTUVWXYZ
abcdefghijklmnopqrstuvwxyz
0123456789&?!$%“”.,/;()

8 point type, 9 point linespace

The alphabet is firmly fixed in the shapes of its letters. Three-year-olds recognize letterforms. Yet there are on the order of 50,000 typefaces in existence, each different. Subtle and not-so-subtle variations in the thickness of the lines, the curves and angles, the shapes of the serifs, the relative sizes of the parts of the letters, and other design features, all add up to individualities. The alphabet is firmly fixed in the shapes of its letters. Three-year-olds recognize letterforms. Yet there are on the order of 50,000 typefaces in existence, each different. Subtle and not-so-subtle variations in the thickness of the lines, the curves and angles, the shapes of the serifs, the relative sizes of the parts of the letters, and other design features, all add up to individualities. The alphabet is firmly fixed in the shapes of its letters. Three-year-olds recognize letterforms. Yet there are on the order of 50,000 typefaces in existence, each different. Subtle and not-so-subtle variations in the thickness of the lines, the curves and angles, the shapes of the serifs, the relative sizes of the parts of the letters, and other design features, all add up to individualities. The alphabet is firmly fixed in the shapes of its letters. Three-year-olds recognize letterforms. Yet there are on the order of 50,000 typefaces in existence, each different. Subtle and not-so-subtle variations in the thickness of the lines, the curves and angles, the shapes of the serifs, the relative sizes of the parts of the letters, and other design features, all add

10 point type, 11 point linespace

The alphabet is firmly fixed in the shapes of its letters. Three-year-olds recognize letterforms. Yet there are on the order of 50,000 typefaces in existence, each different. Subtle and not-so-subtle variations in the thickness of the lines, the curves and angles, the shapes of the serifs, the relative sizes of the parts of the letters, and other design features, all add up to individualities. The alphabet is firmly fixed in the shapes of its letters. Three-year-olds recognize letterforms. Yet there are on the order of 50,000 typefaces in exist-ence, each different. Subtle and not-so-subtle variations in the thickness of the lines, the curves and angles, the shapes of the serifs, the relative sizes of the parts of the letters, and other design features, all add up to individualities. The alphabet is firmly fixed in the shapes of its letters. Three-year-olds recognize letterforms. Yet there are on the order of 50,000 typefaces in exist-ence, each different. Subtle and not so subtle variations in the thickness of the lines, the curves

12 point type, 13 point linespace

The alphabet is firmly fixed in the shapes of its letters. Three-year-olds recognize letterforms. Yet there are on the order of 50,000 typefaces in existence, each different. Subtle and not-so-subtle varia-tions in the thickness of the lines, the curves and angles, the shapes of the serifs, the relative sizes of the parts of the letters, and other design features, all add up to individualities. The alphabet is firmly fixed in the shapes of its letters. Three-year-olds recognize letterforms. Yet there are on the order of 50,000 type-faces in existence, each different. Subtle and not-so-subtle variations in the thick-ness of the lines, the curves and angles, the shapes of the serifs, the relative sizes of the parts of the letters, and other

A softer, gentler typeface. Subtle flares and relaxed curves make this a pleasant change of pace from Helvetica or Optima. It sets evenly, and looks better than most in a block of type.

ABCDEFGHIJKLMNOPQRSTUVWXYZ abcdefghijklmnopqrstuvwxyz 0123456789&?!$%"".,/;()

8 point type, 9 point linespace

The alphabet is firmly fixed in the shapes of its letters. Three-year-olds recognize letterforms. Yet there are on the order of 50,000 typefaces in existence, each different. Subtle and not-so-subtle variations in the thickness of the lines, the curves and angles, the shapes of the serifs, the relative sizes of the parts of the letters, and other design features, all add up to individualities. The alphabet is firmly fixed in the shapes of its letters. Three-year-olds recognize letterforms. Yet there are on the order of 50,000 typefaces in existence, each different. Subtle and not-so-subtle variations in the thickness of the lines, the curves and angles, the shapes of the serifs, the relative sizes of the parts of the letters, and other design features, all add up to individualities. The alphabet is firmly fixed in the shapes of its letters. Three-year-olds recognize letterforms. Yet there are on the order of 50,000 typefaces in existence, each different. Subtle and not-so-subtle variations in the thickness of the lines, the curves and angles, the shapes of the serifs, the relative sizes of the parts of the letters, and other design features, all add up to individualities. The alphabet is firmly fixed in the shapes of its letters. Three-year-olds recognize letterforms. Yet there are on the order of 50,000 typefaces in existence, each different. Subtle and not-so-subtle variations in the thickness of the lines, the curves and angles, the shapes of the serifs, the relative sizes of the parts of the letters, and other design features, all add up to individualities. The alphabet is firmly fixed in the shapes of its letters. Three-year-olds recognize

10 point type, 11 point linespace

The alphabet is firmly fixed in the shapes of its letters. Three-year-olds recognize letterforms. Yet there are on the order of 50,000 typefaces in existence, each different. Subtle and not-so-subtle variations in the thickness of the lines, the curves and angles, the shapes of the serifs, the relative sizes of the parts of the letters, and other design features, all add up to individualities. The alphabet is firmly fixed in the shapes of its letters. Three-year-olds recognize letterforms. Yet there are on the order of 50,000 typefaces in existence, each different. Subtle and not-so-subtle variations in the thickness of the lines, the curves and angles, the shapes of the serifs, the relative sizes of the parts of the letters, and other design features, all add up to individualities. The alphabet is firmly fixed in the shapes of its letters. Three-year-olds recognize letterforms. Yet there are on the order of 50,000 typefaces in existence, each different. Subtle and not-so-subtle variations in the thickness of the lines, the curves and angles, the shapes of the serifs, the

12 point type, 13 point linespace

The alphabet is firmly fixed in the shapes of its letters. Three-year-olds recognize letterforms. Yet there are on the order of 50,000 typefaces in existence, each different. Subtle and not-so-subtle variations in the thickness of the lines, the curves and angles, the shapes of the serifs, the relative sizes of the parts of the letters, and other design features, all add up to individualities. The alphabet is firmly fixed in the shapes of its letters. Three-year-olds recognize letterforms. Yet there are on the order of 50,000 typefaces in existence, each different. Subtle and not-so-subtle variations in the thickness of the lines, the curves and angles, the shapes of the serifs, the relative sizes of the parts of the letters, and other design features, all add up to individualities.

The whole Stone family is masterfully designed to work together, including the italics. There is no annoying visual weight difference. Use freely.

ABCDEFGHIJKLMNOPQRSTUVWXYZ
abcdefghijklmnopqrstuvwxyz
0123456789&?!$%“”.,/;()

8 point type, 9 point linespace

The alphabet is firmly fixed in the shapes of its letters. Three-year-olds recognize letterforms. Yet there are on the order of 50,000 typefaces in existence, each different. Subtle and not-so-subtle variations in the thickness of the lines, the curves and angles, the shapes of the serifs, the relative sizes of the parts of the letters, and other design features, all add up to individualities. The alphabet is firmly fixed in the shapes of its letters. Three-year-olds recognize letterforms. Yet there are on the order of 50,000 typefaces in existence, each different. Subtle and not-so-subtle variations in the thickness of the lines, the curves and angles, the shapes of the serifs, the relative sizes of the parts of the letters, and other design features, all add up to individualities. The alphabet is firmly fixed in the shapes of its letters. Three-year-olds recognize letterforms. Yet there are on the order of 50,000 typefaces in existence, each different. Subtle and not-so-subtle variations in the thickness of the lines, the curves and angles, the shapes of the serifs, the relative sizes of the parts of the letters, and other design features, all add up to individualities. The alphabet is firmly fixed in the shapes of its letters. Three-year-olds recognize letterforms. Yet there are on the order of 50,000 typefaces in existence, each different. Subtle and not-so-subtle variations in the thickness of the lines, the curves and angles, the shapes

10 point type, 11 point linespace

The alphabet is firmly fixed in the shapes of its letters. Three-year-olds recognize letterforms. Yet there are on the order of 50,000 typefaces in existence, each different. Subtle and not-so-subtle variations in the thickness of the lines, the curves and angles, the shapes of the serifs, the relative sizes of the parts of the letters, and other design features, all add up to individualities. The alphabet is firmly fixed in the shapes of its letters. Three-year-olds recognize letterforms. Yet there are on the order of 50,000 typefaces in existence, each different. Subtle and not-so-subtle variations in the thickness of the lines, the curves and angles, the shapes of the serifs, the relative sizes of the parts of the letters, and other design features, all add up to individualities. The alphabet is firmly fixed in the shapes of its letters. Three-year-olds recognize letterforms. Yet there are on the order of 50,000 typefaces in existence, each

12 point type, 13 point linespace

The alphabet is firmly fixed in the shapes of its letters. Three-year-olds recognize letterforms. Yet there are on the order of 50,000 typefaces in exist-ence, each different. Subtle and not-so-subtle variations in the thickness of the lines, the curves and angles, the shapes of the serifs, the relative sizes of the parts of the letters, and other design features, all add up to individu-alities. The alphabet is firmly fixed in the shapes of its letters. Three-year-olds recognize letterforms. Yet there are on the order of 50,000 typefaces in existence, each different. Subtle and not-so-subtle variations in the thick-ness of the lines, the curves and angles, the shapes of the serifs, the

Not quite halfway between Regular and Bold, the Semibold is best for heads, subheads and occasional words within text for emphasis. A very useful face, going well with the rest of the family.

ABCDEFGHIJKLMNOPQRSTUVWXYZ
abcdefghijklmnopqrstuvwxyz
0123456789&?!$%"".,/;()

8 point type, 9 point linespace

The alphabet is firmly fixed in the shapes of its letters. Three-year-olds recognize letterforms. Yet there are on the order of 50,000 typefaces in existence, each different. Subtle and not-so-subtle variations in the thickness of the lines, the curves and angles, the shapes of the serifs, the relative sizes of the parts of the letters, and other design features, all add up to individualities. The alphabet is firmly fixed in the shapes of its letters. Three-year-olds recognize letterforms. Yet there are on the order of 50,000 typefaces in existence, each different. Subtle and not-so-subtle variations in the thickness of the lines, the curves and angles, the shapes of the serifs, the relative sizes of the parts of the letters, and other design features, all add up to individualities. The alphabet is firmly fixed in the shapes of its letters. Three-year-olds recognize letterforms. Yet there are on the order of 50,000 typefaces in existence, each different. Subtle and not-so-subtle variations in the thickness of the lines, the curves and angles, the shapes of the serifs, the relative sizes of the parts of the letters, and other design features, all add up to individualities. The alphabet is firmly fixed in the shapes of its letters. Three-year-olds recognize letterforms. Yet there are on the order of 50,000 typefaces in existence, each different. Subtle and not-so-subtle variations in the thickness of the lines, the curves and angles, the shapes of the serifs, the relative sizes of the parts of the letters,and other design features, all add up to individualities. The alphabet is firmly fixed in the shapes of its letters. Three-

10 point type, 11 point linespace

The alphabet is firmly fixed in the shapes of its letters. Three-year-olds recognize letterforms. Yet there are on the order of 50,000 typefaces in existence, each different. Subtle and not-so-subtle variations in the thickness of the lines, the curves and angles, the shapes of the serifs, the relative sizes of the parts of the letters, and other design features, all add up to individualities. The alphabet is firmly fixed in the shapes of its letters. Three-year-olds recognize letterforms. Yet there are on the order of 50,000 typefaces in existence, each different. Subtle and not-so-subtle variations in the thickness of the lines, the curves and angles, the shapes of the serifs, the relative sizes of the parts of the letters, and other design features, all add up to individualities. The alphabet is firmly fixed in the shapes of its letters. Three-year-olds recognize letterforms. Yet there are on the order of 50,000 typefaces in existence, each different. Subtle and not-so-subtle variations in the thickness of the lines, the curves and angles, the shapes of the serifs, the relative sizes

12 point type, 13 point linespace

The alphabet is firmly fixed in the shapes of its letters. Three-year-olds recognize letterforms. Yet there are on the order of 50,000 typefaces in existence, each different. Subtle and not-so-subtle variations in the thickness of the lines, the curves and angles, the shapes of the serifs, the relative sizes of the parts of the letters, and other design features, all add up to individualities. The alphabet is firmly fixed in the shapes of its letters. Three-year-olds recognize letterforms. Yet there are on the order of 50,000 typefaces in existence, each different. Subtle and not-so-subtle variations in the thickness of the lines, the curves and angles, the shapes of the serifs, the relative sizes of the parts of the letters, and other design features, all add up to individualities. The alphabet is

Complementary, but mainly to other italics. If a whole piece is done in italic, this face comes into play. Otherwise, it is seldom needed, since bold** and **italic is redundant.

ABCDEFGHIJKLMNOPQRSTUVWXYZ
abcdefghijklmnopqrstuvwxyz
0123456789&?!$%“”.,/;()

8 point type, 9 point linespace

The alphabet is firmly fixed in the shapes of its letters. Three-year-olds recognize letterforms. Yet there are on the order of 50,000 typefaces in existence, each different. Subtle and not-so-subtle variations in the thickness of the lines, the curves and angles, the shapes of the serifs, the relative sizes of the parts of the letters, and other design features, all add up to individualities. The alphabet is firmly fixed in the shapes of its letters. Three-year-olds recognize letterforms. Yet there are on the order of 50,000 typefaces in existence, each different. Subtle and not-so-subtle variations in the thickness of the lines, the curves and angles, the shapes of the serifs, the relative sizes of the parts of the letters, and other design features, all add up to individualities. The alphabet is firmly fixed in the shapes of its letters. Three-year-olds recognize letterforms. Yet there are on the order of 50,000 typefaces in existence, each different. Subtle and not-so-subtle variations in the thickness of the lines, the curves and angles, the shapes of the serifs, the relative sizes of the parts of the letters, and other design features, all add up to individualities. The alphabet is firmly fixed in the shapes of its letters. Three-year-olds recognize letterforms. Yet there are on the order of 50,000 typefaces in

10 point type, 11 point linespace

The alphabet is firmly fixed in the shapes of its letters. Three-year-olds recognize letterforms. Yet there are on the order of 50,000 typefaces in existence, each different. Subtle and not-so-subtle variations in the thickness of the lines, the curves and angles, the shapes of the serifs, the relative sizes of the parts of the letters, and other design features, all add up to individualities. The alphabet is firmly fixed in the shapes of its letters. Three-year-olds recognize letterforms. Yet there are on the order of 50,000 typefaces in existence, each different. Subtle and not-so-subtle variations in the thickness of the lines, the curves and angles, the shapes of the serifs, the relative sizes of the parts of the letters, and other design features, all add up to individualities. The alphabet is firmly fixed in the shapes of its letters. Three-year-olds recognize letterforms. Yet

12 point type, 13 point linespace

The alphabet is firmly fixed in the shapes of its letters. Three-year-olds recognize letterforms. Yet there are on the order of 50,000 typefaces in existence, each different. Subtle and not-so-subtle variations in the thickness of the lines, the curves and angles, the shapes of the serifs, the relative sizes of the parts of the letters, and other design features, all add up to individualities. The alphabet is firmly fixed in the shapes of its letters. Three-year-olds recognize letterforms. Yet there are on the order of 50,000 typefaces in existence, each different. Subtle and not-so-subtle variations in the

A very heavy face, use this for very heavy messages: headlines, especially. When used as a subhead, use without punctuation following, as that would gild the lily.

ABCDEFGHIJKLMNOPQRSTUVWXYZ
abcdefghijklmnopqrstuvwxyz
0123456789&?!$%"".,/;()

8 point type, 9 point linespace

The alphabet is firmly fixed in the shapes of its letters. Three-year-olds recognize letterforms. Yet there are on the order of 50,000 typefaces in existence, each different. Subtle and not-so-subtle variations in the thickness of the lines, the curves and angles, the shapes of the serifs, the relative sizes of the parts of the letters, and other design features, all add up to individualities. The alphabet is firmly fixed in the shapes of its letters. Three-year-olds recognize letterforms. Yet there are on the order of 50,000 typefaces in existence, each different. Subtle and not-so-subtle variations in the thickness of the lines, the curves and angles, the shapes of the serifs, the relative sizes of the parts of the letters, and other design features, all add up to individualities. The alphabet is firmly fixed in the shapes of its letters. Three-year-olds recognize letterforms. Yet there are on the order of 50,000 typefaces in existence, each different. Subtle and not-so-subtle variations in the thickness of the lines, the curves and angles, the shapes of the serifs, the relative sizes of the parts of the letters, and other design features, all add up to individualities. The alphabet is firmly fixed in the shapes of its letters. Three-year-olds recognize letterforms. Yet there are on the order of 50,000 typefaces in existence, each different. Subtle and not-so-subtle variations in the thickness of the lines, the curves and angles, the shapes

10 point type, 11 point linespace

The alphabet is firmly fixed in the shapes of its letters. Three-year-olds recognize letterforms. Yet there are on the order of 50,000 typefaces in existence, each different. Subtle and not-so-subtle variations in the thickness of the lines, the curves and angles, the shapes of the serifs, the relative sizes of the parts of the letters, and other design features, all add up to individualities. The alphabet is firmly fixed in the shapes of its letters. Three-year-olds recognize letterforms. Yet there are on the order of 50,000 typefaces in existence, each different. Subtle and not-so-subtle variations in the thickness of the lines, the curves and angles, the shapes of the serifs, the relative sizes of the parts of the letters, and other design features, all add up to individualities. The alphabet is firmly fixed in the shapes of its letters. Three-year-olds recognize letterforms. Yet there are on the order of 50,000 typefaces in existence, each

12 point type, 13 point linespace

The alphabet is firmly fixed in the shapes of its letters. Three-year-olds recognize letterforms. Yet there are on the order of 50,000 typefaces in existence, each different. Subtle and not-so-subtle variations in the thickness of the lines, the curves and angles, the shapes of the serifs, the relative sizes of the parts of the letters, and other design features, all add up to individualities. The alphabet is firmly fixed in the shapes of its letters. Three-year-olds recognize letterforms. Yet there are on the order of 50,000 typefaces in existence, each different. Subtle and not-so-subtle variations in the thickness of the lines, the curves and angles, the shapes of

Provided to fill out the family, and for the very infrequent times that the Bold needs further emphasis. Well-cut, so don't be afraid of it.

ABCDEFGHIJKLMNOPQRSTUVWXYZ
abcdefghijklmnopqrstuvwxyz
0123456789&?!$%“”.,/;()

8 point type, 9 point linespace

The alphabet is firmly fixed in the shapes of its letters. Three-year-olds recognize letterforms. Yet there are on the order of 50,000 typefaces in existence, each different. Subtle and not-so-subtle variations in the thickness of the lines, the curves and angles, the shapes of the serifs, the relative sizes of the parts of the letters, and other design features, all add up to individualities. The alphabet is firmly fixed in the shapes of its letters. Three-year-olds recognize letterforms. Yet there are on the order of 50,000 typefaces in existence, each different. Subtle and not-so-subtle variations in the thickness of the lines, the curves and angles, the shapes of the serifs, the relative sizes of the parts of the letters, and other design features, all add up to individualities. The alphabet is firmly fixed in the shapes of its letters. Three-year-olds recognize letterforms. Yet there are on the order of 50,000 typefaces in existence, each different. Subtle and not-so-subtle variations in the thickness of the lines, the curves and angles, the shapes of the serifs, the relative sizes of the parts of the letters, and other design features, all add up to individualities. The alphabet is firmly fixed in the shapes of its letters. Three-year-olds recognize letterforms. Yet there are on the order of 50,000 typefaces in existence, each different. Subtle and not-so-subtle variations in the thickness of the lines, the curves and angles, the shapes of the serifs,

10 point type, 11 point linespace

The alphabet is firmly fixed in the shapes of its letters. Three-year-olds recognize letterforms. Yet there are on the order of 50,000 typefaces in existence, each different. Subtle and not-so-subtle variations in the thickness of the lines, the curves and angles, the shapes of the serifs, the relative sizes of the parts of the letters, and other design features, all add up to individualities. The alphabet is firmly fixed in the shapes of its letters. Three-year-olds recognize letterforms. Yet there are on the order of 50,000 typefaces in existence, each different. Subtle and not-so-subtle variations in the thickness of the lines, the curves and angles, the shapes of the serifs, the relative sizes of the parts of the letters, and other design features, all add up to individualities. The alphabet is firmly fixed in the shapes of its letters. Three-year-olds recognize letterforms. Yet there are on the the order of 50,000 typefaces in existence, each different.

12 point type, 13 point linespace

The alphabet is firmly fixed in the shapes of its letters. Three-year-olds recognize letterforms. Yet there are on the order of 50,000 typefaces in existence, each different. Subtle and not-so-subtle variations in the thickness of the lines, the curves and angles, the shapes of the serifs, the relative sizes of the parts of the letters, and other design features, all add up to individualities. The alphabet is firmly fixed in the shapes of its letters. Three-year-olds recognize letterforms. Yet there are on the order of 50,000 typefaces in existence, each different. Subtle and not-so-subtle variations in the thickness of the lines, the curves and angles, the shapes of its letters. Three-year-olds recognize

A very readable text face, increasing in popularity. You might suggest this to yuppie clients, or to show you are “with it” in type. Stone Serif is a relaxed face, not as formal as many.

ABCDEFGHIJKLMNOPQRSTUVWXYZ
abcdefghijklmnopqrstuvwxyz
0123456789&?!$%“”.,/;()

8 point type, 9 point linespace

The alphabet is firmly fixed in the shapes of its letters. Three-year-olds recognize letterforms. Yet there are on the order of 50,000 typefaces in existence, each different. Subtle and not-so-subtle variations in the thickness of the lines, the curves and angles, the shapes of the serifs, the relative sizes of the parts of the letters, and other design features, all add up to individualities. The alphabet is firmly fixed in the shapes of its letters. Three-year-olds recognize letterforms. Yet there are on the order of 50,000 typefaces in existence, each different. Subtle and not-so-subtle variations in the thickness of the lines, the curves and angles, the shapes of the serifs, the relative sizes of the parts of the letters, and other design features, all add up to individualities. The alphabet is firmly fixed in the shapes of its letters. Three-year-olds recognize letterforms. Yet there are on the order of 50,000 typefaces in existence, each different. Subtle and not-so-subtle variations in the thickness of the lines, the curves and angles, the shapes of the serifs, the relative sizes of the parts of the letters, and other design features, all add up to individualities. The alphabet is firmly fixed in the shapes of its letters. Three-year-olds recognize letterforms. Yet there are on the order of 50,000 typefaces in existence, each different. Subtle and not-so-subtle variations in the thickness of the lines, the curves and angles, the shapes of the serifs, the relative sizes of the parts of the letters, and other design features, all add up to individualities. The alphabet is firmly fixed in the shapes of

10 point type, 11 point linespace

The alphabet is firmly fixed in the shapes of its letters. Three-year-olds recognize letterforms. Yet there are on the order of 50,000 typefaces in existence, each different. Subtle and not-so-subtle variations in the thickness of the lines, the curves and angles, the shapes of the serifs, the relative sizes of the parts of the letters, and other design features, all add up to individualities. The alphabet is firmly fixed in the shapes of its letters. Three-year-olds recognize letterforms. Yet there are on the order of 50,000 typefaces in existence, each different. Subtle and not-so-subtle variations in the thickness of the lines, the curves and angles, the shapes of the serifs, the relative sizes of the parts of the letters, and other design features, all add up to individualities. The alphabet is firmly fixed in the shapes of its letters. Three-year-olds recognize letterforms. Yet there are on the the order of 50,000 typefaces in existence, each different. Subtle and not-so-subtle variations in the thickness of the lines, the curves and angles, the shapes

12 point type, 13 point linespace

The alphabet is firmly fixed in the shapes of its letters. Three-year-olds recognize letterforms. Yet there are on the order of 50,000 typefaces in existence, each different. Subtle and not-so-subtle variations in the thickness of the lines, the curves and angles, the shapes of the serifs, the relative sizes of the parts of the letters, and other design features, all add up to individualities. The alphabet is firmly fixed in the shapes of its letters. Three-year-olds recognize letterforms. Yet there are on the order of 50,000 typefaces in existence, each different. Subtle and not-so-subtle variations in the thickness of the lines, the curves and angles, the shapes of its letters. Three-year-olds recognize letterforms. Yet there are on the order of 50,000 typefaces

Interestingly, this italic can be used in large text blocks. It retains the salient features of alphanumeric characters better than most, but adds spice.

ABCDEFGHIJKLMNOPQRSTUVWXYZ
abcdefghijklmnopqrstuvwxyz
0123456789&?!$%“”.,/;()

8 point type, 9 point linespace

The alphabet is firmly fixed in the shapes of its letters. Three-year-olds recognize letterforms. Yet there are on the order of 50,000 typefaces in existence, each different. Subtle and not-so-subtle variations in the thickness of the lines, the curves and angles, the shapes of the serifs, the relative sizes of the parts of the letters, and other design features, all add up to individualities. The alphabet is firmly fixed in the shapes of its letters. Three-year-olds recognize letterforms. Yet there are on the order of 50,000 typefaces in existence, each different. Subtle and not-so-subtle variations in the thickness of the lines, the curves and angles, the shapes of the serifs, the relative sizes of the parts of the letters, and other design features, all add up to individualities. The alphabet is firmly fixed in the shapes of its letters. Three-year-olds recognize letterforms. Yet there are on the order of 50,000 typefaces in existence, each different. Subtle and not-so-subtle variations in the thickness of the lines, the curves and angles, the shapes of the serifs, the relative sizes of the parts of the letters, and other design features, all add up to individualities. The alphabet is firmly fixed in the shapes of its letters. Three-year-olds recognize letterforms. Yet there are on the order of 50,000 typefaces in existence, each different. Subtle and

10 point type, 11 point linespace

The alphabet is firmly fixed in the shapes of its letters. Three-year-olds recognize letterforms. Yet there are on the order of 50,000 typefaces in existence, each different. Subtle and not-so-subtle variations in the thickness of the lines, the curves and angles, the shapes of the serifs, the relative sizes of the parts of the letters, and other design features, all add up to individualities. The alphabet is firmly fixed in the shapes of its letters. Three-year-olds recognize letterforms. Yet there are on the order of 50,000 typefaces in existence, each different. Subtle and not-so-subtle variations in the thickness of the lines, the curves and angles, the shapes of the serifs, the relative sizes of the parts of the letters, and other design features, all add up to individualities. The alphabet is firmly fixed in the shapes of its letters. Three-year-olds recognize letterforms. Yet there are on the

12 point type, 13 point linespace

The alphabet is firmly fixed in the shapes of its letters. Three-year-olds recognize letterforms. Yet there are on the order of 50,000 typefaces in existence, each different. Subtle and not-so-subtle variations in the thickness of the lines, the curves and angles, the shapes of the serifs, the relative sizes of the parts of the letters, and other design features, all add up to individualities. The alphabet is firmly fixed in the shapes of its letters. Three-year-olds recognize letterforms. Yet there are on the order of 50,000 typefaces in existence, each different. Subtle and not-so-subtle variations in the thickness of the lines, the curves and angles,

Best set this in small doses to get the most use out of it. It makes a good first impression, but gets old quickly. You’ve probably met people like that.

ABCDEFGHIJKLMNOPQRSTUVWXYZ
abcdefghijklmnopqrstuvwxyz
0123456789&?!$%“”.,/;()

8 point type, 9 point linespace

The alphabet is firmly fixed in the shapes of its letters. Three-year-olds recognize letterforms. Yet there are on the order of 50,000 typefaces in existence, each different. Subtle and not-so-subtle variations in the thickness of the lines, the curves and angles, the shapes of the serifs, the relative sizes of the parts of the letters, and other design features, all add up to individualities. The alphabet is firmly fixed in the shapes of its letters. Three-year-olds recognize letterforms. Yet there are on the order of 50,000 typefaces in existence, each different. Subtle and not-so-subtle variations in the thickness of the lines, the curves and angles, the shapes of the serifs, the relative sizes of the parts of the letters, and other design features, all add up to individualities. The alphabet is firmly fixed in the shapes of its letters. Three-year-olds recognize letterforms. Yet there are on the order of 50,000 typefaces in existence, each different. Subtle and not-so-subtle variations in the thickness of the lines, the curves and angles, the shapes of the serifs, the relative sizes of the parts of the letters, and other design features, all add up to individualities. The alphabet is firmly fixed in the shapes of its letters. Three-year-olds recognize letterforms. Yet there are on the order of 50,000 typefaces in existence, each different. Subtle and not-so-subtle variations in the thickness of the lines, the curves and angles, the shapes

10 point type, 11 point linespace

The alphabet is firmly fixed in the shapes of its letters. Three-year-olds recognize letterforms. Yet there are on the order of 50,000 typefaces in existence, each different. Subtle and not-so-subtle variations in the thickness of the lines, the curves and angles, the shapes of the serifs, the relative sizes of the parts of the letters, and other design features, all add up to individualities. The alphabet is firmly fixed in the shapes of its letters. Three-year-olds recognize letterforms. Yet there are on the order of 50,000 typefaces in existence, each different. Subtle and not-so-subtle variations in the thickness of the lines, the curves and angles, the shapes of the serifs, the relative sizes of the parts of the letters, and other design features, all add up to individualities. The alphabet is firmly fixed in the shapes of its letters. Three-year-olds recognize letterforms. Yet there are on the the order of 50,000 typefaces in existence,

12 point type, 13 point linespace

The alphabet is firmly fixed in the shapes of its letters. Three-year-olds recognize letterforms. Yet there are on the order of 50,000 typefaces in existence, each different. Subtle and not-so-subtle variations in the thickness of the lines, the curves and angles, the shapes of the serifs, the relative sizes of the parts of the letters, and other design features, all add up to individualities. The alphabet is firmly fixed in the shapes of its letters. Three-year-olds recognize letterforms. Yet there are on the order of 50,000 typefaces in existence, each different. Subtle and not-so-subtle variations in the thickness of the lines, the curves and angles, the shapes of its letters.

More staying power than the roman, this face should be used instead of the roman for longer phrases. It’s almost as easy to read, and remains fresh longer.

ABCDEFGHIJKLMNOPQRSTUVWXYZ abcdefghijklmnopqrstuvwxyz 0123456789&?!$%“”.,/;()

8 point type, 9 point linespace

The alphabet is firmly fixed in the shapes of its letters. Three-year-olds recognize letterforms. Yet there are on the order of 50,000 typefaces in existence, each different. Subtle and not-so-subtle variations in the thickness of the lines, the curves and angles, the shapes of the serifs, the relative sizes of the parts of the letters, and other design features, all add up to individualities. The alphabet is firmly fixed in the shapes of its letters. Three-year-olds recognize letterforms. Yet there are on the order of 50,000 typefaces in existence, each different. Subtle and not-so-subtle variations in the thickness of the lines, the curves and angles, the shapes of the serifs, the relative sizes of the parts of the letters, and other design features, all add up to individualities. The alphabet is firmly fixed in the shapes of its letters. Three-year-olds recognize letterforms. Yet there are on the order of 50,000 typefaces in existence, each different. Subtle and not-so-subtle variations in the thickness of the lines, the curves and angles, the shapes of the serifs, the relative sizes of the parts of the letters, and other design features, all add up to individualities. The alphabet is firmly fixed in the shapes of its letters. Three-year-olds

10 point type, 11 point linespace

The alphabet is firmly fixed in the shapes of its letters. Three-year-olds recognize letterforms. Yet there are on the order of 50,000 typefaces in existence, each different. Subtle and not-so-subtle variations in the thickness of the lines, the curves and angles, the shapes of the serifs, the relative sizes of the parts of the letters, and other design features, all add up to individualities. The alphabet is firmly fixed in the shapes of its letters. Three-year-olds recognize letterforms. Yet there are on the order of 50,000 typefaces in existence, each different. Subtle and not-so-subtle variations in the thickness of the lines, the curves and angles, the shapes of the serifs, the relative sizes of the parts of the letters, and other design features, all add up to individualities. The alphabet is firmly fixed in the

12 point type, 13 point linespace

The alphabet is firmly fixed in the shapes of its letters. Three-year-olds recognize letterforms. Yet there are on the order of 50,000 typefaces in existence, each different. Subtle and not-so-subtle variations in the thickness of the lines, the curves and angles, the shapes of the serifs, the relative sizes of the parts of the letters, and other design features, all add up to individualities. The alphabet is firmly fixed in the shapes of its letters. Three-year-olds recognize letterforms. Yet there are on the order of 50,000 typefaces in existence, each different. Subtle and

Almost exclusively to be used for short headlines, or in reverse. Too heavy to use in text. It is designed so it can be set tightly, even touching characters, without reducing legibility appreciably.

ABCDEFGHIJKLMNOPQRSTUVWXYZ abcdefghijklmnopqrstuvwxyz 0123456789&?!$%“”.,/;()

8 point type, 9 point linespace

The alphabet is firmly fixed in the shapes of its letters. Three-year-olds recognize letterforms. Yet there are on the order of 50,000 typefaces in existence, each different. Subtle and not-so-subtle variations in the thickness of the lines, the curves and angles, the shapes of the serifs, the relative sizes of the parts of the letters, and other design features, all add up to individualities. The alphabet is firmly fixed in the shapes of its letters. Three-year-olds recognize letterforms. Yet there are on the order of 50,000 typefaces in existence, each different. Subtle and not-so-subtle variations in the thickness of the lines, the curves and angles, the shapes of the serifs, the relative sizes of the parts of the letters, and other design features, all add up to individualities. The alphabet is firmly fixed in the shapes of its letters. Three-year-olds recognize letterforms. Yet there are on the order of 50,000 typefaces in existence, each different. Subtle and not-so-subtle variations in the thickness of the lines, the curves and angles, the shapes of the serifs, the relative sizes of the parts of the letters, and other design features, all add up to individualities. The alphabet is firmly fixed in the shapes of its letters. Three-year-olds recognize letterforms. Yet there are on the order of

10 point type, 11 point linespace

The alphabet is firmly fixed in the shapes of its letters. Three-year-olds recognize letterforms. Yet there are on the order of 50,000 typefaces in existence, each different. Subtle and not-so-subtle variations in the thickness of the lines, the curves and angles, the shapes of the serifs, the relative sizes of the parts of the letters, and other design features, all add up to individualities. The alphabet is firmly fixed in the shapes of its letters. Three-year-olds recognize letterforms. Yet there are on the order of 50,000 typefaces in existence, each different. Subtle and not-so-subtle variations in the thickness of the lines, the curves and angles, the shapes of the serifs, the relative sizes of the parts of the letters, and other design features, all add up to individualities. The alphabet is firmly fixed in the shapes of its letters. Three-year-olds

12 point type, 13 point linespace

The alphabet is firmly fixed in the shapes of its letters. Three-year-olds recognize letterforms. Yet there are on the order of 50,000 typefaces in existence, each different. Subtle and not-so-subtle variations in the thickness of the lines, the curves and angles, the shapes of the serifs, the relative sizes of the parts of the letters, and other design features, all add up to individualities. The alphabet is firmly fixed in the shapes of its letters. Three-year-olds recognize letterforms. Yet there are on the order of 50,000 typefaces in existence, each different. Subtle and not-so-subtle variations in

As with the other Stone Serif italics, mainly to be used in all-italic pieces, or as emphasis with the Bold, or on its own in single phrases. This face won't be needed often, but is still useful.

ABCDEFGHIJKLMNOPQRSTUVWXYZ
abcdefghijklmnopqrstuvwxyz
0123456789&?!$%“”.,/;()

8 point type, 9 point linespace

The alphabet is firmly fixed in the shapes of its letters. Three-year-olds recognize letterforms. Yet there are on the order of 50,000 typefaces in existence, each different. Subtle and not-so-subtle variations in the thickness of the lines, the curves and angles, the shapes of the serifs, the relative sizes of the parts of the letters, and other design features, all add up to individualities. The alphabet is firmly fixed in the shapes of its letters. Three-year-olds recognize letterforms. Yet there are on the order of 50,000 typefaces in existence, each different. Subtle and not-so-subtle variations in the thickness of the lines, the curves and angles, the shapes of the serifs, the relative sizes of the parts of the letters, and other design features, all add up to individualities. The alphabet is firmly fixed in the shapes of its letters. Three-year-olds recognize letterforms. Yet there are on the order of 50,000 typefaces in existence, each different. Subtle and not-so-subtle variations in the thickness of the lines, the curves and angles, the shapes of the serifs, the relative sizes of the parts of the letters, and other design features, all add up to individualities. The alphabet is firmly fixed in the shapes of its letters. Three-year-olds recognize letterforms. Yet there are on the order of 50,000 typefaces in existence, each different. Subtle and not-so-subtle variations in the thickness of the lines, the curves and angles, the shapes of the serifs, the relative sizes of the parts of the letters, and other design features, all add up to individualities. The alphabet is firmly fixed in the shapes of its letters. Three-year-olds recognize letterforms. Yet there are on the order of

10 point type, 11 point linespace

The alphabet is firmly fixed in the shapes of its letters. Three-year-olds recognize letterforms. Yet there are on the order of 50,000 typefaces in existence, each different. Subtle and not-so-subtle variations in the thickness of the lines, the curves and angles, the shapes of the serifs, the relative sizes of the parts of the letters, and other design features, all add up to individualities. The alphabet is firmly fixed in the shapes of its letters. Three-year-olds recognize letterforms. Yet there are on the order of 50,000 typefaces in existence, each different. Subtle and not-so-subtle variations in the thickness of the lines, the curves and angles, the shapes of the serifs, the relative sizes of the parts of the letters, and other design features, all add up to individualities. The alphabet is firmly fixed in the shapes of its letters. Three-year-olds recognize letterforms. Yet there are on the order of 50,000 typefaces in existence, each different. Subtle and not-so-subtle variations in the thickness of the lines, the curves and angles, the shapes of the serifs, the relative sizes of the parts of

12 point type, 13 point linespace

The alphabet is firmly fixed in the shapes of its letters. Three-year-olds recognize letterforms. Yet there are on the order of 50,000 typefaces in existence, each different. Subtle and not-so-subtle variations in the thickness of the lines, the curves and angles, the shapes of the serifs, the relative sizes of the parts of the letters, and other design features, all add up to individualities. The alphabet is firmly fixed in the shapes of its letters. Three-year-olds recognize letterforms. Yet there are on the order of 50,000 typefaces in existence, each different. Subtle and not-so-subtle variations in the thickness of the lines, the curves and angles, the shapes of the serifs, the relative sizes of the parts of the letters, and other design features, all add up to individualities. The

When in doubt, use Times Roman, which will do for most text applications. It will not convey a free-wheeling spirited diatribe as well as some more flamboyant faces, but it is hard to go wrong with Times. Very very legible.

ABCDEFGHIJKLMNOPQRSTUVWXYZ
abcdefghijklmnopqrstuvwxyz
0123456789&?!$%“”.,/;()

8 point type, 9 point linespace

The alphabet is firmly fixed in the shapes of its letters. Three-year-olds recognize letterforms. Yet there are on the order of 50,000 typefaces in existence, each different. Subtle and not-so-subtle variations in the thickness of the lines, the curves and angles, the shapes of the serifs, the relative sizes of the parts of the letters, and other design features, all add up to individualities. The alphabet is firmly fixed in the shapes of its letters. Three-year-olds recognize letterforms. Yet there are on the order of 50,000 typefaces in existence, each different. Subtle and not-so-subtle variations in the thickness of the lines, the curves and angles, the shapes of the serifs, the relative sizes of the parts of the letters, and other design features, all add up to individualities. The alphabet is firmly fixed in the shapes of its letters. Three-year-olds recognize letterforms. Yet there are on the order of 50,000 typefaces in existence, each different. Subtle and not-so-subtle variations in the thickness of the lines, the curves and angles, the shapes of the serifs, the relative sizes of the parts of the letters, and other design features, all add up to individualities. The alphabet is firmly fixed in the shapes of its letters. Three-year-olds recognize letterforms. Yet there are on the order of 50,000 typefaces in existence, each different. Subtle and not-so-subtle variations in the thickness of the lines, the curves and angles, the shapes of the serifs, the relative sizes of the parts of the letters, and other design features, all add up to individualities. The alphabet is firmly fixed in the shapes of its letters. Three-year-olds recognize letterforms. Yet there are on the order

10 point type, 11 point linespace

The alphabet is firmly fixed in the shapes of its letters. Three-year-olds recognize letterforms. Yet there are on the order of 50,000 typefaces in existence, each different. Subtle and not-so-subtle variations in the thickness of the lines, the curves and angles, the shapes of the serifs, the relative sizes of the parts of the letters, and other design features, all add up to individualities. The alphabet is firmly fixed in the shapes of its letters. Three-year-olds recognize letterforms. Yet there are on the order of 50,000 typefaces in existence, each different. Subtle and not-so-subtle variations in the thickness of the lines, the curves and angles, the shapes of the serifs, the relative sizes of the parts of the letters, and other design features, all add up to individualities. The alphabet is firmly fixed in the shapes of its letters. Three-year-olds recognize letterforms. Yet there are on the order of 50,000 typefaces in existence, each different. Subtle and not-so-subtle variations in the thickness of the lines, the curves and angles, the shapes of the serifs, the relative sizes of the parts of

12 point type, 13 point linespace

The alphabet is firmly fixed in the shapes of its letters. Three-year-olds recognize letterforms. Yet there are on the order of 50,000 typefaces in existence, each different. Subtle and not-so-subtle variations in the thickness of the lines, the curves and angles, the shapes of the serifs, the relative sizes of the parts of the letters, and other design features, all add up to individualities. The alphabet is firmly fixed in the shapes of its letters. Three-year-olds recognize letterforms. Yet there are on the order of 50,000 typefaces in existence, each different. Subtle and not-so-subtle variations in the thickness of the lines, the curves and angles, the shapes of the serifs, the relative sizes of the parts of the letters, and other design features, all add up to individualities. The

Perfectly suited to its roman partner, Times Italic stresses without weakening nor overemphasizing the intent. It is hard to overuse Times Italic, so well designed is it, but it can be done. For the most part, though, use freely.

ABCDEFGHIJKLMNOPQRSTUVWXYZ
abcdefghijklmnopqrstuvwxyz
0123456789&?!$%“”.,/;()

8 point type, 9 point linespace

The alphabet is firmly fixed in the shapes of its letters. Three-year-olds recognize letterforms. Yet there are on the order of 50,000 typefaces in existence, each different. Subtle and not-so-subtle variations in the thickness of the lines, the curves and angles, the shapes of the serifs, the relative sizes of the parts of the letters, and other design features, all add up to individualities. The alphabet is firmly fixed in the shapes of its letters. Three-year-olds recognize letterforms. Yet there are on the order of 50,000 typefaces in existence, each different. Subtle and not-so-subtle variations in the thickness of the lines, the curves and angles, the shapes of the serifs, the relative sizes of the parts of the letters, and other design features, all add up to individualities. The alphabet is firmly fixed in the shapes of its letters. Three-year-olds recognize letterforms. Yet there are on the order of 50,000 typefaces in existence, each different. Subtle and not-so-subtle variations in the thickness of the lines, the curves and angles, the shapes of the serifs, the relative sizes of the parts of the letters, and other design features, all add up to individualities. The alphabet is firmly fixed in the shapes of its letters. Three-year-olds recognize letterforms. Yet there are on the order of 50,000 typefaces in existence, each different. Subtle and not-so-subtle variations in the thickness of the lines, the curves and angles, the shapes of the serifs, the relative sizes of the parts of the letters, and other design features, all add up to individualities. The alphabet is firmly fixed in the shapes of its letters. Three-year-olds

10 point type, 11 point linespace

The alphabet is firmly fixed in the shapes of its letters. Three-year-olds recognize letterforms. Yet there are on the order of 50,000 typefaces in existence, each different. Subtle and not-so-subtle variations in the thickness of the lines, the curves and angles, the shapes of the serifs, the relative sizes of the parts of the letters, and other design features, all add up to individualities. The alphabet is firmly fixed in the shapes of its letters. Three-year-olds recognize letterforms. Yet there are on the order of 50,000 typefaces in existence, each different. Subtle and not-so-subtle variations in the thickness of the lines, the curves and angles, the shapes of the serifs, the relative sizes of the parts of the letters, and other design features, all add up to individualities. The alphabet is firmly fixed in the shapes of its letters. Three-year-olds recognize letterforms. Yet there are on the order of 50,000 typefaces in existence, each different. Subtle and not-so-subtle variations in the thickness of the lines, the curves and angles, the shapes of the serifs, the

12 point type, 13 point linespace

The alphabet is firmly fixed in the shapes of its letters. Three-year-olds recognize letterforms. Yet there are on the order of 50,000 typefaces in existence, each different. Subtle and not-so-subtle variations in the thickness of the lines, the curves and angles, the shapes of the serifs, the relative sizes of the parts of the letters, and other design features, all add up to individualities. The alphabet is firmly fixed in the shapes of its letters. Three-year-olds recognize letterforms. Yet there are on the order of 50,000 typefaces in existence, each different. Subtle and not-so-subtle variations in the thickness of the lines, the curves and angles, the shapes of the serifs, the relative sizes of the parts of the letters, and other design features, all add up to indi-

This is a face created to fill a need. Times Roman is legible, but weak. It gets lost in any complex graphic design, especially with a color treatment. Times Semibold stands up and demands to be read, and will be. Use it when design needs a strong legible face.

ABCDEFGHIJKLMNOPQRSTUVWXYZ
abcdefghijklmnopqrstuvwxyz
0123456789&?!$%“”.,/;()

8 point type, 9 point linespace

The alphabet is firmly fixed in the shapes of its letters. Three-year-olds recognize letterforms. Yet there are on the order of 50,000 typefaces in existence, each different. Subtle and not-so-subtle variations in the thickness of the lines, the curves and angles, the shapes of the serifs, the relative sizes of the parts of the letters, and other design features, all add up to individualities. The alphabet is firmly fixed in the shapes of its letters. Three-year-olds recognize letterforms. Yet there are on the order of 50,000 typefaces in existence, each different. Subtle and not-so-subtle variations in the thickness of the lines, the curves and angles, the shapes of the serifs, the relative sizes of the parts of the letters, and other design features, all add up to individualities. The alphabet is firmly fixed in the shapes of its letters. Three-year-olds recognize letterforms. Yet there are on the order of 50,000 typefaces in existence, each different. Subtle and not-so-subtle variations in the thickness of the lines, the curves and angles, the shapes of the serifs, the relative sizes of the parts of the letters, and other design features, all add up to individualities. The alphabet is firmly fixed in the shapes of its letters. Three-year-olds recognize letterforms. Yet there are on the order of 50,000 typefaces in existence, each different. Subtle and not-so-subtle variations in the thickness of the lines, the curves and angles, the shapes of the serifs, the relative sizes of the parts of the letters, and other design features, all add up to individualities. The alphabet is firmly fixed in the shapes of its letters. Three-year-olds recognize letterforms. Yet there are on

10 point type, 11 point linespace

The alphabet is firmly fixed in the shapes of its letters. Three-year-olds recognize letterforms. Yet there are on the order of 50,000 typefaces in existence, each different. Subtle and not-so-subtle variations in the thickness of the lines, the curves and angles, the shapes of the serifs, the relative sizes of the parts of the letters, and other design features, all add up to individualities. The alphabet is firmly fixed in the shapes of its letters. Three-year-olds recognize letterforms. Yet there are on the order of 50,000 typefaces in existence, each different. Subtle and not-so-subtle variations in the thickness of the lines, the curves and angles, the shapes of the serifs, the relative sizes of the parts of the letters, and other design features, all add up to individualities. The alphabet is firmly fixed in the shapes of its letters. Three-year-olds recognize letterforms. Yet there are on the order of 50,000 typefaces in existence, each different. Subtle and not-so-subtle variations in the thickness of the lines, the curves and angles, the shapes of the serifs, the relative sizes of the parts of

12 point type, 13 point linespace

The alphabet is firmly fixed in the shapes of its letters. Three-year-olds recognize letterforms. Yet there are on the order of 50,000 typefaces in existence, each different. Subtle and not-so-subtle variations in the thickness of the lines, the curves and angles, the shapes of the serifs, the relative sizes of the parts of the letters, and other design features, all add up to individualities. The alphabet is firmly fixed in the shapes of its letters. Three-year-olds recognize letterforms. Yet there are on the order of 50,000 typefaces in existence, each different. Subtle and not-so-subtle variations in the thickness of the lines, the curves and angles, the shapes of the serifs, the relative sizes of the parts of the letters, and other design features, all add up to individualities. The

As with all the Times family italics, this works, but not with its complement. Use the Semibold Italic with Times Roman if you Really want to stress a word or phrase. If it's not that important, this italic does fine with the Semibold.

ABCDEFGHIJKLMNOPQRSTUVWXYZ
abcdefghijklmnopqrstuvwxyz
0123456789&?!$%“”.,/;()

8 point type, 9 point linespace

The alphabet is firmly fixed in the shapes of its letters. Three-year-olds recognize letterforms. Yet there are on the order of 50,000 typefaces in existence, each different. Subtle and not-so-subtle variations in the thickness of the lines, the curves and angles, the shapes of the serifs, the relative sizes of the parts of the letters, and other design features, all add up to individualities. The alphabet is firmly fixed in the shapes of its letters. Three-year-olds recognize letterforms. Yet there are on the order of 50,000 typefaces in existence, each different. Subtle and not-so-subtle variations in the thickness of the lines, the curves and angles, the shapes of the serifs, the relative sizes of the parts of the letters, and other design features, all add up to individualities. The alphabet is firmly fixed in the shapes of its letters. Three-year-olds recognize letterforms. Yet there are on the order of 50,000 typefaces in existence, each different. Subtle and not-so-subtle variations in the thickness of the lines, the curves and angles, the shapes of the serifs, the relative sizes of the parts of the letters, and other design features, all add up to individualities. The alphabet is firmly fixed in the shapes of its letters. Three-year-olds recognize letterforms. Yet there are on the order of 50,000 typefaces in existence, each different. Subtle and not-so-subtle variations in the thickness of the lines, the curves and angles, the shapes of the serifs, the relative sizes of the parts of the letters, and other design features, all add up to individualities. The alphabet is firmly fixed in the shapes of

10 point type, 11 point linespace

The alphabet is firmly fixed in the shapes of its letters. Three-year-olds recognize letterforms. Yet there are on the order of 50,000 typefaces in existence, each different. Subtle and not-so-subtle variations in the thickness of the lines, the curves and angles, the shapes of the serifs, the relative sizes of the parts of the letters, and other design features, all add up to individualities. The alphabet is firmly fixed in the shapes of its letters. Three-year-olds recognize letterforms. Yet there are on the order of 50,000 typefaces in existence, each different. Subtle and not-so-subtle variations in the thickness of the lines, the curves and angles, the shapes of the serifs, the relative sizes of the parts of the letters, and other design features, all add up to individualities. The alphabet is firmly fixed in the shapes of its letters. Three-year-olds recognize letterforms. Yet there are on the order of 50,000 typefaces in existence, each different. Subtle and not-so-subtle variations in the thickness of the lines, the curves and angles, the shapes

12 point type, 13 point linespace

The alphabet is firmly fixed in the shapes of its letters. Three-year-olds recognize letterforms. Yet there are on the order of 50,000 typefaces in existence, each different. Subtle and not-so-subtle variations in the thickness of the lines, the curves and angles, the shapes of the serifs, the relative sizes of the parts of the letters, and other design features, all add up to individualities. The alphabet is firmly fixed in the shapes of its letters. Three-year-olds recognize letterforms. Yet there are on the order of 50,000 typefaces in existence, each different. Subtle and not-so-subtle variations in the thickness of the lines, the curves and angles, the shapes of the serifs, the relative sizes of the parts of the letters, and other design features, all add up to

Strictly a newspaper headline look. You won’t blow any socks off with Times Bold, and it’s not even that easy to read. For sheer “This-is-how-it-is,” though, Times Bold is hard to beat. It epitomizes the authority of the printed word.

ABCDEFGHIJKLMNOPQRSTUVWXYZ
abcdefghijklmnopqrstuvwxyz
0123456789&?!$%“”.,/;()

8 point type, 9 point linespace

The alphabet is firmly fixed in the shapes of its letters. Three-year-olds recognize letterforms. Yet there are on the order of 50,000 typefaces in existence, each different. Subtle and not-so-subtle variations in the thickness of the lines, the curves and angles, the shapes of the serifs, the relative sizes of the parts of the letters, and other design features, all add up to individualities. The alphabet is firmly fixed in the shapes of its letters. Three-year-olds recognize letterforms. Yet there are on the order of 50,000 typefaces in existence, each different. Subtle and not-so-subtle variations in the thickness of the lines, the curves and angles, the shapes of the serifs, the relative sizes of the parts of the letters, and other design features, all add up to individualities. The alphabet is firmly fixed in the shapes of its letters. Three-year-olds recognize letterforms. Yet there are on the order of 50,000 typefaces in existence, each different. Subtle and not-so-subtle variations in the thickness of the lines, the curves and angles, the shapes of the serifs, the relative sizes of the parts of the letters, and other design features, all add up to individualities. The alphabet is firmly fixed in the shapes of its letters. Three-year-olds recognize letterforms. Yet there are on the order of 50,000 typefaces in existence, each different. Subtle and not-so-subtle variations in the thickness of the lines, the curves and angles, the shapes of the serifs, the relative sizes of the parts of the letters, and other design features, all add up to individualities. The alphabet is firmly fixed in the shapes of its letters. Three-year-olds recognize letterforms. Yet there are on the order

10 point type, 11 point linespace

The alphabet is firmly fixed in the shapes of its letters. Three-year-olds recognize letterforms. Yet there are on the order of 50,000 typefaces in existence, each different. Subtle and not-so-subtle variations in the thickness of the lines, the curves and angles, the shapes of the serifs, the relative sizes of the parts of the letters, and other design features, all add up to individualities. The alphabet is firmly fixed in the shapes of its letters. Three-year-olds recognize letterforms. Yet there are on the order of 50,000 typefaces in existence, each different. Subtle and not-so-subtle variations in the thickness of the lines, the curves and angles, the shapes of the serifs, the relative sizes of the parts of the letters, and other design features, all add up to individualities. The alphabet is firmly fixed in the shapes of its letters. Three-year-olds recognize letterforms. Yet there are on the order of 50,000 typefaces in existence, each different. Subtle and not-so-subtle variations in the thickness of the lines, the curves and angles, the shapes of the serifs, the

12 point type, 13 point linespace

The alphabet is firmly fixed in the shapes of its letters. Three-year-olds recognize letterforms. Yet there are on the order of 50,000 typefaces in existence, each different. Subtle and not-so-subtle variations in the thickness of the lines, the curves and angles, the shapes of the serifs, the relative sizes of the parts of the letters, and other design features, all add up to individualities. The alphabet is firmly fixed in the shapes of its letters. Three-year-olds recognize letterforms. Yet there are on the order of 50,000 typefaces in existence, each different. Subtle and not-so-subtle variations in the thickness of the lines, the curves and angles, the shapes of the serifs, the relative sizes of the parts of the letters, and other design features, all add up to

This has limited use. It is lighter and weaker than Times Bold, so if used for emphasis it tends to de-emphasize. It actually works better with Times Semibold than with Times Bold. It **is** ***well cut, and does create the italic stress, but not with Bold.***

ABCDEFGHIJKLMNOPQRSTUVWXYZ
abcdefghijklmnopqrstuvwxyz
0123456789&?!$%“”.,/;()

8 point type, 9 point linespace

The alphabet is firmly fixed in the shapes of its letters. Three-year-olds recognize letterforms. Yet there are on the order of 50,000 typefaces in existence, each different. Subtle and not-so-subtle variations in the thickness of the lines, the curves and angles, the shapes of the serifs, the relative sizes of the parts of the letters, and other design features, all add up to individualities. The alphabet is firmly fixed in the shapes of its letters. Three-year-olds recognize letterforms. Yet there are on the order of 50,000 typefaces in existence, each different. Subtle and not-so-subtle variations in the thickness of the lines, the curves and angles, the shapes of the serifs, the relative sizes of the parts of the letters, and other design features, all add up to individualities. The alphabet is firmly fixed in the shapes of its letters. Three-year-olds recognize letterforms. Yet there are on the order of 50,000 typefaces in existence, each different. Subtle and not-so-subtle variations in the thickness of the lines, the curves and angles, the shapes of the serifs, the relative sizes of the parts of the letters, and other design features, all add up to individualities. The alphabet is firmly fixed in the shapes of its letters. Three-year-olds recognize letterforms. Yet there are on the order of 50,000 typefaces in existence, each different. Subtle and not-so-subtle variations in the thickness of the lines, the curves and angles, the shapes of the serifs, the relative sizes of the parts of the letters, and other design features, all add

10 point type, 11 point linespace

The alphabet is firmly fixed in the shapes of its letters. Three-year-olds recognize letterforms. Yet there are on the order of 50,000 typefaces in existence, each different. Subtle and not-so-subtle variations in the thickness of the lines, the curves and angles, the shapes of the serifs, the relative sizes of the parts of the letters, and other design features, all add up to individualities. The alphabet is firmly fixed in the shapes of its letters. Three-year-olds recognize letterforms. Yet there are on the order of 50,000 typefaces in existence, each different. Subtle and not-so-subtle variations in the thickness of the lines, the curves and angles, the shapes of the serifs, the relative sizes of the parts of the letters, and other design features, all add up to individualities. The alphabet is firmly fixed in the shapes of its letters. Three-year-olds recognize letterforms. Yet there are on the order of 50,000 typefaces in existence, each different. Subtle and not-so-subtle variations in the thickness of the lines, the

12 point type, 13 point linespace

The alphabet is firmly fixed in the shapes of its letters. Three-year-olds recognize letterforms. Yet there are on the order of 50,000 typefaces in existence, each different. Subtle and not-so-subtle variations in the thickness of the lines, the curves and angles, the shapes of the serifs, the relative sizes of the parts of the letters, and other design features, all add up to individualities. The alphabet is firmly fixed in the shapes of its letters. Three-year-olds recognize letterforms. Yet there are on the order of 50,000 typefaces in existence, each different. Subtle and not-so-subtle variations in the thickness of the lines, the curves and angles, the shapes of the serifs, the relative sizes of the parts of the letters,

Notice there is no italic to this face. It is hard to read, hard to set well, and awkward at best. It is part of the Times family, so included here, but the only time it looks half-decent is when set in reverse (white on black).

ABCDEFGHIJKLMNOPQRSTUVWXYZ
abcdefghijklmnopqrstuvwxyz
0123456789&?!$%“”.,/;()

8 point type, 9 point linespace

The alphabet is firmly fixed in the shapes of its letters. Three-year-olds recognize letterforms. Yet there are on the order of 50,000 typefaces in existence, each different. Subtle and not-so-subtle variations in the thickness of the lines, the curves and angles, the shapes of the serifs, the relative sizes of the parts of the letters, and other design features, all add up to individualities. The alphabet is firmly fixed in the shapes of its letters. Three-year-olds recognize letterforms. Yet there are on the order of 50,000 typefaces in existence, each different. Subtle and not-so-subtle variations in the thickness of the lines, the curves and angles, the shapes of the serifs, the relative sizes of the parts of the letters, and other design features, all add up to individualities. The alphabet is firmly fixed in the shapes of its letters. Three-year-olds recognize letterforms. Yet there are on the order of 50,000 typefaces in existence, each different. Subtle and not-so-subtle variations in the thickness of the lines, the curves and angles, the shapes of the serifs, the relative sizes of the parts of the letters, and other design features, all add up to individualities. The alphabet is firmly fixed in the shapes of its letters. Three-year-olds recognize letterforms. Yet there are on the order of 50,000 typefaces in existence, each different. Subtle and not-so-subtle variations in the thickness of the lines, the curves and angles, the shapes of the serifs,

10 point type, 11 point linespace

The alphabet is firmly fixed in the shapes of its letters. Three-year-olds recognize letterforms. Yet there are on the order of 50,000 typefaces in existence, each different. Subtle and not-so-subtle variations in the thickness of the lines, the curves and angles, the shapes of the serifs, the relative sizes of the parts of the letters, and other design features, all add up to individualities. The alphabet is firmly fixed in the shapes of its letters. Three-year-olds recognize letterforms. Yet there are on the order of 50,000 typefaces in existence, each different. Subtle and not-so-subtle variations in the thickness of the lines, the curves and angles, the shapes of the serifs, the relative sizes of the parts of the letters, and other design features, all add up to individualities. The alphabet is firmly fixed in the shapes of its letters. Three-year-olds recognize letterforms. Yet there are on the order of 50,000 typefaces in existence, each different. Subtle and not-so-subtle

12 point type, 13 point linespace

The alphabet is firmly fixed in the shapes of its letters. Three-year-olds recognize letterforms. Yet there are on the order of 50,000 typefaces in existence, each different. Subtle and not-so-subtle variations in the thickness of the lines, the curves and angles, the shapes of the serifs, the relative sizes of the parts of the letters, and other design features, all add up to individualities. The alphabet is firmly fixed in the shapes of its letters. Three-year-olds recognize letterforms. Yet there are on the order of 50,000 typefaces in existence, each different. Subtle and not-so-subtle variations in the thickness of the lines, the curves and angles, the shapes of the serifs, the relative sizes of the

Trump's wide serifs require a loose setting, which requires extra line space, all of which adds up to extravagance. Not for the tight-fisted or tight-minded. Very readable. Very rich.

ABCDEFGHIJKLMNOPQRSTUVWXYZ
abcdefghijklmnopqrstuvwxyz
0123456789&?!$%“”.,/;()

8 point type, 9 point linespace

The alphabet is firmly fixed in the shapes of its letters. Three-year-olds recognize letterforms. Yet there are on the order of 50,000 typefaces in existence, each different. Subtle and not-so-subtle variations in the thickness of the lines, the curves and angles, the shapes of the serifs, the relative sizes of the parts of the letters, and other design features, all add up to individualities. The alphabet is firmly fixed in the shapes of its letters. Three-year-olds recognize letterforms. Yet there are on the order of 50,000 typefaces in existence, each different. Subtle and not-so-subtle variations in the thickness of the lines, the curves and angles, the shapes of the serifs, the relative sizes of the parts of the letters, and other design features, all add up to individualities. The alphabet is firmly fixed in the shapes of its letters. Three-year-olds recognize letterforms. Yet there are on the order of 50,000 typefaces in existence, each different. Subtle and not-so-subtle variations in the thickness of the lines, the curves and angles, the shapes of the serifs, the relative sizes of the parts of the letters, and other design features, all add up to individualities. The alphabet is firmly fixed in the shapes of its letters. Three-year-olds recognize letterforms. Yet there are on the order of 50,000 typefaces in existence, each different. Subtle and not-so-subtle variations in the thickness of the lines, the curves and angles, the shapes of the

10 point type, 11 point linespace

The alphabet is firmly fixed in the shapes of its letters. Three-year-olds recognize letterforms. Yet there are on the order of 50,000 typefaces in existence, each different. Subtle and not-so-subtle variations in the thickness of the lines, the curves and angles, the shapes of the serifs, the relative sizes of the parts of the letters, and other design features, all add up to individualities. The alphabet is firmly fixed in the shapes of its letters. Three-year-olds recognize letterforms. Yet there are on the order of 50,000 typefaces in existence, each different. Subtle and not-so-subtle variations in the thickness of the lines, the curves and angles, the shapes of the serifs, the relative sizes of the parts of the letters, and other design features, all add up to individualities. The alphabet is firmly fixed in the shapes of its letters. Three-year-olds recognize letterforms. Yet there are on the order of 50,000 typefaces in existence, each

12 point type, 13 point linespace

The alphabet is firmly fixed in the shapes of its letters. Three-year-olds recognize letterforms. Yet there are on the order of 50,000 typefaces in existence, each different. Subtle and not-so-subtle variations in the thickness of the lines, the curves and angles, the shapes of the serifs, the relative sizes of the parts of the letters, and other design features, all add up to individualities. The alphabet is firmly fixed in the shapes of its letters. Three-year-olds recognize letterforms. Yet there are on the order of 50,000 typefaces in existence, each different. Subtle and not-so-subtle variations in the thickness of the lines, the curves and angles, the shapes of the serifs, the relative

While the numerals are slightly odd, the rest of this italic stays true to Trump's concept of confident power. It's visually lighter than the roman and the serifs a bit smaller, so it should be set a hair more tightly.

ABCDEFGHIJKLMNOPQRSTUVWXYZ
abcdefghijklmnopqrstuvwxyz
0123456789&?!$%“”.,/;()

8 point type, 9 point linespace

The alphabet is firmly fixed in the shapes of its letters. Three-year-olds recognize letterforms. Yet there are on the order of 50,000 typefaces in existence, each different. Subtle and not-so-subtle variations in the thickness of the lines, the curves and angles, the shapes of the serifs, the relative sizes of the parts of the letters, and other design features, all add up to individualities. The alphabet is firmly fixed in the shapes of its letters. Three-year-olds recognize letterforms. Yet there are on the order of 50,000 typefaces in existence, each different. Subtle and not-so-subtle variations in the thickness of the lines, the curves and angles, the shapes of the serifs, the relative sizes of the parts of the letters, and other design features, all add up to individualities. The alphabet is firmly fixed in the shapes of its letters. Three-year-olds recognize letterforms. Yet there are on the order of 50,000 typefaces in existence, each different. Subtle and not-so-subtle variations in the thickness of the lines, the curves and angles, the shapes of the serifs, the relative sizes of the parts of the letters, and other design features, all add up to individualities. The alphabet is firmly fixed in the shapes of its letters. Three-year-olds recognize letterforms. Yet there are on the order of 50,000 typefaces in existence, each different. Subtle and not-so-subtle variations in the thickness of the lines, the curves and angles, the shapes of the serifs,

10 point type, 11 point linespace

The alphabet is firmly fixed in the shapes of its letters. Three-year-olds recognize letterforms. Yet there are on the order of 50,000 typefaces in existence, each different. Subtle and not-so-subtle variations in the thickness of the lines, the curves and angles, the shapes of the serifs, the relative sizes of the parts of the letters, and other design features, all add up to individualities. The alphabet is firmly fixed in the shapes of its letters. Three-year-olds recognize letterforms. Yet there are on the order of 50,000 typefaces in existence, each different. Subtle and not-so-subtle variations in the thickness of the lines, the curves and angles, the shapes of the serifs, the relative sizes of the parts of the letters, and other design features, all add up to individualities. The alphabet is firmly fixed in the shapes of its letters. Three-year-olds recognize letterforms. Yet there are on the order of 50,000 typefaces in existence, each different. Subtle and not-so-subtle

12 point type, 13 point linespace

The alphabet is firmly fixed in the shapes of its letters. Three-year-olds recognize letterforms. Yet there are on the order of 50,000 typefaces in existence, each different. Subtle and not-so-subtle variations in the thickness of the lines, the curves and angles, the shapes of the serifs, the relative sizes of the parts of the letters, and other design features, all add up to individualities. The alphabet is firmly fixed in the shapes of its letters. Three-year-olds recognize letterforms. Yet there are on the order of 50,000 typefaces in existence, each different. Subtle and not-so-subtle variations in the thickness of the lines, the curves and angles, the shapes of the serifs, the relative sizes of the

More angular and harsh than the regular weight, this doesn’t work as well. It is often preferable to stay with the roman for what would normally be a bold application, as in chapter titles. Okay for subheads.

ABCDEFGHIJKLMNOPQRSTUVWXYZ
abcdefghijklmnopqrstuvwxyz
0123456789&?!$%“”.,/;()

8 point type, 9 point linespace

The alphabet is firmly fixed in the shapes of its letters. Three-year-olds recognize letterforms. Yet there are on the order of 50,000 typefaces in existence, each different. Subtle and not-so-subtle variations in the thickness of the lines, the curves and angles, the shapes of the serifs, the relative sizes of the parts of the letters, and other design features, all add up to individualities. The alphabet is firmly fixed in the shapes of its letters. Three-year-olds recognize letterforms. Yet there are on the order of 50,000 typefaces in existence, each different. Subtle and not-so-subtle variations in the thickness of the lines, the curves and angles, the shapes of the serifs, the relative sizes of the parts of the letters, and other design features, all add up to individualities. The alphabet is firmly fixed in the shapes of its letters. Three-year-olds recognize letterforms. Yet there are on the order of 50,000 typefaces in existence, each different. Subtle and not-so-subtle variations in the thickness of the lines, the curves and angles, the shapes of the serifs, the relative sizes of the parts of the letters, and other design features, all add up to individualities. The alphabet is firmly fixed in the shapes of its letters. Three-year-olds recognize letterforms. Yet there are on the order of 50,000 typefaces in existence, each different. Subtle and not-so-subtle variations in the thickness of the lines, the curves and angles, the shapes of the

10 point type, 11 point linespace

The alphabet is firmly fixed in the shapes of its letters. Three-year-olds recognize letterforms. Yet there are on the order of 50,000 typefaces in existence, each different. Subtle and not-so-subtle variations in the thickness of the lines, the curves and angles, the shapes of the serifs, the relative sizes of the parts of the letters, and other design features, all add up to individualities. The alphabet is firmly fixed in the shapes of its letters. Three-year-olds recognize letterforms. Yet there are on the order of 50,000 typefaces in existence, each different. Subtle and not-so-subtle variations in the thickness of the lines, the curves and angles, the shapes of the serifs, the relative sizes of the parts of the letters, and other design features, all add up to individualities. The alphabet is firmly fixed in the shapes of its letters. Three-year-olds recognize letterforms. Yet there are on the order of 50,000 typefaces in existence, each

12 point type, 13 point linespace

The alphabet is firmly fixed in the shapes of its letters. Three-year-olds recognize letterforms. Yet there are on the order of 50,000 typefaces in existence, each different. Subtle and not-so-subtle variations in the thickness of the lines, the curves and angles, the shapes of the serifs, the relative sizes of the parts of the letters, and other design features, all add up to individualities. The alphabet is firmly fixed in the shapes of its letters. Three-year-olds recognize letterforms. Yet there are on the order of 50,000 typefaces in existence, each different. Subtle and not-so-subtle variations in the thickness of the lines, the curves and angles, the shapes of the serifs, the relative

Again, somewhat harsh. It tries too hard. Give this one only limited play, and only when no alternative is available. It imparts an almost threatening feel of instability in a powerful position. The mad king.

12 point type, 24 point linespace

18 point type, 36 point linespace

Similar Styles

If a client asks for a typeface you don't have, another might serve his purpose just as well. Listed below are seventy-five typefaces and the face in this book which comes closest to the "feel" of each. Bear in mind that these are *similarities*, not *identities*. No typeface has exactly the same emotional impact as any other.

American Typewriter	Souvenir
Antique Olive	Frutiger
Aster	Times
Avenir	Avant Garde
Bauhaus	Avant Garde
Belwe	Souvenir
Bembo	Baskerville
Benguiat	Souvenir
Berkeley	Goudy
Bookman	Century
Candida	Trump
Caslon	Times
Caxton	Clearface
Cheltenham	Century
Clarendon	Memphis
Cochin	Baskerville
Concorde	Clearface
Cooper Black	Souvenir
Corona	Century
Cushing	Clearface
Eras	Frutiger
Excelsior	Century
Fenice	Bodoni
Folio	Stone Sans
Franklin Gothic	Helvetica
Futura	Avant Garde
Galliard	Garamond
Garth Graphic	Trump
Gill Sans	Avant Garde
Glypha	Memphis
Granjon	Baskerville
Hiroshige	Stone Serif
Impressum	Memphis
Italia	Souvenir
Janson	Times
Kabel	Avant Garde
Korinna	Souvenir
Leawood	Trump
Life	Times
Lubalin Graph	Memphis
Lucida	Memphis
Lucida Sans	Stone Sans
Melior	Trump
Meridien	Stone Serif
Minion	Stone Serif
Minister	Garamond
New Caledonia	Baskerville
News Gothic	Helvetica
Novarese	Americana
Olympian	Stone Serif
Perpetua	Baskerville
Plantin	Palatino
Quorum	Optima
Raleigh	Memphis
Rockwell	Memphis
Rotis Serif	Palatino
Rotis Sans Serif	Helvetica
Sabon	Century
Serif Gothic	Avant Garde
Serifa	Memphis
Serpentine	Eurostile
Shannon	Frutiger
Shelley	Snell Roundhand
Spartan	Frutiger
Stempel Schneidler	Clearface
Symbol	Optima
Syntax	Frutiger
Trade Gothic	Helvetica
Univers	Helvetica
Usherwood	Palatino
Utopia	Trump
Versailles	Memphis
Walbaum	Bodoni
Weidemann	Clearface
Weiss	Palatino

Type Font Source Directory

Adobe Systems Inc.
1585 Charleston Rd.
P.O. Box 7900
Mountain View, CA 94039-7900
(415) 961-4400

Agfa Corporation
Agfa Compugraphic Division
90 Industrial Way
Wilmington, MA 01887
(508) 658-5600

Alphatype Corporation
220 Campus Drive
Suite 103
Arlington Heights, IL 60004

Architext Inc.
121 Interpark Blvd.
Suite 1101
San Antonio, TX 78216
(512) 490-2240

Bitstream Inc.
Athenaeum House
215 First Street
Cambridge, MA 02142
(617) 497-6222

Casady & Greene Inc.
22734 Portola Drive
Salinas, CA 93908-1119
(408) 484-9228

C. Centennial Inc.
2 Centennial Drive
Centennial Park
Peabody, MA 01960
(508) 532-5908

Computer Output Printing, Inc.
4828 Loop Central Drive
Houston, TX 77081
(713) 666-0911

Crosfield Lightspeed Inc.
47 Farnsworth Street
Boston, MA 02210
(617) 338-2173

Digital Typeface Corporation
9955 West 69th Street
Eden Prairie, MN 55344
(612) 944-9264

Electra Font Technologies
1601 Trapelo Road
Waltham, MA 02154
(617) 890-1288

The Font Company
12629 North Tatum Blvd.
Suite 210
Phoenix, AZ 85032
(602) 998-9711

The Font Factory
2400 Central Parkway
Suite A
Houston, TX 77092
(713) 682-8973

FontHaus Inc.
15 Perry Avenue
Suite A7
Norwalk, CT 06850

Image Club Graphics Inc.
#5 1902 11th Street Southeast
Calgary, Alberta T2G 2G2
CANADA
(403) 262-8008

Letraset USA Inc.
40 Eisenhower Drive
Paramus, NJ 07652
(201) 845-6100

Linotype-Hell Company
425 Oser Avenue
Hauppauge, NY 11788
(516) 434-2074

Videosoft, Inc.
2103 South Broadway
P.O. Box 165920
Little Rock, AR 72206
(501) 376-2083

Glossary

Ascender The portion of some lower case letters which rises above the x-height: b, d, f, h, k, l. These are very often, though not always, taller than the cap height.

Baseline The imaginary line on which all letters sit.

Cap Height This is the actual size of capital letters in a typeface, expressed as a percentage of point size. Most typefaces have cap heights ranging from 65% to 75%, but some are much taller or shorter.

Descender The portion of some lower case letters which falls below the baseline: g, j, p, q, y.

Font All the characters included in one typeface. This includes punctuation. Some fonts (such as Zapf Dingbats) are not alphanumeric, but other useful characters instead.

Italic A slanted design of a typeface designed to complement the normal vertical design. (See Oblique.)

Kern (verb) To manually adjust space between letters; (noun) the amount of space thus added or subtracted.

Letterspace (verb) To add extra space between letters overall in a line of type; (noun) the amount of space thus added.

Line Length The horizontal measure of a line into which all the characters are supposed to fit.

Line Space The distance from the baseline of a line of type to the baseline of an adjacent line, either above or below it.

Oblique An artificial italic, formed by electronically slanting a normal vertical typeface.

Pica In true printing terms, six picas are just short of one inch. In some systems, six picas equal one inch exactly. Ask the manufacturer.

Point There are twelve points in one pica, in any system.

Point Size see Size.

Roman The normal vertical version of a typeface is called Roman (as opposed to Italic).

Sans Serif see Serif.

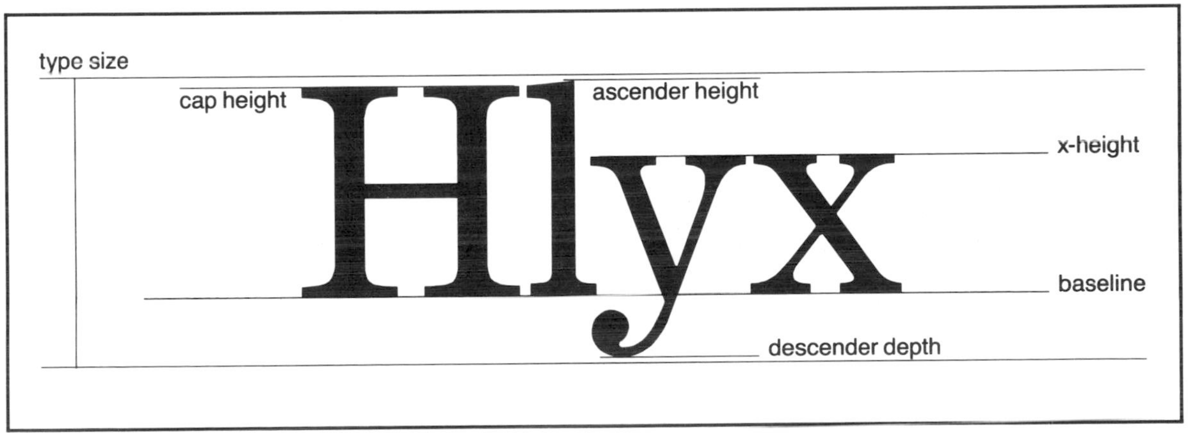

Serif The little feet at the ends of letters are serifs. Typefaces without serifs are called Sans Serif.

Size The Type Size (Point Size) of type is the vertical space allowed for any character of a typeface to fit within. Most typefaces are designed to be a bit smaller, actually, than their point size, so characters on adjacent lines won't touch. Often expressed numerically, as in "10-point type."

Solid Type is "Set Solid" if the point size of a line of type equals the line space to the line above it.

Track The overall tightness or looseness of a line of type; how close the characters are to each other. A higher track number results in tighter type.

Type Size see Size.

White Space The visual amount of space between lines of type. Typefaces with a low x-height have more white space.

Wordspace The space between words. Too little or too much wordspace results in lower legibility.

X-height The size of lower case letters in a typeface, expressed as a percentage of point size. The x-height usually ranges from 40% to 50%.

Index